One Thousand Useful Mohawk Words

by

David Kanatawakhon Maracle
University of Western Ontario, London

AUDIO·FORUM
THE LANGUAGE SOURCE

Guilford, Connecticut

ONE THOUSAND USEFUL MOHAWK WORDS

ISBN: 0-88432-710-8

Published by Audio-Forum
a division of Jeffrey Norton, Publishers, Inc.
On-the-Green, Guilford, CT 06437

PRONUNCIATION

The Mohawk language used in this course is written using the Standard orthography which makes use of 12 letters of the Roman alphabet: **a, e, h, i, k, n, o, r, s, t, w, y,** and glottal marker **'**. The following table provides a listing of the vowels, consonants, and consonant combinations that will be found in written Mohawk. It will be most advantageous to the student of the language to approach a fluent speaker for aid in pronunciation of many of the sounds shown in the tables below, as the English equivalents provided are approximate at best.

PRONUNCIATION TABLE		
Vowels	**Approximate English Equivalent**	**Mohawk Example**
ORAL **a**	as *a* in f*a*ther	**kàsere'** [kà:-se-re'] *car* **ahta'** [áh-ta'] *shoe(s)*
e	as *e* in th*ey*, or *ay* in s*ay*	**wàke'** [wà:-ke'] *I am going* **kenenhskwas** [ke-nénhs-kwas] *I steal*
	as *e* in m*e*t, b*e*t	**kàsere'** [kà:-se-re'] *car* **ohere** [ó-he-reh] *corn stalk*
i	as *ee* in s*ee*, or *ea* in m*ea*t	**ise** [í:-se'] *you* **owira** [o-wí:-ra'] *baby*
o	as *o* in n*o*te, p*o*ke	**okonhsa** [o-kónh-sa'] *face* **okara** [o-ká:-ra'] *story*
NASAL **en**	as a sound similar to *u* in s*u*n when pronounced through the nose.	**owenna** [o-wén:-na'] *word* **kenenhskwas** [ke-nénhs-kwas] *I steal*
on	as a sound similar to *oo* in m*oo*n when pronounced through the nose.	**orònya'** [o-ròn:-ya'] *blue* **ohonte** [ó-hon-teh] *green, grass*

Consonants	Approximate English Equivalent	Mohawk Example
OBSTRUENTS		
k	as *g* in g*ate*: when occurring between vowels, when followed by a vowel, or when occurring before a **w**	**wàke'** [wà:-ke'] *I am going* **kà:sere'** [kà:-se-re'] *car* **ikkwas** [ík-kwas] *I pick*
	as *k* in s*k*ate: when occurring before a consonant	**wakthare'** [wák-tha-re'] *I am talking* **kakhwa** [kák-hwa'] *food*
t	as *d* in *d*og: when occurring between vowels, when followed by a vowel, or when occurring before y	**tàre'** [tà:-re'] *her is coming* **akta** [ák-ta'] *near, beside* **o'tara** [o'-tá:-ra'] *clay* **atyàtawi'** [a-tyà:-ta-wi'] *coat*
	as *t* in *t*ake: when occurring before a consonant	**katstha'** [káts-tha'] *I use it* **ketshenryes** [kets-hén-ryes] *I find* **wa'kkweni'** [wa'k-kwé:-ni'] *I was able*
s	as *s* in *s*ay: when occurring before another consonant, or before a vowel	**wàkatste'** [wà:-kats-te'] *I used it* **ohsera** [óh-se-ra'] *year*
	as a soft *z* sound when occurring after a long stress (ie. see : in bracket samples)	**kàsere'** [kà:-se-re'] *car*
	as *sh* in *sh*e: when occurring before consonant y and in some dialects when occurring before vowel i	**katstahsyons** [kats-táh-syons] *I finish using* **athsyana** [at-hsyá:-na'] *a handful* **ohsìta'** [oh-sì:-ta'] *foot*
SONORANTS		
n	as *n* in *n*ow, *n*ote, *n*ever	**onen** [ó:-nenh] *now, already* **ohna** [óh-na'] *skin*

r	as an *rl* combination: in some dialects it occurs more like an *r*, while in others it may occur more like an *l*	**raksa'a** [rak-sá:-'ah] *boy* **ohere** [ó-he-reh] *corn stalk*
SEMI-VOWELS **w**	as *w* in *w*ay, *w*in. *NOTE: w will change to vowel o when it occurs between consonants*	**wahenron'** [wa-hén:-ron'] *he said* **wàke'** [wà:-ke'] *I am going* **o'wàronk** [o'-wà:-ronk] *meat*
y	as *y* in *y*et, *y*ellow *NOTE: y will change to vowel i when it occurs between consonants*	**oyente** [ó:-yen-teh] *firewood* **yehninons** [yeh-ní:-nons] *she buys* **atyàtawi'** [a-tyà:-ta-wi'] *coat*
ASPIRATES **h**	as *h* in *h*at, *h*ard	**ohere** [ó-he-reh] *corn stalk* **wahenron'** [wa-hén:-ron'] *he said*
	as a puff of air after a vowel, or directly after a consonant before a vowel	**ahta'** [áh-ta'] *shoe(s)* **wakhrorih** [wak-hró:-rih] *I did say*
GLOTTAL **'**	as a stop occurring directly after vowels	**wàkko'** [wà:k-ko'] *I picked* **o'tara** [o'-tá:-ra'] *clay, clan* **wa'tyen'** [wá'-kyen'] *I put down*

NOTE: Both the aspirate and glottal are features of the language that can be best acquired through listening and practice with a fluent speaker.

Consonants	Approximate English Equivalent	Mohawk Example
COMBINATIONS		
hw	as *wh* in *wh*ere	**onhwentsya** [on-hwén-tsya'] *earth* **kahwènkare** [ka-hwèn:-ka-reh] *snowshoes*
kh	as *c* in *c*at, *c* in *c*ow	**khekens** [khé:-kens] *I see her* **wa'khrori'** [wa'-khró:-ri'] *I told*
khw	as *qu* in *qu*een, *qu*iet	**kakhwa** [ká-khwa'] *food*
kw	should be pronounced as a *g* /gate/ plus *w* /way/ combination	**okwaho** [o-kwá-hoh] *wolf* **akwekon** [a-kwé:-konh] *all*
ky	should be pronounced as a *g* /gate/ plus *y* /yet/ combination	**wàkyen'** [wà:-kyen'] *I put down* **anokyen** [a-nó-kyen'] *muskrat*
ny	should be pronounced as a *n* /now/ plus *y* /yet/ combination	**ohnyara** [oh-nyá:-ra'] *throat* **onyare** [ó-nya-reh] *snake*
ry	each consonant should be pronounced separately: *r* as per Mohawk pronunciation, and *y* as in yet.	**wa'kathroryana'** [wa'-kat-hro-ryá:-na'] *I am going to tell about it*
sh	should be pronounced separately as a *s* /say/ plus *h* /hat/ combination.	**ohshehs** [óhs-hehs] *syrup* **enshiken'** [ens-hí:-ken' *I see him again*
sy	as *sh* in *sh*e, *sh*ow, but with more of a *sh* plus *y* combined sound.	**ohsya** [óh-sya'] *palm of the hand* **wahsyen'** [wáh-syen'] *you put down*
th	each consonant in this combination should be pronounced separately: *t* as in *t*ake, *h* as in *h*at	**wakthare'** [wák-tha-re'] *I am speaking* **thonne's** [thón:-ne'] *they are about*

tsy	this combination represents the **j** sound (a sound midway between English *j* and *ch*)	**kanàtsyonk** [ka-nà:-tsyonk] *pail* **tsyatak** [tsyá:-tak] *seven*
	when *tsy* occurs between consonants it will be represented as tsi with a sound similar to *gee*	**otsìtsya** [o-tsì:-tsya'] *flower* **otsinekwar** [o-tsí:-ne-kwar] *yellow*
tshy	this consonant combination provides a sound very similar to the English *ch* as in *church*	**wa'tshyatkahtho'** [wa'-tshyat-káh-tho'] *I saw him*
ty	each consonant in this combination should be pronounced separately: *t* as in *dog*, *y* as in *yet*	**satyen** [sá-tyen] *you sit down!* **atyàtawi'** [a-tyà:-ta-wi'] *coat*
wh	as a soft *f* sound, as pronounced by slightly touching the lower lip to the upper teeth	**ohwhare** [óh-wha-reh] *fur* **o'whahsa** [o'-wháh-sa'] *skirt*

ACCENT

The accented syllable of most verb paradigms that end with a vowel-consonant pattern: **-a'**, **-as**, **-os**, **-ons**, **-ens**, **-is**, or a consonant-s pattern: **-ts**, **-ks**, **-hs**, **-'s**, will most often occur in the second to the last (penultimate) position:

kyenthos [kyént[2]-hos[1]] *I plant*

katorats [ka-tó:[2]-rats[1]] *I hunt*

khninons [khní:[2]-nons[1]] *I buy*

Most verb paradigms that end with **-e'** or **-eh** will have the accented syllable occurring in third to the last position (anti-penultimate):

wa'katorate' [wa'-ka-tó:[3]-ra[2]-te'[1]] *I hunted*

wakhnyoteh [wák[3]-hnyo[2]-teh[1]] *I have erected it*

There are also a few rare occasions where the accent will occur in the fourth to the last syllable (pre-anti-penultimate):

wa'kataweya'te' [wa'-ka-tá:[4]-we[3]-ya'[2]-te'[1]] *I entered*

Examples of accent patterns like the one shown above will have to be dealt with and learned when they occur.

STRESS

Stress in Mohawk always coincides with accent. For every word in the language the syllable that receives the accent will also receive the stress. Stress is defined as short or long.

SHORT STRESS - will occur where the vowel receiving the accent occurs before a consonant combination:

katstha' [káts-tha'] *I use*

wakthare' [wák-tha-re'] *I am speaking*

Short stress will also occur in situations where the accented syllable precedes an h-vowel syllable combination:

káhere [ká-he-reh] *it is sitting up on*

LONG STRESS will occur where the accented syllable and the following syllable are spearated by a single consonant:

katorats [ka-tó:-rats] *I hunt*

wa'kiron' [wa'-kí:-ron'] *I said*

In cases like this the stress will have a *rising tone* quality.

FALLING TONE quality is produced when the accented syllable receiving the stress occurs directly before a **glottal**-consonant, or an **aspirate**-consonant combination.

For example:

where accented syllable with glottal ' occurs before **k**, **t**, or **s** the accented syllable will receive long stress with falling tone.

wa'kken' becomes **wàkken'** [wà:-k-ken'] *I saw it*

atya'tawi' becomes **atyàtawi'** [a-tyà:-ta-wi'] *coat, dress*

ka'sere' becomes **kàsere'** [kà:-se-re'] *car, vehicle*

where accented syllable with aspirate **h** occurs before **n**, **r**, **w**, or **y** the accented syllable will receive long stress with falling tone.

wa'kken' becomes **wàkken'** [wà:-k-ken'] *I saw it*

kanenhra becomes **kanènra** [ka-nèn:-ra'] *team, band*

ka'sere' becomes **kàsere'** [kà:-se-re'] *car, vehicle*

SOME USEFUL GRAMMAR POINTS

On the following pages provide some useful aspects of Mohawk grammar that will make it easier to use this lexicon. The pronominal prefixes, necessary to create verb paradigms, are provided as they would occur with most verbs. A brief description of the Modals is provided, as well as some handy locative suffixes suitable for most nominals.

PRONOMINAL PREFIXES

The following verb paradigms provide a brief look at the pronominal prefixes required with each of the different verb stems found in Mohawk. For convenience of recognition the pronominal prefix has been provided in full for each paradigm.

SUBJECTIVE SERIES

A-STEM

ka	kahtentyes	*I leave*
sa	sahtentyes	*you leave*
ra	rahtentyes	*he leaves*
yon	yonhtentyes	*she leaves*
wa	wahtentyes	*it leaves*
tya	tyahtentyes	*you & I leave*
yakya	yakyahtentyes	*he / she & I leave*
tsya	tsyahtentyes	*you (2) leave*
ya	yahtentyes	*they (2 males) leave*
kya	kyahtentyes	*they (2 females) leave*
tewa	tewahtentyes	*you all & I leave*
yakwa	yakwahtentyes	*they & I leave*
sewa	sewahtentyes	*you all leave*
ron	ronhtentyes	*they (males) leave*
kon	konhtentyes	*they (females) leave*

C-STEM

k	khninons	*I buy*
s	shninons	*you buy*
ra	rahninons	*he buys*
ye	yehninons	*she buys*
ka	kahninons	*it buys*
teni	tenihninons	*you & I buy*
yakeni	yakenihninons	*he / she & I buy*
seni	senihninons	*you (2) buy*

ni	nihninons	*they (2 males) buy*
keni	kenihninons	*they (2 females) buy*
—		
tewa	tewahninons	*you all & I buy*
yakwa	yakwahninons	*they & I buy*
sewa	sewahninons	*you all buy*
rati	ratihninons	*they (males) buy*
konti	kontihninons	*they (females) buy*

NOTE: The 1ˢᵗ person singular of C-Stem verbs will occur as: **k** before verb bases beginning with **h** or **y**; **ke** where the verb base begins with **n, r, w,** or glottal **'**; or **ik** in all cases where the verb base is single syllable (ie. **ikyens** *I lay something down*) and in most cases where the verb base begins with **h, t,** or **k**.

NOTE: The 2ⁿᵈ person singular of C-Stem verbs will occur as: **s** before verb bases beginning with **h, k,** or **t**; **se** where the verb base begins with **n, r, w,** or glottal **'**; or **ihs** in all cases where the verb base is single syllable (ie. **ihseks** *you eat it*); and **ts** in most cases where the verb base begins with **y**.

I-STEM

ki	kiyaks	*I shoot (a bow)*
si	siyaks	*you shoot (a bow)*
ren	renyaks	*he shoots (a bow)*
ye	yeyaks	*she shoots (a bow)*
ken	kenyaks	*it shoots (a bow)*
—		
teni	teniyaks	*you & I shoot (a bow)*
yakeni	yakeniyaks	*he / she & I shoot (a bow)*
seni	seniyaks	*you (2) shoot (a bow)*
ni	niyaks	*they (2 males) shoot (a bow)*
keni	keniyaks	*they (2 females) shoot a bow*
—		
tewen	tewenyaks	*you all & I shoot (a bow)*
yakwen	yakwenyaks	*they & I shoot (a bow)*
sewen	sewenyaks	*you all shoot (a bow)*
rati	ratiyaks	*they (males) shoot (a bow)*
konti	kontiyaks	*they (females) shoot (a bow)*

E/EN-STEM

ken	kennihtyaks	*I put around the neck*
sen	sennihtyaks	*you put around the neck*
ren	rennihtyaks	*he puts around the neck*
yen	yennihtyaks	*she puts around the neck*
wen	wennihtyaks	*it puts around the neck*
—		
tenen	tenennihtyaks	*you & I put around the neck*
yakenen	yakenennihtyaks	*he / she & I put around...*
senen	senennihtyaks	*you (2) put around the neck*
nen	nennihtyaks	*they (2 males) put around...*
kenen	kenennihtyaks	*they (2 females) put around...*
—		
tewen	tewennihtyaks	*you all & I put around...*
yakwen	yakwennityaks	*they & I put around the neck*
sewen	sewennihtyaks	*you all put around the neck*
ronnen	ronnennihtyaks	*they (males) put around...*
konnen	konnennihtyaks	*they (females) put around...*

O/ON-STEM

kon	konnis	*I make*
son	sonnis	*you make*
ron	ronnis	*he makes*
yakon	yakonnis	*she makes*
yon	yonnis	*it makes*
—		
tenon	tenonnis	*you & I make*
yakenon	yakenonnis	*he / she & I make*
senon	senonnis	*you (2) make*
non	nonnis	*they (2 males) make*
kenon	kenonnis	*they (2 females) make*

tyon	tyonnis	*you all & I put make*
yakyon	yakyonnis	*they & I make*
tsyon	tsyonnis	*you all make*
ronnon	ronnonnis	*they (males) make*
konnon	konnonnis	*they (females) make*

OBJECTIVE SERIES

A-STEM

waka	wakahtentyonh	*I have left / did leave*
sa	sahtentyonh	*you have left / did leave*
ro	rohtentyonh	*he has left / did leave*
yako	yakohtentyonh	*she has left / did leave*
yo	yohtentyonh	*it has left / did leave*
yonkya	yonkyahtentyonh	*you & I have left / did leave*
yonkya	yonkyahtentyonh	*he / she & I have left / did leave*
tsya	tsyahtentyonh	*you (2) have left / did leave*
rona	ronahtentyonh	*they (2 males) have left / did leave*
yona	yonahtentyonh	*they (2 females) have left / did leave*
yonkwa	yonkwahtentyonh	*you all & I have left / did leave*
yonkwa	yonkwahtentyonh	*they & I have left / did leave*
sewa	sewahtentyonh	*you all have left / did leave*
rona	ronahtentyonh	*they (males) have left / did leave*
yona	yonahtentyonh	*they (females) have left / did leave*

C-STEM

wak	wakhninonh	*I have bought / did buy*
sa	sahninonh	*you have bought / did buy*
ro	rohninonh	*he has bought / did buy*
yako	yakohninonh	*she has bought / did buy*
yo	yohninonh	*it has bought / did buy*

yonkeni	yonkenihninonh	*you & I have bought / did buy*
yonkeni	yonkenihninonh	*he / she & I have bought / did buy*
seni	senihninonh	*you (2) have bought / did buy*
roti	rotihninonh	*they (2 males) have bought / did buy*
yoti	yotihninonh	*they (2 females) have bought / did...*
yonkwa	yonkwahninonh	*you all & I have bought / did buy*
yonkwa	yonkwahninonh	*they & I have bought / did buy*
sewa	sewahninonh	*you all have bought / did buy*
roti	rotihninonh	*they (males) have bought / did buy*
yoti	yotihninonh	*they (females) have bought / did buy*

NOTE: The 1st person singular of C-Stem verbs occurs as: **wak** before verbs beginning with **h**, **k**, **t**, or **y**; **wake** before verb bases beginning with **n**, **r**, **w**, or glottal '.

I-STEM

waki	wakiyenh	*I did shoot / have shot a bow*
sen	senyenh	*you did shoot / have shot...*
ro	royenh	*he did shoot / have shot...*
yako	yakoyenh	*she did shoot / have shot...*
yo	yoyenh	*it did shoot / have shot...*
yonkeni	yonkeniyenh	*you & I did shoot / have...*
yonkeni	yonkeniyaks	*he / she & I did shoot /...*
seni	seniyaks	*you (2) did shoot / have...*
roti	rotiyenh	*they (2 males) did shoot /...*
yoti	yotiyenh	*they (2 females) did shoot /...*
yonkwen	yonkwenyenh	*you all & I did shoot / have..*
yonkwen	yonkwenyaks	*they & I did shoot / have...*
sewen	sewenyaks	*you all did shoot / have...*
roti	rotiyaks	*they (males) did shoot /...*
yoti	yotiyaks	*they (females) did shoot /...*

E/EN-STEM

waken	**wakennihtyenh**	*I have / did put around the neck*
sawen	**sawennihtyenh**	*you have / did put around the neck*
rawen	**rawennihtyenh**	*he have / did put around the neck*
yakawen	**yakawennihtyenh**	*she have / did put around the neck*
yawen	**yawennihtyenh**	*it have / did put around the neck*
—		
yonkenen	**yonkenennihtyenh**	*you & I have / did put around...*
yonkenen	**yonkenennihtyenh**	*he / she & I have / did put around...*
senen	**senennihtyenh**	*you (2) have / did put around the...*
ronen	**ronennihtyenh**	*they (2 males) have / did put...*
yonen	**yonennihtyenh**	*they (2 females) have / did put...*
—		
yonkwen	**yonkwennihtyenh**	*you all & I have / did put around...*
yonkwen	**yonkwennityenh**	*they & I have / did put around the...*
sewen	**sewennihtyenh**	*you all have / did put around the...*
ronen	**ronennihtyenh**	*they (males) have / did put around...*
yonen	**yonennihtyenh**	*they (females) have / did put...*

O/ON-STEM

wakon	**wakonnih**	*I have made / did make*
son	**sonnih**	*you have made / did make*
raon	**raonnih**	*he has made / did make*
yakaon	**yakaonnih**	*she has made / did make*
yaon	**yaonnih**	*it has made / did make*
—		
yonkenon	**yonkenonnih**	*you & I have made / did make*
yonkenon	**yonkenonnih**	*he / she & I have made / did make*
senon	**senonnih**	*you (2) have made / did make*
ronon	**rononnih**	*they (2 males) have made / did make*
yonon	**yononnih**	*they (2 females) have made / did...*

yonkyon	yonkyonnih	*you all & I put have made / did...*
yonkyon	yonkyonnih	*they & I have made / did make*
tsyon	tsyonnih	*you all have made / did make*
ronon	rononnih	*they (males) have made / did make*
yonon	yononnih	*they (females) have made / did make*

TRANSITIVE SERIES

A-STEM

konya-	konyathroris	*I tell about you*
kwa-	kwathroris	*I tell about you (all)*
riya-	riyathroris	*I tell about him*
kheya-	kheyathroris	*I tell about her / them*
takwa-	takwathroris	*you tell about me / us*
etsheya-	etsheyathroris	*you tell about him*
sheya-	sheyathroris	*you tell about her / them*
rakwa-	rakwathroris	*he tells about me*
shonkwa-	shonkwathroris	*he tells about us*
ya-	yathroris	*he tells about you*
ro-	rothroris	*he tells about him*
shako-	shakothroris	*he tells about her / them*
yonkwa-	yonkwathroris	*she / they tell(s) about me*
yonkhiya-	yonkhiyathroris	*she / they tell(s) about us*
yesa-	yesathroris	*she / they tell(s) about you*
ronwa-	ronwathroris	*she / they tell(s) about him*
yontata-	yontatathroris	*she / they tell(s) about her*
ronwana-	ronwanathroris	*she / they tell(s) about them*

kon-	konhroris	*I tell you*
kwa-	kwahroris	*I tell you (all)*
ri-	rihroris	*I tell him*
khe-	khehroris	*I tell her / them*
—		
tak(e)-	takhroris	*you tell me*
takwa-	takwahroris	*you tell us*
ets(he)-	etshroris	*you tell him*
she-	shehroris	*you tell her / them*
—		
rak(e)-	rakhroris	*he tells me*
shonkwa-	shonkwahroris	*he tells us*
ya-	yahroris	*he tells you*
ro-	rohroris	*he tells him*
shako-	shakohroris	*he tells her / them*
—		
yonk(e)-	yonkhroris	*she / they tell(s) me*
yonkhi-	yonkhihroris	*she / they tell(s) us*
yesa-	yesathroris	*she / they tell(s) you*
ronwa-	ronwahroris	*she / they tell(s) him*
yontat(e)-	yontathroris	*she / they tell(s) her*
ronwati-	ronwatihroris	*she / they tell(s) them*

MODALS

USING THE AORIST

RULES DETERMINING SHAPE OF AORIST MODAL PREFIX:

    wa'-   before pronominals beginning with **k**, **y** (the **y** is deleted)

    wa-   before **h** (where it is the result of masculine pronominals beginning with **r** changing to **h**)

wah-	before 1st person pronominal **ihs / s / se**, and before 3rd person Dual masculine **n(i)-** or **y(a)-**.	
we-	before pronominals beginning with **t**, and 2rd person Dual / Plural in the Subjective series, and all 2nd person pronominals in the Objective series.	
on-	before pronominals beginning with **w**	

AORIST with C-Stem verb bases that begin with **k, t, n, w, y, h** or glottal **'**.

wa'k	**wa'khninon'**	*I bought*
wa'ke *(before verb bases beginning with n, w, or glottal '.)*		
wahs	**wahshninon'**	*you bought*
wahse *(before verb bases beginning with n, w, or glottal '.)*		
wat- *(before verb bases that begin with hs.)*		
waha	**wahahninon'**	*he bought*
wa'e	**wa'ehninon'**	*she bought*
wa'ka	**wa'kahninon'**	*it/IT bought*

weteni	**wetenihninon'**	*we bought*
wa'akeni	**wa'akenihninon'**	*we bought*
weseni	**wesenihninon'**	*you bought*
wahni	**wahnihninon'**	*they bought*
wa'keni	**wa'kenihninon'**	*they bought*

wetewa	**wetewahninon'**	*we bought*
wa'akwa	**wa'akwahninon'**	*we bought*
wesewa	**wesewahninon'**	*you bought*
wahati	**wahatihninon'**	*they bought*
wa'konti	**wa'kontihninon'**	*they bought*

AORIST with A-Stem verb bases (that begin with **a**.

wa'ka	**wa'kahtenti'**	*I left*
wehsa	**wehsahtenti'**	*you left*
waha	**wahahtenti'**	*he left*
wa'on	**wa'onhtenti'**	*she left*
on	**onhtenti'**	*it/IT left*

wetya	wetyahtenti'	*we left*
wa'akya	wa'akyahtenti'	*we left*
wetsya	wetsyahtenti'	*you left*
wahya	wahyahtenti'	*they left*
wa'kya	wa'kyahtenti'	*they left*
— wetewa	wetewahtenti'	*we left*
wa'akwa	wa'akwahtenti'	*we left*
wesewa	wesewahtenti'	*you left*
wahon	wahonhtenti'	*they left*
wa'kon	wa'konhtenti'	*they left*

USING THE FUTURE

RULES DETERMINING SHAPE OF FUTURE MODAL PREFIX:

en   before pronominals beginning with **k**, **y**, and **h** (the result of masculine pronominals beginning with **r** changing to **h**); before pronominals beginning with **t**, and 2nd person Dual and Plural in the Subjective series, and all 2nd person pronominals in the Objective series; before pronominals beginning with **w**

enh   before 1st person pronominal **ihs** / **s** / **se**, and before 3rd person Dual masculine **n(a)-** or **y(a)-**.

FUTURE with C-Stem verb bases that begin with **k**, **t**, **n**, **w**, **y**, **h** or glottal '.

enk	**enkhninon'**	*I will buy*
enke *(before verb bases beginning with n, w, or glottal '.)*		
enhs	**enhshninon'**	*you will buy*
enhse *(before verb bases beginning with n, w, or glottal '.)*		
ent- *(before verb bases that begin with hs.)*		
enha	**enhahninon'**	*he will buy*
enye	**enyehninon'**	*she will buy*
enka	**enkahninon'**	*it/IT will buy*
— **enteni**	**entenihninon'**	*we will buy*
enyakeni	**enyakenihninon'**	*we will buy*
enseni	**ensenihninon'**	*you will buy*

er̀·ni	enhnihninon'	*they will buy*
e: ·ni	enkenihninon'	*they will buy*
ei ·wa	entewahninon'	*we will buy*
enyakwa	enyakwahninon'	*we will buy*
ensewa	ensewahninon'	*you will buy*
enhati	enhatihninon'	*they will buy*
enkonti	enkontihninon'	*they will buy*

FUTURE with A-Stem verb bases (that begin with **a**.

enka	enkahtenti'	*I will leave*
enhsa	enhsahtenti'	*you will leave*
enha	enhahtenti'	*he will leave*
enyon	enyonhtenti'	*she will leave*
enwa	enwahtenti'	*it/IT will leave*
entya	entyahtenti'	*we will leave*
enyakya	enyakyahtenti'	*we will leave*
entsya	entsyahtenti'	*you will leave*
enhya	enhyahtenti'	*they will leave*
enkya	enkyahtenti'	*they will leave*
entewa	entewahtenti'	*we will leave*
enyakwa	enyakwahtenti'	*we will leave*
ensewa	ensewahtenti'	*you will leave*
enhon	enhonhtenti'	*they will leave*
enkon	enkonhtenti'	*they will leave*

USING THE NON-DEFINITE

RULES DETERMINING SHAPE OF NON-DEFINITE MODAL PREFIX:

a   before pronominals beginning with **k, y,** and **h** (where it is the result of masculine pronominals beginning with **r** changing to **h**)

ah   before 1st person pronominal **ihs / s / se**, and before 3rd person Dual masculine **n(a)-** or **y(a)-**.

ae	before pronominals beginning with **t**, and before 2rd person Dual and Plural in the Subjective series, and all 2nd person pronominals in the Objective series.		
aon	before pronominals beginning with **w**		

NON-DEFINITE with C-Stem verb bases that begin with **k, t, n, w, y, h** or glottal ’.

ak	**akhninon’**		*I would buy*
	ake *(before verb bases beginning with n, w, or glottal ’.)*		
ahs	**ahshninon’**		*you would buy*
	ahse *(before verb bases beginning with n, w, or glottal ’.)*		
	at- *(before verb bases that begin with hs.)*		
aha	**ahahninon’**		*he would buy*
aye	**ayehninon’**		*she would buy*
aka	**akahninon’**		*it/IT would buy*
— **aeteni**	**aetenihninon’**		*we would buy*
ayakeni	**ayakenihninon’**		*we would buy*
aeseni	**aesenihninon’**		*you would buy*
ahni	**ahnihninon’**		*they would buy*
akeni	**akenihninon’**		*they would buy*
—			
aetewa	**aetewahninon’**		*we would buy*
ayakwa	**ayakwahninon’**		*we would buy*
aesewa	**aesewahninon’**		*you would buy*
ahati	**ahatihninon’**		*they would buy*
akonti	**akontihninon’**		*they would buy*

NON-DEFINITE with A-Stem verb bases (that begin with **a.**

aka	**akahtenti’**		*I would leave*
ahsa	**ahsahtenti’**		*you would leave*
aha	**ahahtenti’**		*he would leave*
ayon	**ayonhtenti’**		*she would leave*
aon	**aonhtenti’**		*it/IT would leave*
— **aetya**	**aetyahtenti’**		*we would leave*
ayakya	**ayakyahtenti’**		*we would leave*
aetsya	**aetsyahtenti’**		*you would leave*
ahya	**ahyahtenti’**		*they would leave*
akya	**akyahtenti’**		*they would leave*

aetewa	aetewahtenti'	*we would leave*
ayakwa	ayakwahtenti'	*we would leave*
aesewa	aesewahtenti'	*you would leave*
ahon	ahonhtenti'	*they would leave*
akon	akonhtenti'	*they would leave*

PLURALS

The are three possible plural suffixes that can accompany most Mohawk nominals. The plural form that one uses must indicate the animate or inanimate nature of the nominal. In many cases it is also possible to indicate an *alike* or *different* aspect of the plural.

a) WITH ANIMATE NOMINALS

erhar *dog*	+	okonha	→	erharhokonha	*dogs*
raksa *boy*	+	okonha	→	ratiksa'okonha	*boys*

b) WITH INANIMATE NOMINALS

kahyatonhsera *book*	+	okon	→	kahyatonhsera'okonh	*books*
kanata *town*	+	okon	→	kanata'okon	*towns*

c) INDICATING DIFFERENCE - With Animate / Inanimate nominals

kahyatonhsera *book*	+	hson'a	→	kahyatonhserahson'a	*books*
erhar *dog*	+	hson'a	→	erharhson'a	*dogs*

LOCATIVES

a) WITH NOMINALS

kanonhsa *house*	+	-àke	→	kanonhsàke	*on the house*
	+	-akon	→	kanonhsakon	*in the house*
	+	-òkon	→	kanonhsòkon	*under the house*
	+	-akta	→	kanonhsakta	*near the house*

a) WITH PLURALS

kanonhsa *house*	+	-a'kehson	→	kanonhsa'kehson	*on the houses*
	+	-akonhson	→	kanonhsakonhson	*in the houses*
	+	-o'konhson	→	kanonhso'konhson	*under the houses*
	+	-aktanyon	→	kanonhsaktanyon	*near the houses*

POSSESSIVES

WITH A-STEM NOMINALS		WITH C-STEM NOMINALS	
akwa-	akwahta' *my coat*	ake-	akenonhsa *my house*
sa-	sahta' *your coat*	sa-	sanonhsa *your house*
rao-	raohta' *his coat*	rao-	raononhsa *his house*
akao-	akaohta' *her coat*	akao-	akaononhsa *her house*
ao-	aohta' *its coat*	ao-	aononhsa *its house*
onkwa-	onkwahtahkwa'okon *our coats*	onkwa-	onkwanonhsa *our house*
raona-	raonahtahkwa'okon *their coats (M)*	raoti-	raotinonhsa *their house (M)*
aona-	aonahtahkwa'okon *their coats (F)*	aoti-	aotinonhsa *their house (F)*

POSSESSIVES WITH LOCATIVES

ÀKE *on* WITH A-STEM NOMINALS

akwahta'	*with àke*	*becomes*	akwatya'tawi'tsheràke *on my coat*
sahta'	*with àke*	*becomes*	satya'tawi'tsheràke *on your coat*
raohta'	*with àke*	*becomes*	raotya'tawi'tsheràke *on his coat*
akaohta'	*with àke*	*becomes*	akaotya'tawi'tsheràke *on her coat*
aohta'	*with àke*	*becomes*	aotya'tawi'tsheràke *on its coat*

onkwahtahkwa'okon	*with àke*	*becomes*	onkwatya'tawi'tshera'kehson *on our coats*
raonahtahkwa'okon	*with àke*	*becomes*	raonatya'tawi'tshera'kehson *on their coats*
aonahtahkwa'okon	*with àke*	*becomes*	aonatya'tawi'tshera'kehson *on their coats*

ÀKE *on* WITH C-STEM NOMINALS

akenonhsa	*with àke*	*becomes*	akenonhsàke *on my house*
sanonhsa	*with àke*	*becomes*	sanonhsàke *on your house*
raononhsa	*with àke*	*becomes*	raononhsàke *on his house*
akaononhsa	*with àke*	*becomes*	akaononhsàke *on her house*
aononhsa	*with àke*	*becomes*	aononhsàke *on its house*

onkwanonhsa	*with àke*	*becomes*	onkwanonhsa'kehson *on our house*
raotinonhsa	*with àke*	*becomes*	raotinonhsa'kehson *on their house*
aotinonhsa	*with àke*	*becomes*	aotinonhsa'kehson *on their house*

AKON *in* WITH A-STEM NOMINALS

akwahta'	*with **akon***	*becomes*	**akwatya'tawi'tsherakon**	*in my coat*
sahta'	*with **akon***	*becomes*	**satya'tawi'tsherakon**	*in your coat*
raohta'	*with **akon***	*becomes*	**raotya'tawi'tsherakon**	*in his coat*
akaohta'	*with **akon***	*becomes*	**akaotya'tawi'tsherakon**	*in her coat*
aohta'	*with **akon***	*becomes*	**aotya'tawi'tsherakon**	*in its coat*

onkwahtahkwa'akon	*with **akon***	*becomes*	**onkwatya'tawi'tsherakonhson**	*in our coats*
raonahtahkwa'akon	*with **akon***	*becomes*	**raonatya'tawi'tsherakonhson**	*in their coats*
aonahtahkwa'akon	*with **akon***	*becomes*	**aonatya'tawi'tsherakonhson**	*in their coats*

WITH C-STEM NOMINALS

akenonhsa	*with **akon***	*becomes*	**akenonhsakon**	*in my house*
sanonhsa	*with **akon***	*becomes*	**sanonhsakon**	*in your house*
raononhsa	*with **akon***	*becomes*	**raononhsakon**	*in his house*
akaononhsa	*with **akon***	*becomes*	**akaononhsakon**	*in her house*
aononhsa	*with **akon***	*becomes*	**aononhsakon**	*in its house*

onkwanonhsa	*with **akon***	*becomes*	**onkwanonhsakonhson**	*in our house*
raotinonhsa	*with **akon***	*becomes*	**raotinonhsakonhson**	*in their house*
aotinonhsa	*with **akon***	*becomes*	**aotinonhsakonhson**	*in their house*

MOHAWK - ENGLISH

WORD LIST

A

1 **a'are** [á:-'a-reh] *a net;*
    akwa'are [akwá:-'a-reh] *my net;* **sa'are** [sá:-'a-reh] *your net;* **rao'are** [ra-ó:-'a-reh] *his net;* **akao'are** [a-ka-ó:-'a-reh] *her net;* **onkwa'are** [on-kwá:-'a-reh] *our net.* **wa'arakon** [wa-'á:-ra-konh] *in the net.* **ka'aronnis** [ka'-a-rón:-nis] *I make a net;*

2 **a'enna** [a'-én:-na'] *a bow;*
    akwa'enna [a-kwa'-én:-na'] *my bow;* **sa'enna** [sa'-én:-na'] *your bow;* **rao'enna** [ra-o'-én:-na'] *his bow;* **akao'enna** [a-ka-o'-én:-na'] *her bow;* **raona'enna'okon** [ra-o-na'-en-na'-ó:-konh] *their bows.* **akwa'ennàke** [a-kwa'-en-nà:-keh] *on my bow.* **waka'ennayen'** [wa-ka'-én:-na-yen'] *I have a bow.*

3 **a'eren** [a'-é:-ren'] *away off; far away*
    ie. **A'eren niyahare'.** [A'-é:-renh ni-ya-há:-re'] *He went away off (somewhere);* **A'eren ya'akoti'.** [A-é:-ren' ya'-a-kó:-ti'] *She threw it far away.*

4 **a'nowara** [a'-nó:-wa-ra'] *a turtle*

5 **a'nyanawen'** [a'-nyá:-na-wen'] *mitts, mittens; gloves*
    akwa'nyanawen' [a-kwa'-nyá:-na-wen'] *my mitts;* **sa'nyanawen'** [sa'-nyá:-na-wen'] *your mitts;* **rao'nyanawen'** [ra-o'-nyá:-na-wen'] *his mitts;* **akao'nyanawen'** [a-ka-o'-nyá:-na-wen'] *her mitts;* **aona'nyanawen'okon** [a-o-na'-nyá:-na-wen'-ó:-konh] *their mitts.* **akwa'nyanawen'tsheràke** [a-kwa'-nya-na-wen'-tshe-rà:-keh] *on my mitts;* **rao'nyanawen'tsherakon** [a-kwa'-nya-na-wen'-tshe-rá:-konh] *in his mitts.* **kata'nyanawenks** [ka-ta'-nyá-na-wenks] *I put on my mitts;* **kata'nyanawenkhsyons** [ka-ta'-nya-na-wén'k-hsyons] *I take off my mitts.*

6 **a'sehson'a** [a'-seh-són:-'ah] *vegetables*

7 **ahkwennya'** [ah-kwén-nya'] *clothes, clothing*
    akwahkwennya' [a-kwah-kwén-nya'] *my clothes;* **sahkwennya'** [sah-kwén-nya'] *your clothes;* **raohkwennya'** [ra-oh-kwén-nya'] *his clothes;* **akaohkwennya'** [a-ka-oh-kwén-nya'] *her clothes;* **aonahkwennya'okon** [a-o-nah-kwén-nya'-ó:-konh] *their clothes.* **akwahkwennya'tsheràke** [a-kwah-kwen-nya'-tshe-rà:-keh] *on my clothes;* **raohkwennya'tsherakon** [a-kwah-kwen-nya'-tshe-rá:-konh] *in his clothes.* **katahkwennyaks** [ka-tah-kwén-nyaks] *I put on my clothes;* **katahkwennyahsyons** [ka-tah-kwen-nyáh-hsyons] *I take off my clothes.*

8 **ahkwesen** [ah-kwé:-sen'] *a partridge*

9 **ahse'ken** [ah-se'-kén:] *because*

10 **ahsen** [áh-senh] *three*

ahsen nikahyatonhserake [áh-sen' ni-ka-hya-tonh-se-rá:-keh] *three books.*
ahsen nikon [áh-sen' ní;-konh] *three (of them)*; **ahsen nikon ne kahyatonhsera'okon** [áh-sen' ní:-konh ne ka-hya-tonh-se-ra'-ó:-konh] *three of the books.* **ahsen nihati** [áh-sen' ni-há:-tih] *three of them (males)*; **ahsen nihati ne rononkwe** [áh-sen' ni-há:-tih ne ro-nón:-kwe'] *three of the men.* **ahsen nikonti** [áh-sen' ni-kón:-tih] *three of them (female)*; **ahsen nikonti ne kononkwe** [áh-sen' ni-kón:-tih ne ko-nón:-kwe'] *three of the women*; **ahsen nikonti ne erhar** [áh-sen' ni-kón:-tih ne erhar] *three of the dogs.* **Ahsen niwakyen'** [áh-sen' ni-wák-yen'] *I have three*; **Ahsen niwakhyatonhserayen'** [áh-sen' ni-wak-hya-tonh-se-rá-yen'] *I have three books.*

11 **Ahsenhatont** [Ah-sén-ha-tont] *Wednesday*

ie. **shiWahsenhaton'kenha** [shi-Wah-sen-ha-ton'-kén-ha'] *last Wednesday;* **Ahsenhatont nen' ne'e onwa kenh wenhniserate.** [...nen' né:-'eh ón:-wah kenh wenh-ni-se-rá:-teh] *Today is Wednesday;* **Ahsenhatont nen' ne'e thetenre.** [...nen' né:-'eh t-he-tén:-reh] *Yesterday was Wednesday;* **Ahsenhatont nen' ne'e enyorhenne'.** [...nen' né:-'eh en-yór-hen'-ne'] *Tomorrow is Wednesday.*

12 **ahseriye'** [ah-se-rí:-ye'] *a string, rope, thread*

Oh niwahseriye'tòten'. [Oh ni-wah-se-ri-ye'-tò:-ten'] *What kind of rope, string, thread is it?* **niwahseriye'ta'ah** [ni-wah-se-ri-ye'-tá:-'ah] *a short rope;* **wahseriyètehs** [wah-se-ri-yè:-tehs] *a long rope.* **kahseriye'tonnis** [kah-se-ri-ye'-tón:-nis] *I make rope.*

13 **ahsìkwara** [ah-sì:-kwa-rà'] *a spear*

ie. **Wakahsikwaroya'ke'.** [Wa'-kah-si-kwa-ró:-ya'-ke'] *I threw a spear (at it).*

14 **ahsikwe** [áh-si-kweh] *a fork*

akwahsikwe [a-kwáh-si-kweh] *my fork;* **sahsikwe** [sáh-si-kweh] *your fork;* **raohsikwe** [ra-óh-si-kweh] *his fork;* **akaohsikwe** [a-ka-óh-si-kweh] *her fork;* **raonahsikwe'okon** [ra-o-nah-si-kwe'-ó:-konh] *their forks.* **akwahsikwàke** [a-kwah-si-kwà:-keh] *on my fork.* **Oh niwahsikòten'.** [Oh ni-wah-si-kò:-ten'] *What kind of fork is it?* **wahsikowanen** [wah-si-ko-wá:-nenh] *a big fork;* **niwahsikwa'ah** [ni-wah-si-kwá:-'ah] *a small fork.* **wakahsikwayen'** [wa-kah-sí-kwa-yen'] *I have a fork.*

15 **ahsire** [áh-si-reh] *a blanket*

akwahsire [a-kwáh-si-reh] *my blanket;* **sahsire** [sáh-si-reh] *your blanket;* **raohsire** [ra-óh-si-reh] *his blanket;* **akaohsire** [a-ka-óh-si-reh] *her blanket;* **raonahsire'okon** [ra-o-nah-si-re'-ó:-konh] *their blankets.* **akwahsiràke** [a-kwah-si-rà:-keh] *on my blanket.* **Oh niwahsiròten'.** [Oh ni-wah-si-rò:-ten'] *What kind of blanket is it?* **wahsirowanen** [wah-si-ro-wá:-nenh] *a big blanket;*

niwahsira'ah [ni-wah-si-rá:-'ah] *a small blanket*; **yohsirahnetska** [yoh-si-rah-néts-ka'] *a soft blanket*. **wakahsirayen'** [wa-kah-sí-kwa-yen'] *I have a blanket*.

16 **ahskwa** [áhs-kwa'] *a roof*
ahskwàke [ahs-kwà:-keh] *on the roof*; ie. **Ahskwàke tkahere**. [...tká-he-reh] *it is there on the roof*;

17 **ahsohkwa** [ah-sóh-kwa'] *dye; colouring*.
Oh niwahsohkòten. [Oh ni-wah-soh-ko-ten'] *What colour is it?*
Onekwenhtara niwahsohkòten. [O-ne-kwénh-ta-ra' ni-wah-soh-kò:-ten'] *It is red (in colour)*. **Wa'tewathsohkwateni'** .

18 **ahsonhta** [ah-sónh-ta'] *a wall*
ahsonhtàke [ah-sonh-tà:-keh] *on the wall*; ie. **Ahsonhtàke tyohrènton** [...tyo-hrèn:-ton'] *it is hanging on the wall*. **ihsi nonhsonhtati** [íh-si' nonh-sónh-ta-tih] *on the other side of the wall*; **karo nonhsonhtati** [ká-ro' nonh-sónh-ta-tih] *on this side of the wall*; **kahsonhtotha'** [kah-sonh-tót-ha'] *I erect a wall*; **kahsonhtotakwas** [kah-sonh-to-tá-kwas] *I take down a wall*.

19 **ahsonthen** [ah-sónt-henh] *midnight*

20 **ahsonthènne'** [ah-sont-hèn:-ne'] *night-time; at night*
ie. **Eso nikonti ne kontirio kontorats ahsonthènne'.** [É:-soh ni-kón:-tih ne kon-tí:-ri-o' kon-tó:-rats ne ah-sont-hèn:-ne'] *Many animals hunt at night*.

21 **ahstawen** [ah-stá:-wen'] *a rattle*
ie. **Kahstawens.** [Kahs-tá:-wens] *I use a rattle; shake a rattle*.

22 **ahta'** [áh-ta'] *a shoe, shoes, footware*
WITH POSSESSIVES: **akwahta'** [a-kwáh-ta'] *my shoe(s)*; **sahta'** [sáh-ta'] *your shoe(s)*; **raohta'** [ra-óh-ta'] *his shoe(s)*; **akaohta'** [a-ka-óh-ta'] *her shoe(s)*; **aonahtahkwa'okon** [a-o-nah-tah-ó:-konh] *their shoes*. WITH LOCATIVES: **akwahtahkàke** [a-kwah-tah-kà:-keh] *on my shoe(s)*; **raohtahkwakon** [ra-oh-táh-kwa-konh] *in his shoe(s)*. WITH ADJECTIVALS: **wahtahkwakayon** [wah-tah-kwa-ká:-yon'] *old shoe(s)*; **wahtahkwaràse** [wah-tah-kwa-rà:-seh] *new shoe(s)*; **wahtahkwiyo** [wah-tah-kwí:-yoh] *good shoe(s)*. WITH VERBIALS: **Oh nihsahtahkòten'** [Oh nih-sah-tah-kò:-ten'] *What kind of shoe(s) do you have?* **tekarahtaryons** [te-ka-rah-tá-ryons] *I put on my shoe(s)*; **kerahtaryonkwas** [ke-rah-ta-ryón-kwas] *I take off my shoe(s)*.

23 **ahtahkwa'onwe** [ah-tah-kwa'-ón:-weh] *a moccasin(s), traditional footware*
See: **ahta'** *shoe(s), footwear*

24 **ahtatshera** [ah-táts-he-ra'] *a quiver (for arrows)*
WITH POSSESSIVES: **akwahtathsera** [a-kwah-táts-he-ra'] *my quiver*; **sahtatshera** [sah-táts-he-ra'] *your quiver*; **raohtatshera** [ra-oh-táts-he-ra'] *his*

3

quiver, **akaohtatshera** [a-ka-oh-tát-he-ra'] *her quiver*. WITH LOCATIVES:
akwahtatsherakon [a-kwah-tats-he-rá:-konh] *in my quiver*, **akwahtatsheràke**
[a-kwah-tats-he-rà:-keh] *on my quiver*.

25 **akaonha** [a-ká-on-ha'] *she, her (Free Pronoun)*
   Onhka ne'e ne akaonha [Ónh-ka' né:-'eh na-ká-on-ha'] *Who is she?*
   Akaonha ne'e ne sahtsi'a. [A-ká-on-ha' né:-'eh neh sah-tsí:-'ah] *She is your
   sister.*

26 **akaratsi** [a-ká:-ra-tsih] *an elm tree*

27 **ake'nihstenha** [a-ke'-nihs-tén-ha'] *my mother*
   See also: **sa'nihstenha** [sa'-nih-stén-ha'] *your mother*, **ro'nihstenha** [ro'-nih-
   stén-ha'] *his mother*; ie. **Sewatis ro'nihstenha** *John's mother*, **ako'nihstenha**
   [a-ko'-nih-stén-ha'] *her mother*; ie. **Wari ako'nihstenha** *Mary's mother*,
   o'nihstenha [o'-nih-stén-ha'] *it's mother*, **onkwa'nihstenha** [on-kwa'-nih-
   stén-ha'] *our mother*, **raoti'nihstenha** [ra-o-ti'-nih-stén-ha'] *their mother*,
   raoti'nihsten'okonha [ra-o-ti'-nih-sten'-o-kón-ha'] *their mothers*;

28 **akenhake'** [a-kén-ha-ke'] *it / there would be; for it / there to be*
   ie. **Skennen akenhake'.** [Skén:-nenh a-kén-ha-ke'] *There would be peace.* See
   iken' *it is (indeed)*

29 **akennha'kène** [a-kenn-ha'-kè:-neh] *in the summer*
   ie. **Akennha'kène tyotkon yakwatawenhe's.** [...tyót-kon ya-kwa-ta-wén-
   he's] *We always go swimming in the summer.*

30 **akèra** [a-kè:-ra'] *a plate*

31 **akhsotha** [ak-hsót-ha'] *my grandmother*
   sahsotha [sah-sót-ha'] *your grandmother*, **rohsotha** [roh-sót-ha'] *his grandmother*;
   ie. **Sewatis rohsotha** *John's grandmother*, **akohsotha** [a-koh-sót-ha'] *her
   grandmother*; ie. **Wari akohsotha** *Mary's grandmother*, **onkwahsotha** [on-kwah-
   sót-ha'] *our grandmother*, **rotihsotha** [ro-tih-sót-ha'] *their grandmother*,
   roti'nihsothokonha [ro-tih-sot-ho-kón-ha'] *their grandmothers*;

32 **ako'nihstenha** [a-ko'-nihs-tén-ha'] *her mother* (See: **ake'nihstenha** *my mother.*)

33 **akohsotha** [a-koh-sót-ha'] *her grandmother* (See: **akhsotha** *my grandmother.*)

34 **akohtsi'a** [a-koh-tsí:-'ah] *her older sister* (See: **aktsi'a** *my older sister.*)

35 **akokstenha** [a-kok-stén-ha'] *an old woman*
   ne akokstenha [na-koks-tén-ha'] *the old woman*; **kiken' akokstenha** [kí:-
   ken'...] *this old woman*; **thiken' akokstenha** [thí:-ken'...] *that old woman*;
   Onhka nen' ne'e thiken' akokstenha [Ónh-ka' nen' né:-'eh...] *Who is that old
   woman?* **tekenikstenha** [te-ke-niks-tén-ha] *two old women*; **kontiksten'okonha**
   [kon-tiks-ten'-o-kón-ha'] *old women.*

36 **aktsi'a** [ak-tsí:-'ah] *my older sister*
   sahtsi'a [sah-tsí:-'ah] *your older sister;* **rohtsi'a** [roh-tsí:-'ah] *his older sister;*
   ie. **Sewatis rohtsi'a** *John's older sister;* **akohtsi'a** [a-koh-tsí:-'ah] *her older sister;*
   ie. **Wari akohtsi'a** *Mary's older sister;* **onkwahtsi'a** [on-kwah-tsí:-'ah] *our older
   sister;* **rotihtsi'a** [ra-o-tih-tsí:-'ah] *their older sister;* **rotihtsi'okonha** [ro-tih-
   tsi'-o-kón-ha'] *their older sisters;*

37 **akwah** [a-kwáh] *quite; very; just*

   a) **akwah iken' tsi** [kwah í:-ken' tsi] *very*
      ie. **Akwah iken' tsi kowanen.** [...ko-wá:-nenh] *It is very big.*

   b) **akwah ken' nahe'a** [a-kwah ken' na-hé:-'ah] *shortly (ie. time)*
      ie. **Akwah ken' nahe'a tontahahtenti'.** [...ton-ta-hah-tén:-ti'] *He returned
      shortly.*

   c) **akwah ken' nikarìwehs** [a-kwah ken' ni-ka-rì:-wehs] *quite a long time*
      ie. **Akwah ken' nikarìwehs yakohtentyonh.** [...ya-koh-tén-tyonh] *She's
      been gone quite a long time.*

   d) **akwah ken' niyore** [kwah ken' ni-yó:-reh] *quite a ways*
      ie. **Akwah ken' niyore yahothenno'tsheronti'.** [...ya-hot-hen-no'ts-he-
      rón:-ti'] *He threw the ball quite a ways.*

   e) **akwah ken' niyore'a** [akwah ken' ni-yo-ré:-'ah] *just a little ways*
      ie. **Akwah ken' niyore'a ya'akonenyonti'.** [...ya'-a-ko-nen-yón:-ti'] *She
      threw the stone just a little ways.*

   f) **akwah ken' niyohsnore tsi** [tsi ni-yoh-snó:-reh tsi] *just as fast as*
      ie. **Wa'tharahtate' akwah ken' niyohsnore tsi wahakweni'.** [Wa'-t-ha-
      ráh-ta-te'...wa-ha-kwé:-ni'] *He ran just as fast as he could (was able to).*

   g) **akwah ne ok ne** [a-kwah nék neh] *just only*
      ie. **Akwah ne ok ne kiken' wakhninonh.** [...wak-hní:-nonh] *I bought just
      only this (thing).*

   h) **akwah oksa ok** [akwah ók-sa' ok] *just as quick*
      ie. **Akwah oksa ok wa'thatahtsi'.** [...wa'-t-ha-táh-tsi'] *He jumped up just as
      quick.*

   i) **akwah tsi** [kwáh tsi] *quite*
      ie. **Akwah tsi niwa'ah.** [...ni-wá:-'ah] *It's quite small.*

   j) **akwah tsi ok nahòten** [a-kwah tsyok na-hò:-ten'] *everything*
      ie. **Akwah tsi ok nahòten wahonneke' thiken' rononkwe.** [...wa-hón:-
      ne-ke' thí:-ken' ro-nón:-kwe'] *Those men ate everything.*

k) **akwah tsi ok nonwe** [akwah tsyok nón:-weh] *everywhere*
ie. **Akwah tsi ok nonwe yewakesakon ne akwatyàtawi'.** [...ye-wa-ke-sá:-konh na-kwa-tyà:-ta-wi'] *I looked everywhere for my coat.*

38 **akwekon** [a-kwé:-konh] *all; everything; the whole thing*
akwekon ne eksa'okonha [a-kwé:-konh ne ek-sa'-o-kón-ha'] *all of the children;*
akwekon ne katshe'ta'okon [a-kwé:-konh ne kats-he'-ta-ó:-konh] *all of the bottles.* **Akwekon wakhninonh.** [A-kwé:-konh wak-hní:-nonh] *I bought all of it.*

39 **akweks** [á-kweks] *an eagle*

40 **akya'tasetshera** [a-kya'-ta-séts-he-ra'] *my girl friend*
ie. **saya'tasetshera** [sa-ya'-ta-séts-he-ra'] *your girl friend;* **raoya'tasetshera** [ra-o-ya'-ta-séts-he-ra'] *his girl friend;* **raotiya'tasetshera'okonha** [ra-o-ti-ya'-ta-sets-he-ra'-o-kón-ha'] *their girl friends.*

41 **anèntaks** [a-nèn:-taks] *porcupine*

42 **anihsnonhsawi'** [a-nih-snónh-sa-wi'] *a ring*
WITH POSSESSIVES: **akwanihsnonhsawi'** [a-kwa-nih-snónh-sa-wi'] *my ring;*
sanihsnonhsawi' [sa-nih-snónh-sa-wi'] *your ring;* **raonihsnonhsawi'** [ra-o-nih-snónh-sa-wi'] *his ring;* **akaonihsnonhsawi'** [a-ka-o-nih-snónh-sa-wi'] *her ring;* **raonanihsnonhsawi'tshera'okon** [ra-o-na-nih-snonh-sa-wi'ts-he-ra'-ó:-konh] *their rings.* WITH LOCATIVES: **akwanihsnonhsawi'tsheràke** [a-kwa-nih-snonh-sa-wi'ts-he-rà:-keh] *on my ring.* WITH VERBS: **kanihsnonhsawìtha'** [ka-nih-snonh-sa-wì:-t-ha'] *I put on a ring;* **kanihsnonhsawi'tahsyons** [ka-nih-snonh-sa-wi'-táh-syonhs] *I take off a ring.*

43 **anìtas** [a-nì:-tas] *a skunk*

44 **anókyen** [a-nó-kyen'] *a muskrat*

45 **Anonhwarori** [A-non-hwa-ró:-rih] *the Mid-Winter festival*

46 **anonk** [á:-nonk] onions (cooking onions)

47 **anonkshera** [a-nónks-he-ra'] *green onions*

48 **anònwarore'** [a-nòn:-wa-ro-re'] *a hat, bonnet...*
akwanònwarore' [a-kwa-nòn-wa-ro-re'] *my hat;* **sanònwarore'** [sa-nòn-wa-ro-re'] *your hat;* **raonònwarore'** [ra-o-nòn-wa-ro-re'] *his hat;* **akaonònwarore'** [a-ka-o-nòn-wa-ro-re'] *her hat;* **raonanònwarore'okon** [ra-o-na-nonh-wa-ro-re'-ó:-konh] *their hats.* **akwanonhwarore'tsheràke** [a-kwa-nòn-wa-ro-rets-he-rà:-keh] *on my hat;* **raononhwarore'tsherakon** [a-kwah-nonh-wa-roh-rets-he-rá:-konh] *in his hat.* **katenonhwaròroks** [ka-te-nonh-wa-rò:-roks] *I put on my hat;* **katenonhwarohrokshyons** [ka-te-nonh-wa-roh-rok-hsyons] *I take off my hat.*

49 **aonha** [á-on-ha'] *it (Free Pronoun)*

50 **aonsarekon** [a-on-sa-ré-konh] *almost*
Aonsarekon taonkwahsi'tyàkonh [A-on-sa-ré-konh ta-on-kwah-si'-tyà:-konh] *I almost slipped;*

51 **are** [á:-reh] *again*
ie. **Toka' nonwa are yenshrawe'.** [To-ka' nón:-wa' yéns-hra-we'] *Maybe he'll come back again.*

52 **arekho** [á-rek-ho] *not yet*
ie. **Yah arekho teshohtentyonh.** [Yah á-rek-ho tes-hoh-tén-tyonh] *He hasn't returned yet.*

53 **àshare** [à:-sha-reh] *a knife*
akwàshare [a-kwà:-sha-reh] *my knife;* **sàshare** [sà:-sha-reh] *your knife;* **raòshare** [ra-ò:-sha-reh] *his knife;* **akaòshare** [a-ka-ò:-sha-reh] *her knife;* **raona'share'okon** [ra-o-na'-sha-re'-ó:-konh] *their knifes.* **akwa'sharàke** [a-kwa'-sha-rà:-keh] *on my knife.* **Oh niwa'sharòten'.** [Oh ni-wa'-sha-rò:-ten'] *What kind of knife is it?* **wa'sharowanen** [wa'-sha-ro-wá:-nenh] *a big knife;* **niwa'shara'ah** [ni-wa'-sha-rá:-'ah] *a small knife;* **yo'sharo'thiye'** [yo'-sha-ro'-thí:-ye'] *a sharp knife.* **waka'sharayen'** [wa-ka'-sha-rá-yen'] *I have a knife.*

54 **atahkwennya'** [a-tah-kwén-nya'] *an outfit, suit; an ensemble*
akwatahkwennya' [a-kwa-tah-kwén-nya'] *my suit;* **satahkwennya'** [sa-tah-kwén-nya'] *your suit;* **raotahkwennya'** [ra-o-tah-kwén-nya'] *his suit;* **akaotahkwennya'** [a-ka-o-tah-kwén-nya'] *her suit;* **raonatahkwennya'okon** [a-o-na-tah-kwén-nya'-ó:-konh] *their suit.* **akwatahkwennya'tsheràke** [a-kwa'-nya-na-wen'-tshe-rà:-keh] *on my suit;* **raotahkwennya'tsherakon** [a-kwa'-nya-na-wen'-tshe-rá:-konh] *in his suit.* **wakatahkwennyatsherayen'** [wa-ka-tah-kwen-nyats-he-rá:-yen'] *I have a suit.*

55 **atakwari** [a-ta-kwá:-ri'] *a bundle; a package*
ie. **katakwariks** [ka-ta-kwá:-riks] *I wrap up / make up a package, bundle;* **katakwarihsyons** [ka-ta-kwa-ríh-syons] *I unwrap a package, bundle.*

56 **atatawi** [a-ta-tá:-wih] *a gift; a present*

57 **atatken** [a-tát-kenh] *a mirror*

58 **ate'wahsare** [a-te'-wáh-sa-reh] *an earring*
akwate'wahsare [a-kwa-te'-wáh-sa-reh] *my earring(s);* **sate'wahsare** [sa-te'-wáh-sa-reh] *your earring(s);* **raote'wahsare** [ra-o-te'-wáh-sa-reh] *his earring(s);* **akaote'wahsare** [a-ka-o-te'-wáh-sa-reh] *her earring(s);* **raonate'wahsare'okon** [ra-o-na-te'-wah-sa-re'-ó:-konh] *their earrings.* **akwate'wahsaràke** [a-kwa-te'-wah-sa-rà:-keh] *on my earring(s).* **Oh niwate'wahsaròten'.** [Oh ni-wa-te'-wah-

sa-rò:-ten'] *What kind of earrings are they?* **wate'wahsarowanen** [wa-te'-wah-sa-ro-wá:-nenh] *a big earring(s)*; **niwate'wahsara'ah** [ni-wa-te'-sha-rá:-'ah] *a small earring(s)*; **wate'wahsariyo** [wa·te'-wah-sa-rí:-yoh] *nice earring(s)*: **wakate'wahsarayen'** [wa-ka-te'-wah-sa-rá-yen'] *I have earrings.*

⁵⁹ **atekhwàra** [a-tek-hwà:-ra'] *a table*
atekhwahrahne' [a-tek-hwa-hráh-ne'] *on the table*; ie. **Atekhwahrahne yahahsren** [...ya-háhs-ren] *put it (there) on the table.* **atekhwahròkon** [a-tek-hwa-hrò:-konh] *under the table*; ie. **Atekhwahròkon yahahsyen** [...ya-háh-syen] *put it (there) under the table.* **atekhwahrakta** [a-tek-hwa-hrák-ta'] *near the table*; ie. **Atekhwahrakta ya'satyen** [...ya'-sá-tyen] *sit near the table.* **watekhwahratsheriyo** [wa-tek-hwa-hrats-he-rí:-yoh] *a good table.* **watekhwahratsherehs** [wa-tek-hwa-hráts-he-rehs] *a long table*; **niwatekhwahratshera'ah** [ni-wa-tek-hwa-hrats-he-rá:-'ah] *a small table.*

⁶⁰ **aten'ènra** [a-ten'-èn:-ra'] *a fence*
aten'enhràke [a-ten'-en-hrà:-keh] *on the fence*; ie. **Aten'enhràke tkentskwahere' ne tsi'tenha.** [...t-kents-kwá-he-re' ne tsi'-tén-ha'] *There's a bird sitting on the fence.* **aten'ènrakon** [a-ten'-èn:-ra-konh] *within the fence (in the yard).*

⁶¹ **atenentshanha** [a-te-nents-hán-ha'] *a bracelet*
WITH POSSESSIVES: **akwatenentshanha** [a-kwa-te-nents-hán-ha'] *my bracelet*; **satenentshanha** [sa-te-nents-hán-ha'] *your bracelet*; **raotenentshanha** [ra-o-te-nents-hán-ha'] *his bracelet*; **akaotenentshanha** [a-ka-o-te-nents-hán-ha'] *her bracelet.* WITH LOCATIVES: **akwatenentshanhatsheràke** [a-kwa-te-nents-han-hats-he-rà:-keh] *on my bracelet.* WITH VERBS: **katenentshanhaks** [ka-te-nents-hán-haks] *I put on a bracelet*; **katenentshanhahsyons** [ka-te-nents-han-háh-syons] *I take off a bracelet.*

⁶² **atenentshawi'tanha** [a-te-nents-ha-wi'-tán-ha'] *a armband*
WITH POSSESSIVES: **akwatenentshawi'tanha** [a-kwa-te-nents-ha-wi'-tán-ha'] *my armband*; **satenentshawi'tanha** [sa-te-nents-ha-wi'-tán-ha'] *your armband*; **raotenentshawi'tanha** [ra-o-te-nents-ha-wi'-tán-ha'] *his armband*; **akaotenentshawi'tanha** [a-ka-o-te-nents-ha-wi'-tán-ha'] *her armband.* WITH LOCATIVES: **akwatenentshawi'tanhatsheràke** [a-kwa-te-nents-ha-wi'-tan-hats-he-rà:-keh] *on my armband.* WITH VERBS: **katenentshawi'tanhaks** [ka-te-nents-ha-wi'-tán-haks] *I put on a armband*; **katenentshawi'tanhahsyons** [ka-te-nents-ha-wi'tan-háh-syons] *I take off a armband.*

⁶³ **atenentshawìtha** [a-te-nents-ha-wì:-ta'] *a wristband (a bracelet)*
akwatenentshawi'tsheràke [a-kwa-te-nents-ha-wi'ts-he-rà:-keh] *on my wristband;* **satenentshawi'tsheràke** [sa-te-nents-ha-wi'ts-he-rà:-keh] *on your wristband;* **ratenentshawi'tsheràke** [ra-o-te-nents-ha-wi'ts-he-rà:-keh] *on his*

wristband; **akaotenentshawi'tsheràke** [a-ka-o-te-nents-ha-wi'ts-he-rà:-keh] *on her wristband.*

64 **ateniyonta** [a-te-ni-yón:-ta'] *an apron*
WITH POSSESSIVES: **akwateniyonta** [a-kwa-te-ni-yón:-ta'] *my apron;* **sateniyonta** [sa-te-ni-yón:-ta'] *your apron;* **raoteniyonta** [ra-o-te-ni-yón:-ta'] *his apron;* **akaoteniyonta** [a-ka-o-te-ni-yón:-ta'] *her apron.* WITH LOCATIVES: **akwateniyontàke** [a-kwa-te-ni-yon-tà:-keh] *on my apron.*

65 **atennàtshera** [a-ten-nà:-ts-he-ra'] *a lunch; groceries, provisions*
ie. **katenna'tsheronni'** [ka-ten-na'ts-he-rón:-ni'] *I make a lunch;* **katenna'tsherahninons** [ka-ten-na'ts-he-rah-ní:-nons] *I buy a lunch; I buy groceries.*

66 **atenneha** [a-ten-né-ha'] *plantain*

67 **atennits** [a-tén:-nits] *a cane; a walking stick*
WITH POSSESSIVES: **akwatennits** [a-kwa-tén:-nits] *my cane;* **satennits** [sa-tén:-nits] *your cane;* **raotennits** [ra-o-tén:-nits] *his cane;* **akaotennits** [a-ka-o-tén:-nits] *her cane.*

68 **atenon'teksta** [a-te-non'-téks-ta'] *a lid; a cover (for a pail, basket, etc..)*

69 **atenonhwaranha** [a-te-non-hwa-rán-ha'] *a headband*
WITH POSSESSIVES: **akwatenonhwaranha** [a-kwa-te-non-hwa-rán-ha'] *my headband;* **satenonhwaranha** [sa-te-non-hwa-rán-ha'] *your headband;* **raotenonhwaranha** [ra-o-te-non-hwa-rán-ha'] *his headband;* **akaotenonhwaranha** [a-ka-o-te-non-hwa-rán-ha'] *her headband.* WITH LOCATIVES: **akwatenonhwaranhatsheràke** [a-kwa-te-non-hwa-ran-hats-he-rà:-keh] *on my headband.* WITH VERBS: **katenonhwaranhaks** [ka-te-non-hwa-rán-haks] *I put on a head band;* **katenonhwaranhahsyons** [ka-te-non-hwa-ran-háh-yons] *I take off a headband.*

70 **atenoseràke** [a-te-no-se-rà:-keh] *in the yard*
ie. **Atenoseràke tkonne's ne kontiksa'okonha.** [...t-kón:-ne's ne kon-tik-sa'-o-kón-ha'] *The girls are in the yard.*

71 **aterahwènta** [a-te-rah-wèn:-ta'] *a snowsnake*

72 **aterennayent** [a-te-rén:-na-yenht] *a prayer*

73 **athahsteren'** [at-háhs-te-ren'] *pants, slacks...*
akwathahsteren' [a-kwat-háhs-te-ren'] *my pants;* **sathahsteren'** [sat-háhs-te-ren'] *your pants;* **raothahsteren'** [ra-ot-háhs-te-ren'] *his pants;* **akaothahsteren'** [a-ka-ot-háhs-te-ren'] *her pants;* **raonathahsteren'okon** [ra-o-nat-hahs-te-ren'-ó:-konh] *their pants.* **akwathahsteren'tsheràke** [a-kwat-hahs-te-renks-he-rà:-keh] *on my pants;* **raothahsteren'tsherakon** [a-kwat-

hahs-te-renks-he-rá:-konh] *in his pants.* **Oh niwathahsteren'tsheròten'** [Oh ni-wat-hahs-te-ren'ts-he-rò:-ten'] *What kind of pants (are they)?* ie. **wathahsterentsherehs** [wat-hahs-te-rén'ts-he-rehs] *long pants;* **niwathahsteren'tsherehsha** [ni-wat-hahs-te-ren'ts-he-réhs-ha'] *short pants.* **kathahsterenks** [kat-háhs-te-renks] *I put on my pants;* **kathahsterenkhsyons** [kat-hahs-te-rénk-hsyons] *I take off my pants.*

74 **athehsa** [at-héh-sa'] *brown*
   athehsa niwahsohkòten' [at-héh-sa' ni-wah-soh-kò:-ten'] *it is brown (coloured); it is dyed brown.*

75 **athenno'** [at-hén:-no'] *a ball*
   akwathenno' [a-kwat-hén:-no'] *my pants;* **sathenno'** [sat-hén:-no'] *your pants;* **raothenno'** [ra-ot-hén:-no'] *his pants;* **akaothenno'** [a-ka-ot-hén:-no'] *her pants;* **raonathenno'okon** [ra-o-nat-hén:-no'-ó:-konh] *their pants.* **wathenno'tsheràke** [wat-hen-nots-he-rà:-keh] *on the ball;* **Oh niwathenno'tsheròten'** [Oh ni-wat-hén:-no'ts-he-rò:-ten'] *What kind of a ball (is it)?* ie. **ohnekwenhtara niwathenno'tsheròten'** [oh-ne-kwénh-ta-ra' ni-wat-hen-no'ts-he-rò:-ten'] *a red ball;* **wathahsterentsherowanen** [wat-hen-no'ts-he-ro-wá:-nenh] *a large ball;* **niwathenno'tshera'ah** [ni-wat-hen-no'ts-he-rá:-'ah] *a small ball.* **wakathenno'tsheratyes** [wa-kat-hen-no'ts-he-rá-tyes] *I throw a ball;* **kathenno'tsherayenahs** [kat-hen-no'ts-he-ra-yé:-nahs] *I catch a ball.*

76 **àthere** [à:-t-he-reh] *a basket*
   akwàthere [a-kwà:-the-reh] *my basket;* **sàthere** [sà:-the-reh] *your basket;* **raòthere** [ra-ò:-the-reh] *his basket;* **akaòthere** [a-ka-ò:-the-reh] *her basket;* **raona'there'okon** [ra-o-na'-the-re'-ó:-konh] *their baskets.* **akwa'theràke** [a-kwa'-the-rà:-keh] *on my basket.* **Oh niwa'theròten'.** [Oh ni-wa'-the-rò:-ten'] *What kind of basket is it?* **wa'therowanen** [wa'-the-ro-wá:-nenh] *a big basket;* **niwa'thera'ah** [ni-wa'-the-rá:-'ah] *a small basket;* **wa'theriyo** [wa'-the-rí:-yoh] *a nice basket.* **waka'therayen'** [wa-ka'-the-rá-yen'] *I have a basket.*

77 **athseronnya'** [at-hse-rón-nya'] *clothing, a suit (of clothes)*
   akwathseronnya' [a-kwat-hse-rón-nya'] *my clothing;* **sathseronnya'** [sat-hse-rón-nya'] *your clothing;* **raothseronnya'** [ra-ot-hse-rón-nya'] *his clothing;* **akaothseronnya'** [a-ka-ot-hse-rón-nya'] *her clothing.* **akwathseronnya'tsheràke** [a-kwat-hse-ron-nyats-he-rà:-keh] *on my clothing;* **raothseronnya'tsherakon** [a-kwat-hse-ron-nyats-he-rá:-konh] *in his clothing.* **wakathseronnyatsherayen'** [wa-kat-hse-ron-nyats-he-rá:-yen'] *I have a suit of clothes.*

78 **atiron** [a-tí:-ronh] *a raccoon*

79 **Atirontaks** [A-ti-rón:-taks] *the Algonquins*

80 **atkahranha** [at-ka-hrán-ha'] *glasses*
   akwatkahranha [a-kwat-ka-hrán-ha'] *my glasses*; **satkahranha** [sat-ka-hrán-ha'] *your glasses*; **raotkahranha** [ra-ot-ka-hrán-ha'] *his glasses*; **akaotkahranha** [a-ka-ot-ka-hrán-ha'] *her glasses*. **akwatkahranhatsheràke** [a-kwa-tya'-tan-hats-he-rà:-keh] *on my glasses*. **katkahranhaks'** [ka-tya'-tán-haks] *I put on my glasses*; **katkahranhahsyons** [ka-tya'-tan-háh-syons] *I take off my glasses*.

81 **atkerothiya** [at-ke-rot-hí:-ya'] *a comb*

82 **atkònsera** [at-kòn:-se-ra'] *a pillow; a cushion*
   akwatkònsera [a-kwa-tya'-tán-ha'] *my pillow*; **satkònsera** [sa-tya'-tán-ha'] *your pillow*; **raotkònsera** [ra-o-tya'-tán-ha'] *his pillow*; **akaotkònsera** [a-ka-o-tya'-tán-ha'] *her pillow*; **aonatkònseraokon** [a-o-na-tya'-tan-ha'-ó:-konh] *their pillows*. **akwatkònseratsheràke** [a-kwa-tya'-tan-hats-he-rà:-keh] *on my pillow*; **akwatkon'seratsheròkon** [a-kwat-kon'se-rò-konh] *under my pillow*. **wakatkon'serayen'** [wa-kat-kon'-se-rá:-yen'] *I have a pillow.*

83 **ato'tsinehta** [a-to'tsi-néh-ta'] *a skate, skates*
   akwato'tsinehta [a-kwa-to'-tsi-néh-ta'] *my skate(s)*; **sato'tsinehta** [sa-to'-tsi-néh-ta'] *your skate(s)*; **raoto'tsinehta** [ra-o-to'-tsi-néh-ta'] *his skate(s)*; **akaoto'tsinehta** [a-ka-o-to'-tsi-néh-ta'] *her skate(s)*; **raonato'tsinehtaokon** [a-o-na-to'-tsi-neh-ta'-ó:-konh] *their skates*. **akwato'tsinehtatsheràke** [a-kwa-to'-tsi-neh-tats-he-rà:-keh] *on my skate(s)*; **raoto'tsinehtatsherakon** [a-kwa-to'-tsi-neh-tats-he-rá:-konh] *in his skate(s)*. **wakato'tsinehtatsherayen'** [wa-ka-to'-tsi-neh-tath-he-rá:-yen'] *I have skates*; **tekato'tsinehtha'** [te-ka-to'-tsi-néh-tha'] *I skate.*

84 **atoken** [a-tó:-ken'] *an axe*

85 **atokwa** [a-tó-kwa'] *a spoon*
   akwatokwa [a-kwa-tó-kwa'] *my spoon*; **satokwa** [sa-tó-kwa'] *your spoon*; **raotokwa** [ra-o-tó-kwa'] *his spoon*; **akaotokwa** [a-ka-o-tó-kwa'] *her spoon*; **raonatokwaokon** [a-o-na-tó-kwa'-ó:-konh] *their skates*. **Oh niwatokwatsheròten'** [Oh ni-wa-to-kwats-he-rò:-ten'] *What kind of spoon is it?* ie. **watokwatsherowanen** [wa-to-kwats-he-ro-wá:-nenh] *a big spoon*; **niwatokwatshera'ah** [ni-wa-to-kwats-he-rá:-'ah] *a small spoon*. **akwatokwatsheràke** [a-kwa-to-kwats-he-rà:-keh] *on my spoon*; **raotokwatsherakon** [a-kwa-to-kwats-he-rá:-konh] *in his spoon*. **wakatokwatsherayen'** [wa-ka-to-kwats-he-rá:-yen'] *I have a spoon.*

86 **atonnhets** [a-tónn-hets] *a soul; a life*

87 **atosera** [a-tóh-se-ra'] *a tent*
   atoseràke [a-to-se-rà:-keh] *on the tent*; **atoserakon** [a-to-se-rá:-konh] *in the*

tent;   **katoserotha'** [ka-to-se-rót-ha'] *I set up a tent.*

88 **atshòkten** [ats-hò:-k-ten'] *a hoe*

89 **attsihkwa'e** [at-tsih-kwá:-'eh] *a lacrosse game*

90 **attsihstohkwa** [at-tsihs-tóh-kwa'] *a clown*

91 **atya'tanha** [a-tya'-tán-ha'] *a belt*
akwatya'tanha [a-kwa-tya'-tán-ha'] *my belt*;   **satya'tanha** [sa-tya'-tán-ha']
your belt;   **raotya'tanha** [ra-o-tya'-tán-ha'] *his belt*;   **akaotya'tanha** [a-ka-o-
tya'-tán-ha'] *her belt*;   **aonatya'tanhaokon** [a-o-na-tya'-tan-ha'-ó:-konh] *their
belts.*   **akwatya'tanhatsheràke** [a-kwa-tya'-tan-hats-he-rà:-keh] *on my belt*;
raotya'tanhatsherakon [a-kwa-tya'-tan-hats-he-rá:-konh] *in his belt.*
katya'tanhaks' [ka-tya'-tán-haks] *I put on my belt*;   **katya'tanhahsyons** [ka-
tya'-tan-háh-syons] *I take off my belt.*

92 **atyàtawi'** [a-tyà:-ta-wi'] *a coat, dress, shirt, etc...*
akwatyàtawi' [a-kwa-tyà:-ta-wi'] *my coat*;   **satyàtawi'** [sa-tyà:-ta-wi'] *your
coat*;   **raotyàtawi'** [ra-o-tyà:-ta-wi'] *his coat*;   **akaotyàtawi'** [a-ka-o-tyà:-ta-
wi'] *her coat*;   **aonatyàtawi'okon** [a-o-na-tya'-ta-wi'-ó:-konh] *their coats.*
akwatyàtawi'tsheràke [a-kwa-tya'-ta-wi'ts-he-rà:-keh] *on my coat*;
raotyàtawi'tsherakon [a-kwa-tya'-ta-wi'ts-he-rá:-konh] *in his coat.*
katya'tawìtha' [ka-tya'-ta-wì:-t-ha'] *I put on my coat*;   **katya'tawi'tahsyons**
[ka-tya'-ta-wi'-táh-syons] *I take off my coat.*

93 **awerahsa** [a-we-ráh-sa'] *moss*
ie. **yowerahsare** [yo-we-ráh-sa-reh] *it has moss on it*;   **awerahsakon** [a-we-ráh-
sa-konh] *in the moss.*

94 **aweryahsa** [a-wer-yáh-sa'] *heart*
ie.. **Raweryahsahniron** [Ra-wer-yah-sah-ní:-ronh] *He has a sturdy heart*;
Raweryahsiyo [Ra-wer-yah-sí:-yoh] *He has a good heart*;   **Raweryahsaksen**
[Ra-wer-yah-sák-senh] *He has a poor heart*;   **Wa'thaweryahsihsonhkwe'** [Wa-t-
ha-wer-yah-síh-sonh-kwe'] *He has a heart-attack.*

95 **awiyo** [a-wí:-yoh] *it is good*
NOTE: *only the -iyo is used:* ie. **kanonhsiyo** [ka-nonh-sí:-yoh] *a good house*;
wa'shariyo [wa'-s-ha-rí:-yoh] *a good knife*;   **raksa'tiyo** [rak-sa'-tí:-yoh] *a good
boy*;   **yeksa'tiyo** [yek-sa'-tí:-yoh] *a good girl.*

96 **àyok** [à:-yok] *huckleberries*

E

⁹⁷ **e'tho** [é'-thoh] *there; so; enough*
    E'tho wakhninonh [...wak-hní:-nonh] *So I bought it*; **Yah e'tho tewakyen'**
    [Yah é'-thoh te-wák-yen'] *I don't have enough.*

⁹⁸ **e'thòne** [e'-thò:-neh] *at that time; then*
    ie. **E'thòne wahiyenawa'se' ne ayakenikwatako'.** [...wa-hi-yé:-na-wa'-se'
    na-ya-ke-ni-kwa-tá:-ko'] *At that time / then I helped him fix it.*

⁹⁹ **eh** [éh] *there* (see: **e'tho**)

   a) **eh ki' nonwe** [eh ki' nón:-weh] *right there*
      ie. **Eh ki' nonwe ya'khnyoten'.** [...ya'k-hnyó:-ten'] *I stood it up right there.*

   b) **eh niyore n(i)-** [eh ni-yó:-reh n(i)-] *so*
      Eh niyore nahohteronne' [...na-hóh-te-ron'-ne'] *He got so scared*

   c) **eh niyore tsi** [tsi ni-yó:-reh tsi] *that's as far as*
      Eh niyore tsi yahare'. [...ya-há:-re'] *That's as far as he went.*

   d) **eh niyohsnore tsi** [eh ni-yoh-snó:-reh tsi] *that's as fast as*
      Eh niyohsnore tsi wahakweni' taharahtate'. [...wa-ha-kwé:-ni' ta-ha-
      ráh-ta-te'] *That's as far as he could run.*

   e) **eh nonkati** [eh non-ká:-tih] *that way; over that way; in that direction*
      Eh nonkati niyahare' [...ni-ya-há:-re'] *He went in that direction / he went
      (over) that way.*

   f) **eh nonwe** [eh nón:-weh] *there; at that place*
      Eh nonwe thoyo'tenhs [...tho-yó-tenhs] *He works there.*

   g) **eh nonwe tsi niwat** [eh non-weh tsi ní:-wat] *thereabouts*
      Eh nonwe tsi niwat karhakon yehatorats [...kar-há:-konh ye-ha-tó:-
      rats] *He's hunting thereabouts in the woods.*

¹⁰⁰ **ehsa** [éh-sa'] *a black ash tree*

¹⁰¹ **eksa'a** [ek-sá:'ah] *a child*
    ie. **raksa'a** [rak-sá:-'ah] *male child - boy*; **yeksa'a** [yek-sá:-'ah] *female child -
    girl*; **Wakeksàtayen'.** [wa-kek-sà:-ta-yen'] *I have a child / children*;
    Wakeksa'tiyos [wa-kek-sa'-tí:-yohs] *I have good children.*

¹⁰² **eksa'okonha** [ek-sa'-o-kón-ha'] *children (non-specific, generic)*
    ie. **ratiksa'okonha** [ra-tik-sa'-o-kón-ha'] *male children - boys*;
    kontiksa'okonha [kon-tik-sa'-o-kón-ha'] *female children - girls.*

103 en'nahsa [en'-náh-sa'] *tounge*
   ken'nahsàke [ken'-nah-sà:-keh] *on my tounge*; **sen'nahsàke** [sen'-nah-sà:-keh]
   on your tounge; **ren'nahsàke** [ren'-nah-sà:-keh] *on his tounge*; **ye'nahsàke** [ye'-
   nah-sà:-keh] *on her tounge*.

104 enhnekeri [enh-né-ke-rih] *hay; grain*

105 enhskat [énhs-kat] *one*
   when used with objects: **skahyatonhserat** [ska-hya-tónh-se-rat] *one book*;
   sewathenno'tsherat [se-wat-hen-nò:ts-he-rat] *one ball*; **tsyohserat** [tsyóh-se-
   rat] *one year*. When used with people or animals: **shayàtat ronkwe** [sha-yà:-
   tat rón-kwe'] *one man*; **tsyeyàtat yakonkwe** [tsye-yà:-tat ya-kón:-kwe'] *one
   woman*; **skayàtat erhar** [ska-yà:-tat ér-har] *one dog*. See also: **skathne**
   [enhs-kát-hne'] *together*; **skathson** [skát-hsonh] *each one*.

106 enkenhake [en-kén-ha-ke'] *it / there will be*
   ie. **Skennen enkenhake'.** [Skén:-nenh en-kén-ha-ké'] *There will be peace.*
   See: **iken'** *it is (indeed)*

107 Ennihska [En-níh-ska'] *February*

108 Ennihskowa [En-nihs-kó:-wa'] *March*

109 ennihsnonhsawi' [en-nih-snónh-sa-wi'] *a ring*
   akwennihsnonhsawi' [a-kwen-nih-snónh-sa-wi'] *my ring*; **sennihsnonhsawi'**
   [sen-nih-snónh-sa-wi'] *your ring*; **raonihsnonhsawi'** [ra-o-nih-snónh-sa-wi']
   his ring; **akaonihsnonhsawi'** [a-ka-o-nih-snónh-sa-wi'] *her ring*.
   akwennihsnonhsawi'tsheràke [a-kwen-nih-snonh-sa-wi'ts-he-rà:-ke] *on my
   ring*. **Wakennihsnonhsawìtha'** [Wa-ken-nih-snonh-sa-wì:-t-ha'] *I have a ring /
   I'm wearing a ring.*

110 ennihtyakstha [en-nih-tyáks-tha'] *necklace*
   akwennihstyakstha [a-kwen-nih-tyáks-t-ha'] *my necklace*; **sennihstyakstha**
   [sen-nih-tyáks-t-ha'] *your necklace*; **raonihstyakstha** [ra-o-nih-tyáks-t-ha'] *his
   necklace*; **akaonihstyakstha** [a-ka-o-nih-tyáks-t-ha'] *her necklace*.
   sennihstyakstatsheràke [sen-nih-tyaks-tats-he-rà:-keh] *on your necklace*.
   Kennihtyaks [ken-níh-tyaks] *I put a necklace around my neck*; **Wakennihtyenh**
   [Wa-ken-níh-tyenh] *I have on a necklace*.

111 ennitskwàra [en-nits-kwà:-ra'] *a chair*
   ennitskwahrahne' [en-nits-kwa-hrah-ne'] *on the chair*. ie. **Ennitskwahrahne'**
   yahahsren [...ya-háhs-ren] *put it (there) on the chair*; **Ennitskwahròkon**
   ya'satyen [...ya'-sá-tyen] *sit it (there) under the chair*. **akwennitskwàra** [a-
   kwen-nits-kwà:-ra'] *my chair*; **sennitskwàra** [sen-nits-kwà:-ra'] *your chair*;
   raonitskwàra [ra-o-nits-kwà:-ra'] *his chair*; **akaonitskwàra** [a-ka-o-nits-
   kwà:-ra'] *her chair*; **raonennitskwahra'okon** [ra-o-nen-nits-kwa-hra'-ó:-

konh] *their chairs.*

112 **ens** [ens] *usually, customarily; as a rule*
  ie. **Niya'tewenhniserake ens royo'tens.** [Ni-ya'-te-wenh-ni-se-rá:-keh ens ro-yó'-tens] *He usually works every day.*

113 **entye nikare** [en-tyeh ní:-ka-reh] *in the afternoon*
  ie. **Enyorhenne' entye nikare enyakwahninònra'.** [En-yór-hen'-ne' en-tye ní:-ka-reh en-ya-kwah-ni-nòn:-ra'] *Tomorrow in the afternoon we are going shopping.*

114 **enyorhenne'** [en-yór-hen'-ne'] *tomorrow*
  ie. **Enyorhenne' enwakyo'tensha'** [...en-wa-kyo'-téns-ha'] *Tomorrow I am going to work.*

115 **erhar** [ér-har] *a dog*
  aketshenen erhar [a-kets-hé:-nenh ér-har] *my dog*; **satshenen erhar** [sats-hé:-nenh...] *your dog*; **raotshenen erhar** [ra-ots-hé:-nenh...] *his dog*; **akaotshenen erhar** [a-ka-ots-hé:-nenh...] *her dog*; **onkwatshenen erhar** [on-kwats-hé:-nenh...] *our dog*; **raonatshenen erhar** [ra-o-nats-hé:-nenh...] *their dog*. **kanahskwiyo erhar** [ka-nahs-kwí:-yoh...] *a good dog*; **kanahskwaksen erhar** [ka-nahs-kwák-sen'...] *a bad dog*; **kahserohen erhar** [kah-se-ró-henh...] *a vicious dog*; **erharkenha** [er-har-kén-ha'] *a dead dog*; **erharhokonha** [er-har-ho-kón-ha'] *dogs.* **Erhar wakenahskwayen'** [...wa-ke-náhs-kwa-yen'] *I have a dog.*

116 **eris** [é:-ris] *a puppy*

117 **eri** [é:-rih] *a cherry, cherries*

118 **eso** [é:-soh] *many; a lot*
  eso nikon [é:-soh ní:-konh] *there are many (of them)*; **sotsi eso** [só-tsih é:-soh] *too many*; **Sotsi ne'e eso** [Só-tsih né:-'eh é:-soh] *That's too many.* With objects: **eso niwenhniserake** [...ni-wenh-ni-se-rá:-keh] *many days*; **eso nikatshètake** [...ni-kats-hè:-ta-keh] *many bottles.* With people and animals: **eso nihati rononkwe** [...ni-há:-tih ro-nón:-kwe'] *many men*; **eso nihati ne rononkwe** [...ne ro-nón:-kwe'] *many of the men*; **eso nikonti kononkwe** [...ni-kón:-tih ko-nón:-kwe'] *many women*; **eso nikonti ne kononkwe** [...ne ko-nón:-kwe'] *many of the women*; **eso nikonti takohs** [...ta-kóhs] *many cats*; **eso nikonti ne takohs** [...ne ta-kóhs] *many of the cats.* With verbs: **Eso niwakyen'** [...ni-wák-yen'] *I have many / lots.*

119 **etshe'kenha** [ets-he'-kén-ha'] *your younger brother* (See: **ri'kenha**)

120 **etshiteniyen'a** [ets-hi-te-ni-yén:-ah] *our son* (See: **riyen'a**)

121 **etshitewa'kenha** [ets-hi-te-wa'-kén-ha'] *our younger brother* (See: **ri'kenha**)

122 **etshyen'a** [ets-hyén:-ah] *your son* (See: **riyen'a**)

15

H

123 **hen'en** [hén:-'enh] *yes*

124 **hanyon** [há-nyonh] *come on*
ie. **Hanyon, to itewe!** [Há-nyonh, tó: í-te-we] *Come on, let's go.*

125 **hao ki' wahi** [há-o' ki' wá-hih] *okay (then)!*

I

126 **i'i** [í:-'ih] *I, me; we, us (Free Pronoun)*
This word is used for purposes of emphasis or clarity: **I'i wakhninonh** [i':-'ih wak-hní:-nonh] *I bought it (as opposed to someone else buying it)*; **Wahakhrori' ne i''i.** [Wa-hak-hró:-ri' ne í:-'ih] *He told me (as opposed to someone else;* **Raktsi'a tahnon ne i'i kanatakon ya'akene'.** [Rak-tsí:-'ah tah-non' ne í:-'ih ka-ná:-ta-konh ya'-á:-ke-ne'] *My older brother and I (as well as myself) went to town.*

127 **ikare** [í:-ka-reh] *it contains / is contained within / has the appearance of*
ie. **kahnekare** [kah-né:-ka-reh] *it has water in it*; **yonawatstare** [yo-na-wáts-ta-reh] *it has mud on it (it's muddy)*; etc...

128 **ikhawe'** [ík-ha-we'] *I have / carry (on myself)* (C-Stem verb - Subj.)
wàkhawe' [wà:-k-ha-we'] *I carried on myself*; **wakhaweh** [wák-ha-weh] *I have carried / did carry on myself.* With nominals: **ikhyatonhserenhawe'** [ik-hya-tonh-se-rén-ha-we'] *I am carrying a book*; **iktsi'tsyenhawe'** [ik-tsi'-tsyén-ha-we'] *I am carrying flowers.*

129 **ihsi** [íh-si'] *on the other side*
ie. **ihsi na'kanonhsati** [...na'-ka-nónh-sa-tih] *the other side of the house*; **ihsi na'ohahati** [...na'-o-há-ha-tih] *the other side of the road*; **ihsi na'kanyatarati** [...na'-ka-nya-ta-rá:-tih] *the other side of the lake*; **ihsi na'kahyonhati** [...na'-ka-hyón-ha-tih] *the other side of the river*; **ihsi nonta'ènrati** [...non-ta'-èn:-ra-tih] *the other side of the fence*; **ihsi na'kahehtati** [...na'ka-héh-ta-tih] *the other side of the field*; **ihsi na'karhati** [...na'-kár-ha-tih] *the other side of the woods.* (see: karo)

a) **ihsi nonwe** [ih-si' nón:-weh] *over on the other side*
ie. **Ihsi nonwe thoyo'te'.** [...tho-yó-te'] *He is working on the other side.*

b) **ihsi nonkati** [ih-si' non-ká:-tih] *toward the other side*
   ie. **Ihsi nonkati ya'konne'.** [...ya'-kón:-ne'] *They are going toward the other side.*

130 **ihsta'a** [ihs-tá:-'ah] *my aunt, your aunt, etc... (genral term for aunt)*

131 **ike'** [í:-ke's] *I am going / walking*
   ie. **Ohahàke ike'.** [O-ha-hà:-keh í:-ke'] *I am going / walking on the road*; **wàke'** [wà:-ke'] *I went*; **wakenonh** [wa-ké:-nonh] *I have gone / did go.* (see: take'; yake')

132 **ike's** [í:-ke's] *I am about* (E-Stem verb - Subj.)
   ie. **Kanonhsakon ike's.** [Ka-nónh-sa-konh í:-ke's] *I am (about) in the house*; **ike'skwe'** [í:-ke's-kwe'] *I was about:* ie. **Kanatakon yeke'skwe'** [ka-ná:-ta-konh yé:-ke's-kwe'] *I was (there) in town*; **enkèseke'** [en-kè:-se-ke'] *I will be about:* ie. **Kanatakon yenkèseke'** [ka-ná:-ta-konh yen-kè:-se-ke'] *I will be about (there) in town / I will stay in town*; **akèseke'** [a-kè:-se-ke'] *I would be about:* ie. **Kanatakon yakèseke'** [ka-ná:-ta-konh ya-kè:-se-ke'] *I would be about (there) in town / I would stay in town*;

133 **ikehre'** [í:-ke-hre'] *I want to / think that / have the opinion that* (E-Stem verb - Subj.)
   wàkehre' [wà:-ke-hre'] *I wanted to...*; **wakèrenh** [wa-kè:-renh] *I have wanted to...* In sentence constructions you would have: **Ikehre' akatorate'.** [Í-ke-hre' a-ka-tó:-ra-te'] *I want to hunt*; **Ikehre' ki' rentorha' onhte.** [Í-ke-hre' ki' ren-tór-ha' ónh-teh] *I think that he's lazy.*

134 **ikeks** [í:-keks] *I eat (s.t.)* E-Stem verb - Subj.)
   wàkeke' [wà:-ke-ke'] *I ate (something)*; **wakekonh** [wa-ké:-konh] *I have eaten / I did eat (something).* With nominals: **ke'wàraks** [ke'-wà:-raks] *I eat meat*; **kàyaks** [kà:-yaks] *I eat fruit*; **kenenhstaks** [ke-nénhs-taks] *I eat corn*; **kyentaks** [kyén:-taks] *I eat wood*; **khontaks** [k-hón:-taks] *I eat grass*; **kitsyaks** [kí-tsyaks] *I eat fish*; **iktsi'nonhtaks** [ik-tsi'-nónh-taks] *I eat insects.*

135 **iken'** [í:-ken'] *for; it is (indeed)*
   ie. **Tsi tkatsyenhayens iken'** [Tsit ka-tsyén-ha-yens í:-ken'] *It is (indeed) the (a) Council house*; **kenhne'** [kénh-ne'] *it was (indeed):* ie. **Tsi yonteweyenhstahkwa kenhne'** [Tsi yon-te-we-yenhs-táh-kwa' kénh-ne'] *It was (indeed) the (a) school*; **enkenhake'** [en-kén-ha-ke'] *it will be / there will be*; **akenhake'** [a-kén-ha-ke'] *it would be / there would be*; **kenhak** [kén-hak] *let there be:* ie. **Skennen kenhak** [Skén-nen kén-hak] *Let there be peace.*

136 **ikenonhne'** [í:-ke-nonh-ne'] *I watch over; guard* (C-Stem verb - Subj.)
   wa'kenònna' [wa'-ke-nòn:-na'] *I watched over; guarded*; **wakenonhneh** [wa-ké:-nonh-ne'] *I have watched over; have guarded.*

137 **ikete'** [í:-ke-teh] *I am standing* (C-Stem verb - Subj.)
ketahkwe' [ké-tah-kwe'] *I was standing*; **enketake'** [en-ké-ta-ke'] *I will be standing*; **aketake'** [a-ké-ta-ke'] *I would be standing*.

138 **ikhnenyehs** [ik-hnén:-yehs] *I am tall* (C-Stem verb - Subj.)
rahnenyehs [rah-nén:-yehs] *he is tall*; **yehnenyehs** [yeh-nén:-yehs] *she is tall*.
ie. **Senha ikhnenyehs tsi niyoht ne raonha.** [Sén-ha' ik-hnén:-yehs] tsi ní:-yoht ne rá-on-ha'] *I am taller than he*; **Eh nikhnenyehs tsi niyoht ne ise.** [Eh nik-hnén:-yehs tsi ní:-yoht ní:-se'] *I am as tall as you.* (see: nikhnenyehsha')

139 **ikhnerenks** [ík-hne-renks] *I tie s.t. to; attach s.t. to* (C-Stem verb - Subj.)
wàkhnerenke' [wà:-k-hne-ren-ke'] *I tied s.t. to...*; **wakhnerenh** [wák-hne-renh] *I have tied to / did tie to...*

140 **ikhseres** [ík-hse-res] *I follow; pursue* (C-Stem verb - Subj.)
wàkhsere' [wà:-k-hse-re'] *I followed; pursued*; **wakhsereh** [wák-hse-reh] *I have followed; have pursued.*

141 **ikhserohen** [ik-hse-ró-hen'] *I am ugly, ill-tempered* (C-Stem verb - Subj.)
ikhserohenhne' [ik-se-so-hénh-ne'] *I was ugly, ill-tempered*; **enkhserohenke'** [enk-hse-ró-hen'ke'] *I will be ugly, ill-tempered*; **akhserohenke'** [ak-hse-ró-hen'ke'] *I would be ugly, ill-tempered*;

142 **ikhseronnis** [ik-hse-rón:-nis] *I arrange / dress / fix s.t. up* (C-Stem verb - Subj.)
ikhseronni' [ik-hse-rón:-ni'] *I am arranging...*; **wa'khseronni'** [wa'-k-hse-rón:-ni'] *I arranged...*; **wakhseronnih** [wak-hse-rón:-nih] *I have arranged / did arrange....*

143 **ikhsònne'.** [ik-hsòn:-ne'] *behind me; at my back*
Also: **ithsònne'** [it-hsòn:-ne'] *behind you...*; **rahsònne'** [rah-sòn:-ne'] *behind him...*; **yehsònne'** [yeh-sòn:-ne'] *behind her...*; **onkwahsonhnehson** [on-kwah-sonh-néh-sonh] *behind us...*; **ratihsonhnehson** [ra-tih-sonh-néh-sonh] *behind them....* (see: ohswa)

144 **ikhswenhs** [ík-hswenhs] *I detest, hate* (C-Stem verb - Subj.)
wàkhswen' [wà:-k-hswen'] *I detested, hated*; **wakhswenhonh** [wak-hswén-honh] *I have detested, hated / did detest, hate.*

145 **ikka'ènyons** [ik-ka'-èn:-yons] *I examine* (C-Stem verb - Subj.)
wa'kka'ènyon' [wa'-k-ka'-èn:-yon'] *I examined*; **wakka'ènyonh** [wak-ka'-èn:-yonh] *I did examine / have examined*; **Yah tewakka'ènyonh** [yah te-wak-ka'-èn:-yonh] *I didn't examine (it).*

146 **ikkens** [ík-kens] *I see* (C-Stem verb - Subj.)
wàkken' [wà:-k-ken'] *I saw:* ie. **Erhar wàkken'** [Ér-har wà:-k-ken'] *I saw a dog;* **wakkenh** [wák-kenh] *I did see / have seen:* ie. **Onen wakkenh** [Ó-nenh wák-kenh] *I have already seen;* **Yah tewakkenh** [yah te-wák-kenh] *I didn't see .*

147 **ikkwatakwas** [ik-kwa-tá-kwas] *I fix s.t. up* (C-Stem verb - Subj.)
   wa'kkwatako' [wa'-k-kwa-tá:-ko'] *I fixed it*; **wakkwatakwenh** [wak-kwa-tá-kwenh] *I have fixed / did fix it*; **Yah tewakkwatakwenh** [yah te-wak-kwa-tá-kwenh] *I didn't fix it*;

148 **ikkwètarons** [ik-kwè:-ta-rons] *I cut a slice (of something)* (C-Stem verb - Subj.)
   wa'kkwètare' [wa'-k-kwè:-ta-re'] *I sliced it*; **wakkwètaronh** [wak-kwè:-ta-ronh] *I have cut / did cut a slice*; **ikkwe'taronnyon'** [ik-kwe'-ta-rón-nyon'] *I am slicing (cutting slices) it up.* See also: **kena'tarakwètarons** [ke-na'-ta-ra-kwè:-ta-rons] *I cut a slice of bread*; **kena'tarakwe'taronnyon'** [ke-na'-ta-ra-kwe'-ta-rón-nyon'] *I am slicing bread.*

149 **iktahkwas** [ik-táh-kwas] *I take out of* (C-Stem verb - Subj.)
   wa'ktahko' [wa'-k-táh-ko'] *I took out of*; **waktahkwenh** [wak-táh-kwenh] *I have taken out of / did take out of*; **yah tewaktahkwenh** [Yah te-wak-táh-kwenh] *I didn't take out of.*

150 **iktakhe's** [ik-ták-he's] *I run* (C-Stem verb - Subj.)
   iktakhenontye's [ik-tak-he-nón-tye's] *I am run about*; **iktakhenontye'** [ik-tak-he-nón-tye'] *I am running about*; **wa'ktakhenontye'** [wa'-k-tak-he-nón-tye'] *I was running about.* See also: **Tohsa stakhe'** [Tóh-sah sták-he'] *Don't run around!*

151 **ikya'ks** [í-kya'ks] *I cut s.t. off / from* (C-Stem verb - Subj.)
   wàkya'ke' [wà:-kya'-ke'] *I cut s.t. off...*; **wakyàkonh** [wa-kyá:-konh] *I have cut / did cut off, from.*

152 **ikyens** [ík-yens] *I set, lay, put s.t. down* (C-Stem verb - Subj.)
   wàkyen' [wà:-kyen'] *I set, laid, put something down*: ie. **Ohson'karàke yàkyen'** [Oh-son'-ka-rà:-keh yà:-kyen'] *I laid something down (there) on the floor*; **wakyenh** [wák-yenh] *I have set, put / did set, put something down*: ie. **Yah thiyewakyenh** [Yah thi-ye-wák-yenh] *I didn't put, set it down.*

153 **inon** [í:-nonh] *far*
   ie. **Inon yahoti'** [í:-nonh ya-hó:-ti'] *He threw it far.*

   a) **inon niyore** [i-nonh ni-yó:-reh] *far away; in the distance*
      ie. **Inon niyore kerhi'takta ithrate'.** [...ker-hi'-ták-ta' ít-hra-te'] *He is standing in the distance beside a tree.*

   b) **inon nonkati** [í:-nonh non-ká:-tih] *far away, into the distance*
      ie. **Inon nonkati niyahonne'.** [...ni-ya-hón:-ne'] *They went off into the distance.*

154 **ise** [í:-seh] *you (Free Pronoun)*
   This word is used for the purpose of emphasis or clarity (often used with commands): **Ise satketsko!** [Í:-se' sat-kéts-ko] *You set up!* **Ise ken sawenk.** [Í:-se' kén sá:-wenk] *Is it yours (rather than someone else's).*

155 **iyenhs** [í:-yenhs] *it is long*

ie. **Sotsi iyenhs** [Só-tsih í:-yenhs] *It's too long;* **Akwah iken tsi iyenhs** [a-kwah í:-ken' tsi í:-yenhs] *It's very long.* **Yah eh teyenhs** [yah eh té:-yenhs] *It's not long enough.* With nominals: **wahseriyètehs** [wah-se-ri-yè:-tehs] *a long rope;* **yohahehs** [yo-há-hehs] *it's a long path;* **kanonhsehs** [ka-nónh-sehs] *a longhouse.* (see: niyenhsha')

K

156 **ka'** [ká'] *where*

WITH NOMINALS: **Ka' ne ya'niha.** [Ka' ne ya'-ní-ha'] *Where is your father?*
WITH VERBS: **Ka' wahse'.** [Ka' wáh-se'] *Where are you going?*

a) **ka' nonwe** [ka' nón:-weh] *where is it?; where?*

As a question: **Ka' nonwe royo'te'.** [...ro-yó'-te'] *Where is he working?* With questions: **Sateryentare ken ka' nonwe thoyo'te'.** [Sa-ter-yén:-ta-reh kén ka' nón:-weh t-ho-yó'-te'] *Do you know where he works.* With negatives: **Yah tewakateryentare ka' nonwe thoyo'te'.** [Yah te-wa-ka-ter-yén:-ta-reh ka' nón:-weh t-ho-yó'-te'] *I don't know where he works.*

b) **ka' nikayen'** [ka' ni-ká:-yen'] *which one*

Ka' nikayen' tesatonhwentsyoni. [...te-sa-ton-hwen-tsyó:-ni'] *Which one do you want?*

c **ka' nonwe tsi niwat** [ka' non-weh tsi ní:-wat] *whereabouts*

Ka' nonwe tsi niwat yahayen' ne akwatyàtawi'. [...ya-há:-yen' na-kwa-tyà:-ta-wi'] *Whereabouts did he put my coat.*

d **ka' ok nonwe** [ka'k nón:-weh] *somewhere*

Ka' ok nonwe kanatakon thoyo'tenhs. [...ka-ná:-ta-konh t-ho-yó'-tenhs] *He works somewhere in town.*

157 **ka'nahkwa** [ka'-náh-kwa'] *a barrel*

Ka'nahkwakon [ka'-náh-kwa-konh] *in the barrel:* ie. **Ok nahòten ka'nahkwakon ikare.** [Ok na-hò:-ten' ka'-náh-kwa-konh í:-ka-reh] *There's something inside the barrel.*

157 **ka'senhtha'** [ka'-sénh-t-ha'] *I lower something down* (A-Stem - Subj.)

wa'kàsenhte' [wa'-kà:-senh-te'] *I lowered something down;* **waka'senhtonh** [wa-ka'-sénh-tonh] *I have lowered / did lower something down.*

158 **ka'tarihàtha'** [ka'-ta-ri-hà:-t-ha'] *I heat something up* (A-Stem - Subj.)
wa'ka'tariha'te' [wa'-ka'-ta-rí:-ha'-te'] *I heated something up*;
waka'tarihàtonh [wa-ka'-ta-ri-hà:-tonh] *I have heated / did heat s.t. up.*

159 **ka'wahrakehrìta** [ka'-wa-hra-ke-hrì:-ta'] *fried meat*
ie. **ke'wahrakehrìta's** [ke'-wa-hra-ke-hrì:-ta's] *I fry meat.*

160 **kahehta** [ka-héh-ta'] *a field (for growing crops)*
ie. **kahehtakon** [ka-héh-ta-konh] *in the field*; **kahehtakonhson** [ka-heh-ta-kónh-sonh] *out in the field / in the fields*; **tsi tkahehtayen'** [tsit-ka-héh-ta-yen'] *to the field / where the field is*; **kahehtiyo** [ka-heh-tí:-yoh] *a good field*; **kahehtaksen** [ka-heh-ták-senh] *a poor field*; **sha'tekahehtihen** [sha'-te-ka-heh-tí:-henh] *in the middle of the field.* **Wakhehtayen'.** [Wak-héh-ta-yen'] *I have a field*; **Khehtahninons** [k-heh-tah-ní:-nons] *I buy a field*; **Kathehtahninons** [kat-heh-tah-ní:-nons] *I sell a field.*

161 **kahènta** [ka-hèn:-ta'] *a meadow; a pasture field*
ie. **kahèntakon** [ka-hèn:-ta-konh] *in the meadow, pasture*; **kahen'takonhson** [ka-hen'-ta-kónh-sonh] *out in the meadow, pasture / in the meadow, pastures*; **tsi tkahèntayen'** [tsit-ka-hèn:-ta-yen'] *to the meadow, pasture / where the meadow, pasture is*; **kahen'tiyo** [ka-hen'-tí:-yoh] *a good meadow, pasture*; **kahen'taksen** [ka-hen'-ták-senh] *a poor meadow, pasture*; **sha'tekahen'tihen** [sha'-te-ka-hen'-tí:-henh] *in the middle of the meadow, pasture.* **Wakhèntayen'.** [Wak-hèn:-ta-yen'] *I have a meadow, pasture*; **Khen'tahninons** [k-hen'-tah-ní:-nons] *I buy a meadow, pasture*; **Kathen'tahninons** [kat-hen'-tah-ní:-nons] *I sell a meadow, pasture.*

162 **kahere** [ká:-he-reh] *it (inanimate) is sitting up on something*
ie. **Atekhwarahne kahere.** [A-tek-hwa-ráh-ne' ká-he-reh] *It's (sitting up) on the table*; **Yohswen'karohare kahere.** [Yohs-wen'-ka-ró-ha-reh...] *It's (sitting up) on the shelf.* With nominals: **Kanonhsahere** [ka-nonh-she-reh] *a house (sitting up)*; **Yonontahere** [yo-non-tá-he-reh] *a hill / mountain (sitting up), ie. a visible hill.*

163 **kahik** [ká-hik] *fruit*
WITH VERBS: **kahyakwas** [ka-hyá-kwas] *I pick fruit*; **kàyaks** [ká:-yaks] *I eat fruit*; WITH ADJECTIVALS: **wahyowanen** [wa-hyo-wá:-nen] *a large fruit*; **niwahyowa'ah** [ni-wa-hyo-wá:-'ah] *a small fruit*; **wahyawekon** [wa-hya-wé-konh] *good tasting fruit.*

164 **kahkwihsrons** [kah-kwíhs-rons] *I try harder; put effort into* (A-Stem - Subj.)
wa'kahkwihsron' [wa'-kah-kwíhs-ron'] *I tried harder...*; **wakahkwihsronh** [wa-kah-kwíhs-ronh] *I have tried harder....*

165 **kahneka'shatste** [kah-ne-ka'-s-háts-teh] *liquor, whisky*

166 **kahnekakon** [kah-ne-ká-konh] *a soda pop, a soft drink*

167 **kahnenna'takehrìta** [kah-nen-na'-ta-ke-hrì:-ta'] *fried potatoes*
   ie. **ikhnenna'takehrìta's** [ik-hnen-na'-ta-ke-hrì:-ta's] *I fry potatoes.*

168 **Kahnyen'kehàka** [Kah-nyen'-ke-hà:-kah] *the Mohawk nation*

169 **kahonre** [ká-hon-reh] *a gun, a rifle*
   akhonre [ák-hon-reh] *my gun, rifle*; **sahonre** [sá-hon-reh] *your gun, rifle*;
   raohonre [rá-o-hon-reh] *his gun, rifle*; **akaohonre** [a-ká-o-hon-reh] *his gun,
   rifle*. **Wakhonrayen'** [wak-hón:-ra-yen'] *I have a gun, rifle.*

170 **kahontaksen** [ka-hon-ták-senh] *a weed*

180 **kahòntsi** [ka-hòn:-tsih] *black; dark coloured*
   With nominals: **kahyatonhserahòntsi** [ka-hya-tonh-se-ra-hòn:-tsih] *a black
   book*; **katsi'tenhserahòntsi** [ka-tsi'-tenh-se-ra-hòn:-tsih] *a black bird*. Also:
   kahon'tsihstha' [ka-hon'-tsíhst-ha'] *it makes black; blackening.*

181 **kahonweya** [ka-hon-wé:-ya'] *boat*
   ie. **ne kahonweya** [ne ka-hon-wé:-ya'] *the boat*; **thiken' kahonweya** [thí:-
   ken'...] *that boat*; **kiken' kahonweya** [kí:-ken'...] *this boat*. With Possessive:
   akhonweya [ak-hon-wé:-ya'] *my boat*; **sahonweya** [sa-hon-wé:-ya'] *your boat*;
   raohonweya [ra-o-hon-wé:-ya'] *his boat*; **akaohonweya** [a-ka-o-hon-wé:-ya']
   her boat; **onkwahonweya** [on-kwa-hon-wé:-ya'] *our boat*; **raotihonweya** [ra-
   o-ti-hon-wé:-ya'] *their boat*; **raotihonweya'okon** [ra-o-ti-hon-we-ya'-ó:-konh]
   their boats. With Locatives: **kahonweyakon** [ka-hon-wé:-ya-konh] *in the boat*;
   kahonweyahne' [ka-hon-we-yáh-ne'] *by boat*; **kahonweyàke** [ka-hon-we-yà:-
   keh] *on the boat*. With verbs: **wakhonwayen'** [wak-hón:-wa-yen'] *I have a boat*;
   ikhonweyahninons [ik-hon-we-yah-ní:-nons] *I buy a boat.*

182 **kahronkas** [ka-hrón:-kas] *I hear (of something)* (A-Stem - Subj.)
   wa'kàronke' [wa'-kà:-ron-ke'] *I heard (of something)*; **wakahronkenh** [wa-ka-
   hrón:-kenh] *I have heard / did hear (of something).* ie. **Wa'kàronke' tsi tontàre'.**
   [Wa'-kà:-ron-ke' tsi ton-tà:-re'] *I heard that he came back.*

183 **kahronkha'** [ka-hrónk-ha'] *I understand a language* (A-Stem - Subj.)
   kahronkhahkwe' [ka-hrónk-hah-kwe'] *I used to understand...*;
   enkahronkhake' [en-ka-hrónk-ha-ke'] *I will understand...*; **akahronkhake'** [a-
   ka-hro'nk-ha-ke'] *I would / for me to understand....*

184 **kahryèna** [ka-hryè:-na'] *a load, a burden; a heavy pack*
   ie. **kahryehnowanen** [kah-ryeh-no-wá:-nenh] *a heavy burden, load*;
   wakhryènayen' [wak-hryè:-na-yen'] *I have a burden, load*; **wakhryehnakehte'**
   [wak-hryeh-na-kéh-te'] *I am lugging about a heavy load, burden.*

185 **kahsehtha'** [kah-séht-ha'] *I hide something* (A-Stem - Subj.)
   wa'kahsehte' [wa'-káh-seh-te'] *I hid something*; **wakahsehtonh** [wa-kah-séh-

tonh] *I have hidden / did hide something.*

186 **kahserakon** [kah-se-rá-konh] *it smells good (to eat)*

187 **kahseta's** [kah-sé:-ta's] *I count, calculate* (A-Stem - Subj.)
wa'kahsete' [wa'-káh-se-te'] *I counted...*; **wakahsetonh** [wa-kah-sé:-tonh] *I have counted / did count....*

188 **kahshakha'** [kahs-hák-ha'] *I cough* (A-Stem - Subj.)
wa'kahshake' [wa'-káhs-ha-ke'] *I coughed*; **wakahshakenh** [wa-kahs-há:-kenh] *I have coughed / did cough.*

189 **kahsherhonni** [kahs-her-hón:-nih] *doughnuts*

190 **kahstha'** [káhst-ha'] *it is useful*
kahstahkwe' [káhs-tah-kwe'] *it was useful*; **enkahstake'** [en-káhs-ta-ke'] *it will be useful*; **akahtstake'** [a-káhs-ta-ke'] *it would be useful / for it to be useful.*

191 **kahstowa** [kahs-tó:-wa'] *a headdress (Iroquoian style)*

192 **kahswàtha'** [kahs-wà:-t-ha'] *I extinguish, put out a fire, light* (A-Stem - Subj.)
wa'kahswa'te' [wa'-káhs-wa'-te'] *I extinguished...*; **wakahswàtonh** [wa-kahs-wà:-tonh] *I have extinguished / did extinguish....*

193 **kahtentyes** [kah-tén-tyes] *I leave / depart* (A-Stem - Subj.)
wa'kahtenti' [wa'-kah-tén:-ti'] *I left / departed*; **wakahtentyonh** [wa-kah-tén-tyonh] *I have departed / did depart; I have left / did leave; I am away.*

194 **kahtha'kenra** [kah-tha'-kén:-ra'] *a soft maple tree*

195 **kahwatsire** [ka-hwá:-tsi-reh] *a family*
akhwatsire [ak-hwá:-tsi-reh] *my family*; **sahwatsire** [sa-hwá:-tsi-reh] *your family*; **raohwatsire** [ra-o-hwá:-tsi-reh] *his family*; **akaohwatsire** [a-ka-o-hwá:-tsi-reh] *her family.* **Wakhwatsirayen'** [Wak-hwa-tsí:-ra-yen'] *I have a family*; **Wakhwatsirowanen** [wak-hwa-tsi-ro-wá:-nenh] *I have a big family*; **niwakhwatsira'ah** [ni-wak-hwa-tsi-rá:-'ah] *i have a small family.*

196 **kahwe** [káh-weh] *coffee*

197 **kahwènkare** [ka-hwèn:-ka-reh] *snowshoe(s)*

198 **kahwetsheronnyàtha** [kah-wets-he-ron-nyà:-t-ha'] *a coffeepot*

199 **kahwihsta'eks** [kah-wihs-tá:-'eks] *a clock*

200 **kahyakwas** [ka-hyá-kwas] *I pick fruit* (A-Stem - Subj.)
wa'kahyako' [wa'-ka-hyá:-ko'] *I picked fruit*; **wakahyakwenh** [wa-ka-hyá-kwenh] *I have picked / did pick fruit.*

201 **kahyaton** [ka-hyá:-tonh] *it is written*
kahyatònne' [ka-hya-tòn:-ne'] *it was written*; **enkahyatonhake'** [en-ka-hya-tón-ha-ke'] *it will be written*; **akahyatonhake'** [a-ka-hya-tón-ha-ke'] *it would be written / for it to be written.*

202 **kahyatonhsera** [ka-hya-tónh-se-ra'] *a book, paper*
ie. **ne kahyatonhsera** [ne ka-hya-tónh-se-ra'] *the book*; **thiken' kahyatonhsera** [thí:-ken'...] *that book*; **kiken' kahyatonhsera** [kí:-ken'...] *this book.* With Possessive: **akhyatonhsera** [ak-hya-tónh-se-ra'] *my book*; **sahyatonhsera** [sa-hya-tónh-se-ra'] *your book*; **raohyatonhsera** [ra-o-hya-tónh-se-ra'] *his book*; **akaohyatonhsera** [a-ka-o-hya-tónh-se-ra'] *her book*; **onkwahyatonhsera'okon** [on-kwa-hya-tonh-se-ra'-ó:-konh] *our books*; **raotihyatonhsera'okon** [ra-o-ti-hya-tonh-se-ra'-ó:-konh] *their books.* With Locatives: **kahyatonhserakon** [ka-hya-tonh-se-rá:-konh] *in the book*; **kahyatonhseràke** [ka-hya-tonh-se-rà:-keh] *on the book.* With verbs: **wakhyatonhserayen'** [wak-hya-tonh-se-rá:-yen'] *I have a book*; **khyatonhserahninons** [khya-tonh-se-rah-ní:-nons] *I buy a book.*

203 **kahyatonhseratokenhti** [ka-hya-tonh-se-ra-to-kénh-tih] *a Bible; a holy book*

204 **kahyonha** [ka-hyón-ha'] *a stream, a river; moving water*
With Locatives: **kahyonhakon** [ka-hyón-ha-konh] *in the stream...*; **kahyonhakta** [ka-hyon-hák-ta'] *beside the stream...*; **kahyonhaktatye'** [ka-hyon-hak-tá-tye'] *along the stream...*; **kahyonhakonhson** [ka-hyon-ha-kónh-sonh] *out in the stream....* With Adjectivals: **kahyonhowanen** [ka-hyon-ho-wá:-nenh] *a large stream... / a river*; **nikahyonha'ah** [ni-ka-hyon-há:-'ah] *a small stream / a creek.* In a verb phrase: **ya'tekhyàyaks** [ya'-tek-hyà:-yaks] *I cross over a stream....*

205 **kahyonhowanen** [ka-hyon-ho-wá:-nen] *a river* (see: kahyonha)

206 **kakhare** [kák-ha-reh] *a skirt*

207 **kakhwa** [kák-hwa'] *food, nourishment*
ie. **kekhonnis** [kek-hón:-nis] *I make food (I cook)*; **kekhwaweyenhon** [kek-hwa-we-yén-honh] *I know how to cook.* With Adjectivals: **kakhwiyo** [kak-hwí:-yoh] *good food*; **kakhwaksen** [kak-hwák-senh] *poor / bad food.* **erhar aotihkwa** [ér-har a-o-tík-hwa'] *dog food.*

208 **kakhwawihstonhtha** [kak-hwa-wihs-tónt-ha'] *a refrigerator*

209 **kakonhsa** [ka-kónh-sa'] *a mask; a face*

210 **kaksa** [kák-sa'] *a dish*
With Locatives: **kaksàke** [kak-sà:-keh] *on the dish*; **kaksakta** [kak-sák-ta'] *beside the dish*; **kaksòkon** [kak-sò:-konh] *under the dish.* With Adjectivals:

kaksowanen [kak-so-wá:-nenh] *a large dish / a platter*.

211 **kakwe'taratshera** [ka-kwe'-ta-ráts-he-ra'] *a slice*
skakwe'taratsherat [ska-kwe'-ta-ráts-he-rat] *one slice*;
tekakwe'taratsherake [te-ka-kwe'-ta-rats-he-rá:-keh] *two slices*; **eso**
nikakwe'taratsherake [é:-soh ni-ka-kwe'-ta-rats-he-rá:-keh] *many / lots of*
slices. With a verb: **Wisk niwakkwe'taratsherayen'**. [Wihsk ni-wak-kwe'-
ta-rats-he-rá:-yen'] *I have five slices*.

212 **kanahkwa** [ka-náh-kwa'] *a marriage; a household*
kanahkwiyo [ka-nah-kwí:-yoh] *a good marriage / household*; **kanahkwaksen**
[ka-nah-kwák-senh] *a poor marriage / household*; **kenahkwaweyenhonh** [ke-nah-
kwa-we-yén-honh] *I am a good housekeeper*; **kenahkwatshenryes** [ke-nah-
kwats-hén-ryes] *I look for a partner (for marriage)*.

213 **kanahskwa** [ka-náhs-kwa'] *a domestic animal*
ie. **wakenahskwayen'** [wa-ke-náhs-kwa-yen'] *I have a domestic animal*: ie.
Erhar wakenahskwayen'. [Ér-har...] *I have a dog*.

214 **kanakare** [ka-ná:-ka-reh] *a pole*

215 **kanakta** [ka-nák-ta'] *bed, place*
With Locatives: **kanaktàke** [ka-nak-tà:-keh] *on the bed*; **kanaktòkon** [ka-nak-
tò:-konh] *under the bed*; **Eh tkanaktayen'** [Eh t-ka-nák-ta-yen'] *there's a bed*
(there); **Kenh kanaktayen'** [Kenh ka-nák-ta-yen'] *Here is a bed (here)*. With
Possessives: **akenakta** [a-ke-nák-ta'] *my bed*; **sanakta** [sa-nák-ta'] *your bed*;
raonakta [ra-o-nák-ta'] *his bed*; **akaonakta** [a-ka-o-nák-ta'] *her bed*; **aonakta**
[a-o-nák-ta'] *its bed*. As an expression: **Wakenaktote** [Wa-ke-nák-to-teh] *I*
have time (to do something); **Yah tewakenaktote** [Yah te-wa-ke-nák-to-teh] *I don't*
have time (to do something).

216 **kanànon** [ka-nà:-nonh] *it is full*
With nominals: **ka'nahkwanànon** [ka'-nah-kwa-nà:-nonh] *a barrel full*;
kayaranànonh [ka-ya-ra-nà:-nonh] *a bag full*; **karontotsheranànon** [ka-ron-
tots-he-ra-nà:-nonh] *a box full*; **kana'tsyanànon** [ka-na'-tsya-nà:-nonh] *a pail*
full.

217 **kanata** [ka-ná:-ta'] *a town, a village*
kanatakon [ka-ná:-ta-konh] *in the town*; **kanatakta** [ka-na-ták-ta'] *near / beside*
the town; **kanatahere** [ka-na-tá-he-reh] *a town sitting up (on a hill, ridge, bank*;
sha'tekanatihen [s-ha'-te-ka-na-tí:-henh] *in the middle of the town*; **kanathen**
[ka-nát-henh] *mid-town, downtown*; **akta tsi tkanatayen'** [ák-ta' tsit ka-ná:-ta-
yen'] *next to the town*. With Adjectivals: **kanatowanen** [ka-na-to-wá:-nenh] *a*
large town / a city; **nikanata'ah** [ni-ka-na-tá:-'ah] *a small town / a village, hamlet*.

218 kanàtaronk [ka-nà:-ta-ronk] *bread*
    ie. **kana'taronkhonwe** [ka-na'-ta-ronk-hón:-weh] *home-made bread;*
    kana'tarakwètaron [ka-na'-ta-ra-kwè:-ta-ronh] *sliced bread.* With verbs:
    wakena'tarayen' {wa-ke-na'-ta-rá:-yen'] *I have (some) bread;*
    kena'tarahninons [ke-na'-ta-rah-ní:-nons] *I buy (some) bread;*
    kena'tarakwètarons [ke-na'-ta-ra-kwè:-ta-rons] *I slice (some) bread;*
    kena'taronnis [ke-na'-ta-rón:-nis] *I make (some) bread;* **kenàtaraks** [ke-nà:-ta-
    raks] *I eat bread.*

219 kanathen [ka-nát-henh] *mid-town; downtown* (See: kanata)

220 kanatowanen [ka-na-to-wá:-nenh] *a city* (See: kanata)

221 kanàtsyonk [ka-nà:-tsyonk] *a pail, bucket*
    ie. **kanàtsyakon** [ka-nà:-tsya-konh] *in the pail;* **kana'tsyanànon** [ka-na'-tsya-
    nà:-nonh] *a pail full;* **wakenàtsyayen'** [wa-ke-nà:-tsya-yen'] *I have a pail...;*
    kena'tsyenhawe' [ke-na'-tsyén-ha-we'] *I am carrying a pail....*

222 kaneka [ká-ne-kah] *anywhere*
    Onhka ok ken kaneka tkonne's. [Onh-kak kén ká-ne-kah t-kón:-ne's] *Is
    there anybody there anywhere?* **Yah kaneka tehonne's.** [Yah ká-ne-kah te-hón:-
    ne's] *They are not anywhere.*

223 kanekòta [ka-ne-kò:-ta'] *a ladder*
    ie. **kaneko'tàke** [ka-ne-ko'-tà:-keh] *on the ladder*

224 kanen [ká:-nenh] *seed(s)*

225 kanena [ka-nè:-na'] *a costume, a uniform*

226 kanenhstohare [ka-nenh-stó-ha-reh] *lyed corn soup*

227 kanènra [ka-nèn:-ra'] *a band, troupe, group*
    ie. **kanenhrowanen** [ka-nen-hro-wá:-nenh] *a large crowd / a congregation;*
    kanènrehs [ka-nèn:-rehs] *a long line / a procession;* **yotinenhrowanen** [yo-ti-
    nen-hro-wá:-nenh] *a committee;* **niyotinenhra'ah** [ni-yo-ti-nen-hrá:-'ah] *a sub-
    committee;* **kenenhronnis** [ke-nen-hrón:-nis] *I organize a committee, club.*

228 kanerahta'kerha [ka-ne-rah-ta'-kér-ha'] *(loose-leaf) tea*

229 kaneron [ká-ne-ron] *a white ash tree*

230 kanheks [kán-heks] *a ribbon; silk*

231 kanhoha [kan-hó-ha'] *door*
    With Locatives: **kanhohàke** [kan-ho-hà:-keh] *on the door;* **kanhohakta** [kan-
    ho-hák-ta'] *near / beside the door;* **tsi kanhokàronte** [tsi kan-ho-kà:-ron-teh] *at /
    to the doorway.* With verbs: **kenhohaya'ks** [ke-n-ho-há:-ya'ks] *I knock on the*

door; **kenhohakahrontha'** [ke-n-ho-ha-ka-hrónt-ha'] *I make an opening for a door*; **kenhohàreks** [ke-n-ho-hà:-reks] *I push the door open / closed.*

232 **kanhya** [kán-hya'] *a stick*

233 **kaniyonta** [ka-ni-yón:-ta] *a minnow*

234 **kannenna'kène** [ka-nen-na'-kè:-neh] *in the fall*
Kanenna'kène' niya'teyohserake yakwanenhstayenthokwas. [...ni-ya'-te-yoh-se-rá:-keh ya-kwa-nenhs-ta-yent-hkwas] *Every year in the fall we harvest the corn.*

235 **kanohares** [ka-nó-ha-rehs] *a washing machine*

236 **kanon'onhserakeras** [ka-non'-onh-se-rá-ke-rahs] *cucumber(s)*

237 **kanon'tihsa** [ka-non'-tíh-sa'] *buttermilk*

238 **kanonhsa** [ka-nónh-sa'] *a house, building*
ie. **kanonhsakon** [ka-nónh-sa-konh] *in the house*; **kanonhsakta** [ka-nonh-sák-ta'] *near the house*; **kanonhsòkon** [ka-nonh-sò:-konh] *under the house*; **kanonhsaktatye'** [ka-nonh-sak-tá-tye'] *along the side of the house*; **ihsi na'kanonhsati** [íh-si' na'-ka-nónh-sa-tih] *on the other side of the house*; **karo na'kanonhsati** [ká-ro' na'-ka-nónh-sa-tih] *on this side of the house*; **ohenton tsi tkanonhsote** [o-hén:-tonh tsit ka-nónh-so-teh] *in front of the house*; **ohnàken tsi tkanonhsote** [oh-nà:-kenh tsit ka-nónh-so-teh] *behind the house*; **akwah thikanonhsakwekon** [kwah t-hi-ka-nonh-sa-kwé:-konh] *all around the house.* With verbs: **kenonhsahninons** [ke-nonh-sah-ní:-nons] *I buy a house*; **katenonhsahninons** [ka-te-nonh-sah-ní:-nons] *I sell a house*; **wakenonhsayen'** [wa-ke-nónh-sa-yen'] *I have a house*; **katenonhsanihas** [ka-te-nonh-sa-ní-has] *I rent a house*; **kenonhsanihas** [ke-nonh-sa-ní-has] *I lease a house.*

239 **kanonhsehs** [ka-nónh-sehs] *a longhouse*

240 **Kanonhsehsneha** [Ka-nonh-sehs-né-ha'] *the Longhouse (way of life & belief)*

241 **kanonnya** [ka-nón-nya'] *a dance*
ie. **kenonnyaweyenhon** [ke-non-nya-we-yén-honh] *I am a good dancer*; (See: tekenonnyahkwa')

242 **kanòntara** [ka-nòn:-ta-ra'] *soup*
kanon'tarakon [ka-non'-ta-rá:-konh] *in the soup.* **kenon'tarathsoris** [ke-non'-ta-rat-hsó-ris] *I eat soup*; **kenon'taronnis** [ke-non'-ta-rón:-nis] *I make soup.*

243 **kanontatsi** [ka-nón:-ta-tsih] *a catepillar*

244 **kanoron** [ka-nó:-ronh] *it is expensive, dear; hard to come by*
ie. **Sotsi kanoron** [só-tsih ka-nó:-ronh] *it's too expensive*; **akwah iken' tsi**

27

kanoron [kwah í:-ken' tsi ka-nó:-ron'] *it very expensive*; **Nikanoron na'a** [Ni-ka-nó:-ronh ná:-'ah] *It's so expensive!* With nominals: **kanonsanoron** [ka-nonh-sa-nó:-ron] *an expensive house*; **watya'tawi'tsheranoron** [wa-tya'-ta-wi'ts-he-ra-nó:-ron] *an expensive coat, shirt, dress*; **kakhwanoron** [kak-hwa-nó:-ron] *expensive food*.

²⁴⁵ **kanyatare** [ka-nyá:-ta-reh] *a lake*
ie. **kanyataràke** [ka-nya-ta-rà:-keh] *on the lake*; **kanyatara'kehson** [ka-nya-ta-ra'-kéh-sonh] *out on the lake*; **sha'tekanyatarihen** [sha'-te-ka-nya-ta-rí-henh] *in the middle of the lake*; **kanyatarhen** [ka-nya-tár-henh] *in mid-lake*.

²⁴⁶ **kànyote** [kà:-nyo-teh] *it is standing upright*
kahnyotehkwe' [kah-nyó:-teh-kwe'] *it was standing upright*; **enkahnyoteke'** [en-kah-nyó:-te-ke'] *it will be standing upright*; **akahnyoteke'** [a-kah-nyó:-te-ke'] *it would be standing upright / for it to be standing upright*. With nominals: **kerhitote** [ker-hì:-to-teh] *a tree (standing upright)*; **kanonhsote** [ka-nónh-so-teh] *a house (standing upright)*.

²⁴⁷ **karahsto** [ka-hráhs-toh] *a drawing*

²⁴⁸ **karenna** [ka-rén:-na'] *a song, a chant*
ne karenna [ne ka-rén:-na'] *the song*; **thiken' karenna** [thí:-ken'...] *that song*; **kiken' karenna** [kí:-ken'...] *this song*; **karenna'okon** [ka-ren-na'-ó:-konh] *songs (of a similar type)*; **karennahson'a** [ka-ren-nah-són:-'ah] *songs (of different types)*. (see: katerennotha')

²⁴⁹ **karhakon** [kar-há:-konh] *in the woods*
ie. **karhakonhson** [kar0ha-kónh-sonh] *out in the woods*. **Ya'tekaterhawe'ehstha'** [ya'-te-ka-ter-ha-we'-éhst-ha'] *I enter into the woods*; **Ya'tekaterhohetstha'** [ya'-te-ka-ter-ho-hétst-ha'] *I go through the woods*.

²⁵⁰ **karhakonha** [kar-ha-kón-ha'] *a hawk*

²⁵¹ **karihonni** [ka-ri-hón:-nih] *the reason is...*
ie. **Ne'e karihonni eh nahatyere'.** [Né:-'eh ka-ri-hón:-nih eh na-há-tye-re'] *That is the reason he did it.*

²⁵² **karihstakenra** [ka-rihs-ta-kén:-ra'] *tin*

²⁵³ **karihstatsi** [ka-ríhs-ta-tsih] *metal*
ie. **karihstàke** [ka-rihs-tà:-keh] *on the metal (ie. on the stove)*; **karihstatatye'** [ka-rihs-ta-tá-tye'] *on the rails / railway track*; **tekarihstòraraks** [te-ka-rihs-tò:-ra-raks] *a typewriter (ie. it squeezes the metal)*; **yonterihstayentahkwa** [yon-te-rihs-ta-yen-táh-kwa'] *a trap*; **karihstakenra** [ka-rihs-ta-kén:-ra'] *tin, pewter*; **yorihstahniron** [yo-rihs-tah-ní:-ronh] *steel*; **nikarihstatenhsha** [ni-ka-rihs-ta-ténhs-ha'] *sheet-metal*. With verbs: **kerihstayens** [ke-ríhs-ta-yens] *I set traps*; **kerihstìseres** [ke-rihs-tì:-se-rehs] *I survey / am a surveyor*; **kerihstonni** [ke-rihs-

tón:-ni'] *I am a blacksmith / metal-worker*; **tekerihstòraraks** [te-ke-rihs-tò:-ra-raks] *I type.*

254 **karihstohare** [ka-rihs-tó-ha-reh] *shovel*

255 **Karihstyahne** [Ka-rihs-tyáh-ne'] *Christianity*

256 **karihton** [ka-ríh-tonh] *a red oak*

257 **karihwènta's** [ka-ri-hwèn:-ta's] *it wears out*
wa'karihwèntane' [wa'-ka-ri-hwèn:-ta'-ne'] *it wore out*; **yorihwen'ta'onh** [yo-ri-hwen'-tá:-'onh] *it have worn out / it is worn out.*

258 **Karihwiyo** [Ka-ri-hwí:-yoh] *the Handsome Lake religion*

259 **kario** [ká-ri-o'] *a wild animal*
ne kario [ne ká-ri-o'] *the wild animal*; **thiken' kario** [thí:-ken'...] *that wild animal*; **kiken' kario** [kí:-ken'...] *this wild animal*; **kontirio** [kon-tí:-ri-o'] *wild animals.* With numericals: **skayàtat kario** [ska-yà:-tat...] *one wild animal*; **tekeniyahsen tekenirio** [te-ke-ni-yáh-senh te-ke-ní:-ri-o'] *two wild animals*; **ahsen nikonti kontirio'okonha** [áh-sen' ni-kón:-tih kon-ti-ri-o'-o-kón-ha'] *three wild animals.* **kario'tsheranakere'** [ka-ri-o'ts-he-ra-ná-ke-re'] *there are plenty of wild animals*; **kario'tsheranakerehkwe'** [ka-ri-o'ts-he-ra-ná-ke-reh-kwe'] *there were plenty of wild animals.*

260 **karis** [ká:-ris] *a sock, socks*

261 **karìwehs** [ka-rì:-wehs] *a long time*
Karìwehs tsi rohtentyonh. [Ka-rì:wehs tsi roh-tén-tyonh] *He's been gone a long time.*

262 **karo** [ká-ro'] *on this side*
ie. **karo na'kanonhsati** [...na'-ka-nónh-sa-tih] *this side of the house*; **karo na'ohahati** [...na'-o-há-ha-tih] *this side of the road*; **karo na'kanyatarati** [...na'-ka-nya-ta-rá:-tih] *this side of the lake*; **karo na'kahyonhati** [...na'-ka-hyón-ha-tih] *this side of the river*; **karo nonta'ènrati** [...non-ta'-èn:-ra-tih] *this side of the fence*; **karo na'kahehtati** [...na'ka-héh-ta-tih] *this side of the field*; **karo na'karhati** [...na'-kár-ha-tih] *this side of the woods.* (see: ihsi)

a) **karo nonwe** [ka-ro' nón:-weh] *over on this side*
ie. **Karo nonwe royo'te'.** [Ka-ro' nón:-weh ro-yó'-te'] *He's working on this side.*

b) **karo nonkati** [ka-ro' non-ká:-tih] *toward this side; over this way*
ie. **Karo nonkati tahonne'.** [Ka-ro' non-ká:-tih ta-hón:-ne'] *They are coming toward this side.*

263 **karonta** [ka-rón:-ta'] *a log; a tree trunk*
    karontàke [ka-ron-tà:-keh] *on the log, tree trunk;* **karontakon** [ka-rón:-ta-konh]
    in the log, tree trunk; **karontowanen** [ka-ron-to-wá:-nenh] *a large log, tree trunk.*

264 **karontats** [ka-rón:-tats] *I shoot* (A-Stem - Subj.)
    wa'karontate' [wa'-ka-rón:-ta-te'] *I shot;* **wakarontatonh** [wa-ka-ron-tá:-
    tonh] *I have shot / did shoot.*

265 **karontotshera** [ka-ron-tóts-he-ra'] *a box*
    With Locatives: **karontotsheràke** [ka-ron-tots-he-rà:-keh] *on the box;*
    karontotsherakon [ka-ron-tots-he-rá:-konh] *in the box;* **karontotsherakta**
    [ka-ron-tots-he-rák-ta'] *beside the box.* With Adjectival: **karontotsherowanen**
    [ka-ron-tots-he-ro-wá:-nenh] *a large box;* **nikarontotshera'ah** [ni-ka-ron-tòts-
    he-rá:-'ah] *a small box;* **karontotsheranànon** [ka-ron-tots-he-ra-nà:-nonh] *a
    box full.*

266 **karonware** [ka-rón:-wa-reh] *wire; a nail, a needle*

267 **karònya** [ka-ròn:-ya'] *sky*
    karonhyàke [ka-ron-hyà:-keh] *in the sky;* **tsi tkarònyate** [tsit ka-ròn-ya-teh]
    to the sky; **karonhyakon** [ka-ron-hyá:-konh] *in heaven.* (see: orònya)

268 **kàsere'** [kà:-se-re'] *car, vehicle, wagon*
    ne kàsere' [ne kà:-se-re'] *the car;* **thiken' kàsere'** [thí:-ken'...] *that car;*
    kiken' kàsere' [kí:-ken'...] *this car.* With Possessives: **akèsere'** [a-kè:-se-
    re'] *my car;* **sàsere'** [sà:-se-re'] *your car;* **raòsere'** [ra-ò:-se-re'] *his car;*
    akaòsere' [a-ka-ò:-se-re'] *her car.* With Locatives: **ka'seretsherakon** [ka'-
    se-rets-he-rá:-konh] *in the car;* **ka'seretsheròkon** [ka'-se-rets-he-rò:-konh]
    under the car; **ka'seretsheràke** [ka'-se-rets-he-rà:-keh] *on the car.* With Verbs:
    wake'seretsherayen' [wa-ke'-se-rets-he-rá:-yen'] *I have a car;*
    ke'seretsherahninons [ke'-se-rets-he-rah-ní:-nons] *I buy a car;*
    katate'seretsherahninons [ka-ta-te'-se-rets-he-rah-ní:-nons] *I sell my car;*
    kate'seretsherohares [ka-te'-se-rets-he-ró-ha-res] *I was my car.*

269 **katahsehtha'** [ka-tah-séht-ha'] *I hide (myself)* (A-Stem - Subj.)
    wa'katahsehte' [wa-ka-táh-seh-teh] *I hid...;* **wakatahsehtonh** [wa-ka-tah-
    séh-tonh] *I have hid / did hide....*

270 **katakwariks** [ka-ta-kwá:-riks] *I wrap s.t. up; I make up a package, bundle*
    (A-Stem Subj.) **wa'katakwarike'** [wa'-ka-ta-kwá:-ri'ke'] *I wrapped s.t. up...;*
    wakatakwarih [wa-ka-ta-kwá:-rih] *I have wrapped / did wrap....* (See: **atakwari**)

271 **katakterihonnyennis** [ka-ta-te-ri-hon-nyén:-nis] *I read (to myself)* (A-Stem verb)
    wa'katerihonnyen' [wa'-ka-ta-te-ri-hón:-nyen'] *I read...;*
    wakatakterihonnyennih [wa-ka-ta-te-ri-hon-nyén:-nih] *I did read / have read....*

30

272 **katatis** [ka-tá:-tis] *I speak / talk* (A-Stem - Subj.)
wa'katati' [wa'-ka-tá:-ti'] *I spoke*; **wakatatih** [wa-ka-tá:-tih] *I have spoken / did speak.*

273 **katawenhs** [ka-tá:-wenhs] *I swim* (A-Stem - Subj.)
wa'katawen' [wa'-ka-tá:-wen'] *I swam*; **wakatawenhonh** [wa-ka-ta-wén-honh] *I have swum / did swim.*

274 **katawèyàtha'** [ka-ta-we-yà:-t-ha'] *I enter* (A-Stem - Subj.)
wa'kataweya'te' [wa'-ka-tá-we-ya'-te'] *I entered*; **wakataweyàtonh** [wa-ka-ta-we-yà:-tonh] *I have entered / did enter.* (See: **tkataweyàtha'**; **yekataweyàtha'**)

275 **kate'nyentenhs** [ka-te'-nyén:-tenhs] *I try, attempt* (A-Stem - Subj.)
wa'kate'nyenten' [wa'-ka-te'-nyén:-ten'] *I tried / attempted*; **wakate'nyenten'onh** [wa-ka-te'-nyen-tén:-'onh] *I have tried / did try....*

276 **kate'nyentenhstha'** [ka-te'-nyen-ténhst-ha'] *I measure / weight something* (A-Stem - Subj.) **wa'kate'nyentenhste'** [wa'-ka-te'-nyén:-tenhs-te'] *I measured...*; **wakate'nyentenhstonh** [wa-ka-te'-nyen-ténhs-tonh] *I have measured / did measure....*

277 **katehswàtha'** [ka-tehs-wà:-t-ha'] *I smell (sniff at) something* (A-Stem - Subj.)
wa'katehswa'te' [wa'-ka-téhs-wa'-te'] *I smelled (sniffed)...*; **wakatehswàtonh** [wa-ka-tehs-wà:-tonh] *I have smelled / did smell....*

278 **katekhonnis** [ka-tek-hón:-nis] *I eat (what I've cooked)* (A-Stem - Subj.)
wa'katekhonni' [wa'-ka-tek-hón:-ni'] *I ate...*; **wakatekhonnih** [wa-ka-tek-hón:-nih] *I have eaten / did eat...; I am eating.*

279 **katekwas** [ka-té-kwas] *I run away* (A-Stem - Subj.)
wa'kateko' [wa'-ka-té:-koh] *I ran away*; **wakatekwenh** [wa-ka-té-kwenh] *I have run away / did run away.*

280 **katenhninons** [ka-tenh-ní:-nons] *I sell* (A-Stem - Subj.)
wa'katenhninon' [wa'-ka-tenh-ní:-non'] *I sold*; **wakatenhninonh** [wa-ka-tenh-ní:-nonh] *I have sold / did sell.*

281 **katenhs** [ká:-tenhs] *it is thick*
Sotsi katenhs. [Só-tsih ká:-tenhs] *it's too thick*; **Akwah iken' tsi katenhs.** [Kwah í:-ken' tsi ká:-tenhs] *it's very thick*; **Yah e'tho tekatenhs.** [Yah é-t-hoh te-ká:-tenhs] *it's not thick enough.* With nominals: **kahswen'karatenhs** [kah-swen'-ka-rá:-tenhs] *a thick board*; **wahsiratenhs** [wah-si-rá:-tenhs] *a thick blanket.*

282 **katennihskwahtha'** [ka-ten-nihs-kwáht-ha'] *I take my time* (A-Stem - Subj.)
wa'katennihskwahte' [wa'-ka-ten-níhs-kwah-te'] *I took my time*; **wakatennihskwahtonh** [wa-ka-ten-nihs-kwáh-tonh] *I have taken / did take my time.*

283 **katerahya'tahkwa'** [ka-te-ra-hya'-táh-kwa'] *I am obstinate* (A-Stem - Subj.)
wa'akterahyàtahkwe' [wa'-ka-te-ra-hyà:-tah-kwe'] *I was obstinate*;
wakaterahya'kwahkwenh [wa-ka-te-ra-hya'-táh-kwenh] *I have been obstinate.*

284 **katerakwas** [ka-te-rá-kwas] *I keep* (A-Stem - Subj.)
wa'katerako' [wa'-ka-te-rá:-ko'] *I kept*; **wakaterakwenh** [wa-ka-te-rá-kwenh] *I have kept / did keep.*

285 **katerennotha'** [ka-te-ren-nót-ha'] *I sing* (A-Stem - Subj.)
wa'katerennoten' [wa'-ka-te-ren-nó:-ten'] *I sang*; **wakaterennoteh** [wa-ka-te-rén:-no-teh] *I have sung / did sing.*

286 **katerharats** [ka-ter-há:-rats] *I am expecting, hoping for* (A-Stem - Subj.)
wa'katerharate' [wa'-ka-ter-há:-ra-te'] *I was expecting, hoping for*;
wakaterhare [wa-ka-tér-ha-reh] *I have been expecting, hoping for.*

287 **katerihwayenhstha'** [ka-te-ri-hwa-yénhst-ha'] *I study* (A-Stem - Subj.)
wa'katerìwayenhste' [wa'-ka-te-rì:-wa-yenhs-te'] *I studied*;
wakaterihwayenhstonh [wa-ka-te-rih-wa-yénhst-ha'] *i have studied / did study.*

288 **kateriyos** [ka-te-rí:-yos] *I fight* (A-Stem - Subj.)
wa'kateriyo' [wa'-ka-te-rí:-yo'] *I fought*; **wakateriyoh** [wa-ka-te-rí:-yoh] *I have fought / did fight; I am fighting.*

289 **kateròroks** [ka-te-rò:-roks] *I watch (something going on)* (A-Stem - Subj.)
wa'kateròroke' [wa'-ka-te-rò:-ro-ke'] *I watched...*; **wakateròronh** [wa-ka-te-rò:-ronh] *I have watched / did watch....*

290 **katèseres** [ka-tè:-se-res] *I drag something* (A-Stem - Subj.)
wa'katèsere' [wa'-ka-tè:-se-re'] *I dragged...*; **wakatèsereh** [wa-ka-tè:-se-reh] *I have dragged / did drag...*

291 **kateweyenhstha'** [ka-te-we-yénhst-ha'] *I practice* (A-Stem - Subj.)
wa'kateweyenhste' [wa'-ka-té:-we-yenhs-te'] *I practiced*;
wakateweyenhstonh [wa-ka-te-we-yénhs-tonh] *I have studied / did study.*

292 **kateweyèntons** [ka-te-we-yèn:-tons] *I take care / look after; I put away / conserve* (A-Stem - Subj.) **wa'kateweyènton'** [wa'-ka-te-we-yèn:-ton'] *I took care of...*; **wakateweyèntonh** [wa-ka-te-we-yèn:-tonh] *I have taken care of / did take care of....*

293 **kathontats** [kat-hón:-tats] *I consent* (A-Stem - Subj.)
wa'kathontate' [wa'-kat-hón:-ta-te'] *I consented*; **wakathontatonh** [wa-kat-hon-tá:-tonh] *I have consented / did consent.*

294 **kathseronnis** [kat-hse-rón:-nis] *I get dressed up* (A-Stem - Subj.)
kathseronni' [kat-hse-rón:-ni'] *I am getting dressed up*; **wa'kathseronni'** [wa'-kat-hse-rón:-ni'] *I got dressed up*; **wakathseronnih** [wa-kat-hse-rón:-nih] *I have gotten dressed up / did get dressed up.*

295 **kathsnenhtha'** [kaths-nénh-t-ha'] *I descend* (A-Stem - Subj.)
wa'kathsnenhte' [wa'-kat-hsnenh-te'] *I descended*; **wakathsnenhtonh** [wa-kat-hsnénh-tonh] *I have descended / did descend.*

296 **kathsokwas** [kat-hsó-kwas] *I smoke* (A-Stem - Subj.)
wa'kathsoko' [wa'-kat-hsó:-ko'] *I smoked*; **wakathsokwenh** [wa-kat-hsó-kwenh] *I have smoked / did smoke.*

297 **kathsoris** [kat-hsó:-ris] *I eat soup* (A-Stem - Subj.)
wa'kathsori' [wa'-kat-hsó:-ri'] *I ate soup*; **wakathsorih** [wa-kat-hsó:-rih] *I have eaten soup / did eat soup.*

298 **kati** [ká-ti'] *so then; consequently*
ie. **Oh kati nahòten sahninonh.** [Oh ká-ti' na-hò:-ten' sah-ní:-nonh] *So then what did you buy*; **Oh kati nonwa nihsatyerha'.** [Oh ká-ti' nón:-wah nih-sa-tyér-ha'] *So then what are you doing now?*

299 **katita's** [ka-tí-ta's] *I get into (a vehicle)* (A-Stem - Subj.)
wa'katita' wa'-ka-tí-ta'] *I got into...*; **wakatitenh** [wa-ka-tí-tenh] *I have gotten into....*

300 **katitahkwas** [ka-ti-táh-kwas] *I get out (of a vehicle)* (A-Stem - Subj.)
wa'katitahko' [wa'-ka-ti-táh-ko'] *I got out...*; **wakatitahkwenh** [wa-ka-ti-táh-kwenh] *I have gotten out / did get out....*

301 **katkahthos** [kat-káh-t-hos] *I see / look* (A-Stem - Subj.)
wa'katkahtho' [wa'-kat-káht-ho'] *I saw; looked*; **wakatkahthonh** [wa-kat-káht-honh] *I did see / have seen; I have looked / did look.*

302 **katkarhatenyes** [kat-kar-ha-té-nyes] *I turn around* (A-Stem - Subj.)
wa'katkarhateni' [wa'-kat-kar-ha-té:-ni'] *I turned around*; **wakatkarhatenyonh** [wa-kat-kar-ha-té-nyonh] *I have turned / did turn around....*

303 **katkawas** [kat-ká:-was] *I quit / let go of* (A-Stem - Subj.)
wa'katkawe' [wa'-kát-ka-we'] *I quit / let go*; **wakatkawenh** [wa-kat-ká:-wenh] *I have quit / did quit; I have let go of / did let go of.* ie. **Wakatkawenh tsi katshokwas.** [Wa-kat-ká:-wenh tsi kats-hó-kwas] *I have quit smoking.*

304 **katke** [kát-keh] *when? whenever*
ie. **Katke entsisahtenti'.** [Kát-keh en-tsi-sah-tén:-ti'] *When are you going home?*
a) **katke ok** [kát-kok] *sometime*
ie. **Katke ok thetenre tontàre'.** [Kát-kok the-tén:-reh ton-tà:-re'] *He came back sometime yesterday.*

305 **katkènse's** [kat-kèn:-se's] *I taste / examine / look at* (A-Stem - Subj.)
wa'katken'se' [wa'-kát-ken'-se'] *I tasted / examined / looked at*; **wakatkènseh** [wa-kat-kèn:-seh] *I have tasted / examined / looked; I did taste / examine / look at.*

306 **katketskwas** [kat-kéts-kwas] *I get up* (A-Stem - Subj.)
wa'katketsko' [wa'-kat-kéts-ko'] *I got up*; **wakatketskwenh** [wa-kat-kéts-kwenh] *I have gotten up / I did get up.*

307 **katkwatakwas** [kat-kwa-tá-kwas] *I get fixed up* (A-Stem - Subj.)
wa'katkwatako' [wa-kat-kwa-tá:-ko'] *I got fixed up*; **wakatkwatakwenh** [wa-kat-kwa-tá-kwenh] *I have gotten fixed up / I did get fixed up.*

308 **katkwenyes** [kat-kwé-nyes] *I win; succeed* (A-Stem - Subj.)
wa'katkweni' [wa'-kat-kwé:-ni'] *I won, succeeded*; **wakatkwenyonh** [wa-kat-kwé-nyonh] *I have won, did win....*

309 **katkwìtha'** [kat-kwì:-t-ha'] *I move over* (A-Stem - Subj.)
wa'katkwi'te' [wa'-kát-kwi'-te'] *I moved over*; **wakatkwìtonh** [wa-kat-kwì:-tonh] *I have move over.*

310 **katòktha'** [ka-tò:-k-t-ha'] *I run out of / short of* (A-Stem - Subj.)
wa'katòkten [wa'-ka-tò:-k-ten] *I ran out of...*; **wakato'kteh** [wa-ká:-to'k-teh] *I have run out / did run out of....*

311 **katon'** [ká:-ton'] *I say / am saying* (A-Stem - Subj.)
This verb is very irregular: **wa'kiron'** [wa'-kí:-ron'] *I said*; **wakenh** [wá:-kenh] *I have said / did say....*

312 **katonhkarya'ks** [ka-tonh-kár-ya'ks] *I am hungry* (A-Stem - Subj.)
wa'katonhkarya'ke' [wa'-ka-tonh-kár-ya'-ke'] *I was hungry*;
wakatonhkaryàkonh [wa-ka-tonh-kar-yà:-konh] *I have been hungry.*

313 **katorats** [ka-tó:-rats] *I hunt* (A-Stem - Subj.)
wa'katorate' [wa'-ka-tó:-ra-te'] *I hunted*; **wakatoratonh** [wa-ka-to-rá:-tonh] *I have hunted / did hunt.*

314 **katorihshenhs** [ka-to-ríhs-henhs] *I rest* (A-Stem - Subj.)
wa'katorihshen' [wa'-ka-to-ríhs-hen'] *I rested*; **wakatorihshenhenh** [wa-ka-to-rihs-hén-henh] *I have rested / did rest.*

315 **katoris** [ka-tó:-ris] *I drive* (A-Stem - Subj.)
wa'katori' [wa'-ka-tó:-ri'] *I drove*; **wakatorih** [wa-ka-tó:-rih] *I have driven / did drive.*

316 **katshe'** [káts-he'] *a bottle, jar*
WITH LOCATIVES: **katshe'tàke** [kats-he'-tà:-keh] *on the bottle...*; **katshètakon** [kats-hè:-ta-konh] *in the bottle....* WITH VERBS: **waketshètayen'** [wa-kats-hè:-ta-yen'] *I have a bottle*; **ketshe'tenhawe'** [kets-he'-tén-ha-we'] *I have a bottle (with me).*

317 **katshe' kahik** [káts-he' ká-hik] *a pear, pears*

318 katshenen [kats-hé:-nen] *a domestic animal; a pet*
ie. **ne katshenen** [ne kats-hé:-nenh] *the animal, pet*; **thiken' katshenen** [thí:-ken'...] *that animal, pet*; **kiken' katshenen** [kí:-ken'...] *this animal, pet*; **kontitshenen'okonha** [kon-tits-he-nen'-o-kón:-'ah] *animals, pets*. Using with animals to make possessive: **aketshenen erhar** [a-kets-hé:-nenh ér-har] *my dog*; **satshenen erhar** [sats-hé:-nenh...] *your dog*; **raotshenen erhar** [ra-ots-hé:-nenh...] *his dog*; **akaotshenen erhar** [a-ka-ots-hé:-nenh...] *her dog*; **onkwatshenen erhar** [on-kwats-hé:-nenh...] *our dog*. With verbs: **Erhar wakenahskwayen'**. [Ér-har wa-ke-náhs-kwa-yen'] *i have a dog*.

319 katsi'tsyakeras [ka-tsi'-tsyá-ke-rahs] *beer*

320 katsi'tsyayenthon [ka-tsi'-tsya-yént-honh] *a flower bed*

321 katstha' [káts-t-ha'] *I use / make use of* (A-Stem - Subj.)
wàkatste' [wà:-kats-te'] *I used*; **wakatstonh** [wa-káts-tonh] *I have used / I did use; I am using.*

322 katste'nyarons [kats-te'-nyá:-rons] *I apply myself to / devote myself to* (A-Stem - Subj.) **wa'katste'nyaron'** [wa'-kats-te'-nyá:-ron'] *I applied myself...*; **wakatste'nyaronh** [wa-kats-te'-nyá:-ronh] *I have applied / did apply myself....*

323 kattokha' [kat-tók-ha'] *I am wise; reasonable* (A-Stem - Subj.)
kattokhahkwe' [kat-tók-hah-kwe'] *I was wise...*; **enkattokhake'** [en-kat-tók-ha-ke'] *I will be wise...*; **akattokhake'** [a-kat-tók-ha-ke'] *I would be / for me to be wise....*

324 katya'tyonni' [ka-tya'-tyón:-ni'] *I am laying down* (A-Stem - Subj.)
katya'tyonnihahkwe' [ka-tya'-tyon-ní-hah-kwe'] *I was laying down*; **enkatya'tyonnihake'** [en-ka-tya'-tyon-ní-ha-ke'] *I will be laying down*; **akatya'tyonnihake'** [a-ka-tya'-tyon-ní-ha-ke'] *I would be laying down / for me to be laying down.*

325 katyens [ká-tyens] *I sit down* (A-Stem - Subj.)
wa'katyen' [wa'-ká-tyen'] *I sat down*; **wakatyenh** [wa-ká-tyenh] *I have sat down / I did sit down.*

326 katyesàtha' [ka-tye-sà:t-ha'] *I damage something* (A-Stem - Subj.)
wa'katyesahte' [wa'-ka-tyé:-sah-te'] *I damaged...*; **wakatyesahtonh** [wa-ka-tye-sáh-tonh] *I have damaged / did damage....*

327 kawennokwas [ka-wen-nó-kwas] *a radio*

328 kawera'shatste [ka-we-ra'-sháts-teh] *a strong wind, Also: There is a strong wind*

329 kawerons [ká-we-rons] *I pour; I spill* (A-Stem - Subj.)
wa'kaweron' [wa'-ká-we-ron'] *I poured / spilled*; **wakaweronh** [wa-ká-we-ronh] *I have spilled, poured / I did spill, pour.*

330 **kaya'takeras** [ka-ya'-tá-ke-rahs] *a goat*

331 **kaya'tarha** [ka-ya'-tár-ha'] *a television*

332 **kaya'tonni** [ka-ya'-tón:-nih] *doll*
With Possessive: **akya'tonni** [a-kya'-tón:-nih] *my doll*; **saya'tonni** [sa-ya'-tón:-nih] *your doll*; **raoya'tonni** [ra-o-ya'-tón:-nih] *his doll*; **akaoya'tonni** [a-ka-o-ya'-tón:-nih] *her doll*.

333 **kaya'tyonni** [ka-ya'-tyón:-nih] *it (animate) is laying down on something*
kaya'tyonnihahkwe' [ka-ya'-tyon-ní-hah-kwe'] *it was laying down*; **enkaya'tyonnihake'** [en-ka-ya'tyon-ní-ha-ke'] *it will be laying down*; **akaya'tyonnihake'** [a-ka-ya'tyon-ní-ha-ke'] *it would be laying / for it to be laying....*

334 **kayare** [ká:-ya-reh] *a bag*
ie. **ikyarenhawe'** [ik-ya-rén-ha-we'] *I carry a bag*; **wakyarakehte'** [wak-ya-ra-kéh-te'] *I lug a bag about.*

335 **kayàtare** [ka-yà:-ta-reh] *a picture (ie. photograph)*
akyàtare [kyà:-ta-reh] *a picture of me*; **sayàtare** [sa-yà:-ta-reh] *a picture of you*; **rayàtare** [ra-yà:-ta-reh] *a picture of him*; **yeyàtare** [ye-yà:-ta-reh] *a picture of her.*

336 **kayen'** [ká:-yen'] *it is laying down on something*
kayentahkwe' [ka-yén:-tah-kwe'] *it was laying...*; **enkayentake'** [en-ka-yén:-ta-ke'] *it will be laying...*; **akayentake'** [a-ka-yén:-ta-ke'] *it would be laying / for it to be laying.*

337 **kayènkwire** [ka-yèn:-kwi-reh] *an arrow; arrows*

338 **kayeri** [ka-yé:-rih] *four*
ie. **kayeri nikon** [...ní:-konh] *(there's) four of them (onjects)*; **kayeri nikonti** [...ni-kón:-tih] *(there's) four of them (female / animal)*; **kayeri nihati** [...ni-há:-tih] *(there's) four of them (male).* **kayeri-yawenre** [...-ya-wén:-reh] *fourteen*; **kayeri-niwahsen** [...-ni-wáh-senh] *fourty.* **kayeri nikatshètake** [...ni-kats-hè:-ta-keh] *four bottles*; **kayeri niwakyen'** [...ni-wák-yen'] *I have four*; **kayeri niwaketshètayen'** [...ni-wa-kets-hè:-ta-yen'] *I have four bottles.*

339 **Kayerihatont** [Ka-ye-rí-ha-tont] *Thursday*
shiKayerihaton'kenha [Shi-ka-ye-ri-ha-ton'-kén-ha'] *last Thursday.*

340 **kayo'tenhsera** [ka-yo'-ténh-se-ra'] *a job; work, employment*

341 **Kayonkwe'hàka** [Ka-yon-kwe'-hà:-kah] *the Cayuga nation*

342 **ke'nikhons** [ke'-ník-hons] *I sew / mend* (C-Stem - Subj.)
wa'ke'nikhon' [wa'-ke'-ník-hon'] *I sewed*; **wake'nikhonhonh** [wa-ke'-nik-

hón:-'onh] *I have sewed; did sew.*

343 **ke'skontha'** [ke'-skónt-ha'] *I roast something* (C-Stem - Subj.)
wa'ke'skonten' [wa'-ke'-skón:-ten'] *I roasted...*; **wakèskonteh** [wa-kè:-skon-teh] *I have roasted / did roast something.*

344 **kehrihtha'** [ke-hríht-ha'] *I cook* (C-Stem - Subj.)
wa'kèrihte' [wa'-kè:-rih-te'] *I cooked*; **wakehrihtonh** [wa-ke-ríh-tonh] *I have cooked / did cook.*

345 **kehyàra's** [ke-hyà:-ra's] *I remember* (E-Stem - Subj.)
wa'kehyarane' [wa'-ke-hyà:-ra'-ne'] *I remembered*; **wakehyahra'onh** [wa-ke-hya-hrá:-'onh] *I have remembered / did remember.*

346 **kekhonnis** [kek-hón:-nis] *I cook* (C-Stem - Subj.)
kekhonni' [kek-hón:-ni'] *I am cooking*; **wa'kekhonni'** [wa'-kek-hón:-ni'] *I cooked*; **wakekhonnih** [wa-kek-hón:-nih] *I have cooked / did cook.*

347 **ken** [kén] *?*
Satshennonni ken. [Sats-hen-nón:-ni' kén] *Are you happy?*
Kahyatonhserowanen ken sayen'. [ka-hya-tonh-se-ro-wá:-nenh kén sá:-yen'] *Do you have a big book?*

348 **ken'** [ken'] *about; so*

a) **ken' nonwe t-** [ken' nón:-weh t-] *over there*
ie. **Ken' nonwe thonatawentye'.** [Ken' nón:-weh t-ho-na-ta-wén-tye']
They are swimming about over there.

b) **ken' ok nikarihwehsha'** [ken'k ni-ka-ri-hwéhs-ha'] *just a short time, while*
ie. **Ken' ok nikarihwehsha yehonahtentyonh.** [Ken' ni-ka-ri-hwéhs-ha' ye-ho-nah-tén-tyonh] *They were away just (only) a short time (while).*

c) **ken' niyore'a** [ken' ni-yo-ré:-'ah] *about so far; a short ways off (away)*
ie. **Ken' niyore'a eh yahàre'.** [Ken' ni-yo-ré:-'ah eh ya-hà:-re'] *He went a short ways off (away).*

349 **kenakeres** [ke-ná-ke-res] *I live in a place* (C-Stem - Subj.)
kenakere' [ke-ná-ke-re'] *I am living...*; **wa'kenakere'** [wa'-ke-ná-ke-re'] *I lived...*; **wakenakereh** [wa-ke-ná-ke-reh] *I have lived....*

350 **kenenhskwas** [ke-nénhs-kwas] *I steal* (C-Stem - Subj.)
wa'kenenhsko' [wa'-ke-nénhs-ko'] *I stole*; **wakenenhskwenh** [wa-ke-nénhs-kwenh] *I have stolen / did steal.*

351 **kenennyo'kwanenhstha'** [ke-nen-nyo'-kwa-nénhst-ha'] *I freeze something* (C-Stem - Subj.) **wa'kenennyòkwanenhste'** [wa'-ke-nen-nyò:-kwa-nenhs-te'] *I froze something*; **wakenennyo'kwanenhstonh** [wa-ke-nen-nyo'-kwa-nénhs-tonh] *I have frozen / did freeze something.*

352 kenh [kénh] *here; this*
  kenh kanatakon [kenh ka-ná-ta-koh] *here in town / in this town*; **kenh katshètakon** [kenh kats-hè:-ta-konh] *in this bottle.*

  a) **kenh ki' nonwe** [eh ki' nón:-weh] *right here*
     ie. **Kenh ki' nonwe ohson'karàke wàkyen'.** [Kenh ki' nón:-weh wà:-k-yen'] *I put it down right here on the floor.*

  b) **kenh nonkati** [ken non-ká:-tih] *this way; over this way; in this direction*
     ie. **Kenh nonkati nontahsawe** [Kenh non-ká:-tih non-táhs-ha-we] *Bring it over this way.*

  c) **kenh nonwe** [tsi nón:-weh] *here*
     ie. **Kenh nonwe tahahawe'.** [Kenh nón:-weh ta-há-ha-we'] *He brought it here.*

  d) **kenh nonwe tsi niwat** [kenh non-weh tsi ní:-wat] *hereabouts*
     ie. **Kenh nonwe tsi niwat ratinakere'.** [...ra-ti-ná-ke-re'] *They live hereabouts.*

  e) **kenh wenhniserate** [kenh wenh-ni-se-rá:-teh] *today*
     ie. **Enyokennore' katke ok kenh wenhniserate.** [En-yo-kén:-no-re' kát-kek...] *it will rain sometime today.*

353 kenhak [kén-hak] *let it be*
  ie. **Skennen kenhak** [Skén:-nenh kén-hak] *Let there be peace!*

354 kenhkwitène' [kenh-kwi-tè:-ne'] *in the spring*
  Kenhkwitène tentkonne' ne kahonk. [Kenh-kwi-tè:-ne' tent-kón:-ne' ne ká-honk] *In the spring the geese will come back.*

355 kenhnàta [kenh-nà:-ta'] *a purse; a handbag*

356 kenhne' [kénh-ne'] *it was (indeed)*
  ie. **Tsi yetsyenhayentahkwa kenhne'.** [Tsi ye-tsyen-ha-yen-táh-kwa' kénh-ne'] *It was a council house.*

357 kenhotonkwas [ke-n-ho-tón-kwas] *I open (a door)* (C-Stem - Subj.)
  wa'kenhotonko' [wa'-ke-n-ho-tón:-ko'] *I opened (a door)*; **wakenhotonkwenh** [wa-ke-n-ho-tón-kwenh] *I have opened / did open....*

358 kenhotons [ke-n-hó:-tons] *I close (a door)* (C-Stem - Subj.)
  wa'kenhoton' [wa'-ke-n-hó:-ton'] *I closed (a door)*; **wakenhotonh** [wa-ke-n-hó:-ton'] *I have closed / did close....*

359 keniyontarhos [ke-ni-yon-tár-hos] *I lock (a door)* (C-Stem - Subj.)
  wa'keniyontarho' [wa'-ke-ni-yon-tár-ho'] *I locked...*; **wakeniyontarhonh** [wa-ke-ni-yon-tár-honh] *I have locked / did lock....*

360 **keniyontahrakwas** [ke-ni-yon-ta-hrá-kwas] *I unlock (a door)* (C-Stem - Subj.)
wa'keniyontahrako' [wa'-ke-ni-yon-ta-hrá:-ko'] *I unlocked...*;
wakeniyontahrakwenh [wa-ke-ni-yon-ta-hrá-kwenh] *I have unlocked / did unlock....*

361 **kennakere** [ken-ná:-ke-reh] *it is plentiful*
kennakerehkwe' [ken-ná-ke-reh-kwe'] *it was plentiful*; **enkennakereke'** [en-ken-ná-ke-re-ke'] *it will be plentiful*; **akennakereke'** [a-ken-ná-ke-re-ke'] *it would be plentiful / for it to be plentiful.* With nominals: **kentsyanakere** [ken-tsya-ná-ke-re'] *fish are plentiful*; **kario'tanakere** [ka-ri-o'-ta-ná-ke-re'] *wild animals are plentiful*; **katsi'tenhseranakere** [ka-tsi'-tenh-se-ra-ná-ke-re'] *birds are plentiful.*

362 **kènne'** [kèn:-ne'] *it was (indeed)* (See: kenhne')

363 **kennihtya'ks** [ken-níh-tya'ks] *I put around my neck* (En-Stem - Subj.)
wa'kennihtya'ke' [wa'-ken-níh-tya'-ke'] *I put around my neck*; **wakennihtyenh** [wa-ken-níh-tyenh] *I have put / did put around my neck.*

364 **kennonhtonnyonhs** [ken-nonh-tón-nyonhs] *I think about (something)* (En-Stem - verb) **kennonhtonnyon'** [ken-nonh-tón-nyon'] *I am thinking about...*;
wa'kennonhtonnyonhwe' [wa'-ken-nonh-tón-nyonh-we'] *I thought about...*;
wakennonhtonnyonhonh [wa-ken-nonh-ton-nyón-honh] *I have thought / did think about....*

365 **kenohares** [ke-nó-ha-res] *I wash (s.t.)* (C-Stem - Subj.)
kenonhare' [ke-nó-ha-re'] *I am washing...*; **wa'ke-nohare'** [wa'-ke-nó-ha-re'] *I washed...*; **wakenonhareh** [wa-ke-nó-ha-reh] *I have washed... / did wash....*

366 **kenònwaks** [ke-nòn:-waks] *I am fond of...* (C-Stem - Subj.)
wa'kenònwake' [wa'-ke-nòn:-wa-ke'] *I was fond of...*; **wakenònweh** [wa-ke-nòn:-weh] *I have been fond of....*

367 **kenònwe's** [ke-nòn:-we's] *I like* (C-Stem - Subj.)
wa'kenònwene' [wa'-ke-nòn:-we'-ne'] *I liked*; **wakenonhwe'onh** [wa-ke-non-hwé-'onh] *I have liked / I did like.*

368 **kenraken** [ken-rá:-ken'] *white; light coloured*
With nominals: **kanonhsaraken** [ka-nonh-sa-rá:-ken'] *a white house*; or **kanonhsakenra** [ka-nonh-sa-kén:-ra'] *a white house*: Both may be used.
Renhnakenra [renh-na-kén:-ra'] *he is white / fair-skinned.*

369 **Kentenha** [Ken-tén-ha'] *October*

370 **kentenhkowa** [Ken-tenh-kó:-wah] *November*

371 **kèntho** [kèn:-t-hoh] *here; in this place, spot*
Shiyohserate wahanenhstayentho' ne kèntho. [Shi-yoh-se-rá:-teh wa-ha-

nenhs-ta-yént-ho' ne kèn:-t-hoh] *Last year he planted corn here (in this place, spot).*

372 kentskare [kénts-ka-reh] *a carpet, floor matt*

373 kentskote [kénts-ko-teh] *it (animate) is sitting upright on something*
kentskotehkwe' [kents-kó:-teh-kwe'] *it was sitting upright...*; **enkentskoteke'**
[en-kents-kó:-te-ke'] *it will be sitting upright...*; **akentskoteke'** [a-kents-kó:-te-
ke'] *it would be sitting upright... / for it to be sitting upright....*

374 kentskwahere [kénts-kwá-he-reh] *it (animate) is sitting up on something*
kentskwaherehkwe' [kents-kwá-he-reh-kwe'] *it was sitting up on*;
enkentskwahereke' [en-kents-kwá-he-re-ke'] *it will be sitting up on*;
akentskwahereke' [a-kents-kwá-he-re-ke'] *it would be sitting up on / for it to·be
sitting up on.*

375 kentsyokwas [ken-tsyó-kwas] *a heron*

376 kentsyonk [kén-tsyonk] *a fish*
ie. **kentsyanakere'** [ken-tsya-ná-ke-re'] *there are plenty of fish*;
kentsyanakerehkwe' [ken-tsya-ná-ke-reh-kwe'] *there were plenty of fish.*
Kitsyenyenahs [ki-tsyen-yé:-nahs] *I catch fish*; **kitsyaks** [kí:-tsyaks] *I eat fish.*

377 kènye' [kèn:-ye'] *oil*
kenhyenare [ken-hyé:-na-re'] *there's oil in it*; **kenhyenanànon** [ken-hye-na-
nà:-nonh] *it's full of oil.*

378 kerahstha' [ke-ráhst-ha'] *I draw* (C-Stem - Subj.)
wàkerahste' [wà:-ke-rahs-te'] *I drew*; **wakerahstonh** [wa-ke-ráhs-tonh] *I have
drawn / I did draw.*

379 kerakewas [ke-ra-ké:-was] *I wipe / clean off* (C-Stem - Subj.)
wa'kerakewe' [wa'-ke-rá:-ke-we'] *I wiped...*; **wakerakewenh** [wa-ke-ra-ké:-
wenh] *I have wiped / did wipe....*

380 kerakwas [ke-rá-kwas] *I choose* (C-Stem - Subj.)
wa'kerako' [wa'-ke-rá:-ko'] *I chose*; **wakerakwenh** [wa-ke-rá-kwenh] *I have
chosen / did choose.*

381 kerathenhs [ke-rát-henhs] *I climb up / ascend* (C-Stem - Subj.)
wa'kerathen' [wa'-ke-rát-hen'] *I ascended*; **wakerathen'onh** [wa-ke-rat-hén:-
'onh] *i have ascended / did ascend.*

382 kerennha's [ke-rénn-ha's] *I get used to* (C-Stem - Subj.)
wa'kerennhane' [wa'-ke-rénn-ha'-ne'] *I got used to*; **wakerennha'onh** [wa-
ke-renn-há:-'onh] *i have gotten used; I am used to.*

383 kerhite [kér-hi'-teh] *a tree; a fruit tree*
With Locatives: **kerhi'tàke** [ker-hi'-tà:-keh] *on / in the tree*; **kerhìtakon** [ker-
hì:-ta-konh] *in the tree*; **kerhi'takta** [ker-hi'-tàk-ta'] *beside the tree*;

kerhi'tòkon ker-hi'-tò:-konh] *under the tree.* Locatives with Plurals: **kerhi'ta'kehson** [ker-hi'-ta'-kéh-sonh] *in the trees;* **kerhi'to'konhson** [ker-hi'-to'-kónh-sonh] *under the trees;* **kerhi'takonhson** [ker-hi'-ta-kónh-sonh] *(out) in the trees.* Also: **kerhìtote** [ker-hì:-to-teh] *a standing tree;* **kerhi'toton** [ker-hi'-tó:-tonh] *standing trees;* **akta tsi tkerhìtote** [ák-ta' tsit ker-hì:-to-teh] *next to the tree:* ie. **Akta tsi tkerhìtote ithrate'.** [...ít-hra-te'] *He's standing next to the tree.*

384 **kerhòroks** [ker-hò:-roks] *I cover something* (C-Stem - Subj.) **wa'kerhòroke'** [wa'-ker-hò:-ro-ke'] *I covered...;* **wakerhòronh** [wa-ker-hò:-ronh] *I have covered / did cover....*

385 **kerihenhs** [ke-rí-henhs] *I allow / let* (C-Stem - Subj.) **wa'kerihen'** [wa'-ke-rí-hen'] *I allowed / let;* **wakerihenhonh** [wqa-ke-ri-hén-honh] *I have allowed / did allow....*

386 **kerios** [ké-ri-ohs] *I kill something* (C-Stem - Subj.) **wa'kerio'** [wa'-ké-ri-o'] *I killed something;* **wakerioh** [wa-ké-ri-oh] *I have killed / did kill something.*

387 **keròroks** [ke-rò:-roks] *I gather up* (C-Stem - Subj.) **wa'keròroke'** [wa'-ke-rò:-ro-ke'] *I gathered up;* **wakeròronh** [wa-ke-rò:-ronh] *I have gathered / did gather up.*

388 **kesaks** [ké:-saks] *I look for / looking for* (E-Stem - Subj.) **wa'kesake'** [wa'-ké:-sa-ke'] *I looked for;* **wakesakonh** [wa-ke-sá:-konh] *I have looked for / did look for.*

389 **keta's** [ké-ta's] *I put inside of* (E-Stem - Subj.) **wa'keta'** [wa'-ké-ta'] *I put inside of;* **waketenh** [wa-ké-tenh] *I have put / did put inside of.*

390 **ketshenryes** [kets-hénr-yes] *I find* (C-Stem - Subj.) **wa'ketshenri'** [wa'-kets-hén:-ri'] *I found;* **waketshenryonh** [wa-kets-hén-ryonh] *I have found / did find.*

391 **kewennahnotha'** [ke-wen-nah-nót-h a'] *I read (aloud)* (C-Stem - Subj.) **wa'kewennahnoten'** [wa'-ke-wen-nah-nó:-ten'] *I read (aloud);* **wakewennànoteh** [wa-ke-wen-nà:-no-teh] *I have read / did read (aloud).*

392 **keweyenhon** [ke-we-yén-honh] *I am good; have a knack for (doing)* (C-Stem - Subj.) **keweyenhònne'** [ke-we-yen-hòn:-ne'] *I was good at;* **enkeweyenhonhake'** [en-ke-we-yen-hón-ha-ke'] *I will be good at;* **akeweyenhonhake'** [a-ke-we-yen-hón-ha-ke'] *I would be / for me to be good at.* WITH INCORPORATED ELEMENTS: **kenonnyaweyenhon** [ke-non-nya-we-yén-honh] *I am a good dancer;* **kekhonnyaweyenhon** [kek-hon-nya-we-yén-honh] *I am a good cook;* **katoratsheraweyenhon** [ka-to-rats-he-ra-we-yén-honh] *I am a*

good hunter.

393 keweyente [ke-we-yén:-teh] *I know how to (do something)* (C-Stem - Subj.)
keweyentehkwe' [ke-we-yén:-teh-kwe'] *I knew how to...*; **enkeweyenteke'** [en-ke-we-yén:-te-ke'] *I will know how to...*; **akeweyenteke'** [a-ke-we-yén:-te-ke'] *I would be / for me to know how to....* WITH VERBS: **Keweyente ne takenonnyahkwe'.** [...ne ta-ke-nón-nyah-kwe'] *I know how to dance*; **Keweyente ne akekhonni'.** [...na-kek-hón:-ni'] *I know how to cook*; **Keweyente ne akatorate'.** [...na-ka-tó:-ra-te] *I know how to hunt.*

394 keweyentehta's [ke-we-yen-téh-ta's] *I learn* (C-Stem - Subj.)
wa'keweyentehtane' [wa'-ke-we-yen-téh-ta'-ne'] *I learned*; **wakeweyentehta'onh** [wa-ke-we-yen-teh-tá:-'onh] *I have learned / did learn.*

395 keyahre' [kè:ya-hre'] *I am remembering* (E-Stem - Subj.)
kehyarehkwe' [ke-hyá:-reh-kwe'] *I was remembering*; **enkehyareke'** [en-ke-hyá:-re-ke'] *I will be remembering*; **akehyareke'** [a-ke-hyá:-re-ke'] *I would be / for me to be remembering.*

396 khahrakwas [k-ha-hrá-kwas] *I take down (from hanging)* (C-Stem - Subj.)
wa'khahrako' [wa'-k-ha-hrá:-ko'] *I took down...*; **wakhahrakwenh** [wak-ha-hrá-kwenh] *I have taken down / did take down....*

397 kharha' [k-hár-ha'] *I hang something up* (C-Stem - Subj.)
wa'khàren' [wa'-k-hà:-ren'] *I hung...up*; **wakhareh** [wák-ha-reh] *I have hung...up.*

398 khawis [k-há:-wis] *I carry (with myself)* (C-Stem - Subj.)
wa'khawi' [wa'-k-há:-wi'] *I carried...*; **wakhawih** [wak-há:-wih] *I have carried / did carry....*

399 khe'kenha [khe'-kén-ha'] *my younger sister*
she'kenha [s-he'-kén-ha'] *your younger sister*; **shako'kenha** [s-ha-ko'-kén-ha'] *his younger sister*; **yontatkenha** [yon-tat-kén-ha'] *her younger sister*; **yakhi'kenha** [yak-hi'-kén-ha'] *our younger sister.*

400 khehretsyarons [k-he-hre-tsyá:-rons] *I encourage her / them* (E-Stem - Trans.)
wa'khehretsyaron' [wa'k-he-hre-tsyá:-ron'] *I encouraged her / them*; **khehretsyaronh** [k-he-hre-tsyá:-ronh] *I have encouraged / did encourage her / them.*

401 khehroris [k-heh-ró:-ris] *I tell her / them* (C-Stem - Trans.)
wa'khehrori' [wa'-k-heh-ró:-ri'] *I told her / them*; **khehrorih** [k-heh-ró:-rih] *I have told / did tell her / them.*

402 khehseres [k-héh-se-res] *I follow her / them* (C-Stem - Trans.)
wa'khehsere' [wa'-k-héh-se-re'] *I followed her / them*; **khehsereh** [k-héh-se-reh] *I have followed / did follow her / them.*

403 **khekahrewahtha'** [k-he-ka-hre-wáht-ha'] *I hurt her / them* (C-Stem - Trans.)
wa'khekahrewahte' [wa'-he-ka-hré:-wah-te'] *I hurt her / them;*
khekahrewahtonh [k-he-ka-hre-wáh-tonh] *I have hurt / did hurt her / them.*

404 **kheken** [khe-kén:] *instead* (See: khere' ken'en)

405 **khekens** [k-hé:-kens] *I see her / them* (C-Stem - Trans.)
wa'kheken' [wa'-k-hé:-ken'] *I saw her / them;* **khekenh** [k-hé:-kenh] *i have seen / did see her / them.*

406 **khena'tonnis** [k-he-na'-tón:-nis] *I show her / them* (C-Stem - Trans.)
wa'khena'tonhahse' [wa'-k-he-na'-tón-hah-se'] *I showed her / them;*
khena'tonnih [k-he-na'-tón:-nih] *I have shown / did show her / them.*

407 **khenontens** [k-he-nón:-tens] *I feed her / them* (C-Stem - Trans.)
wa'khenonte' [wa'-k-hé:-non-te'] *I fed her / them;* **khenontenh** [k-he-nón:-tenh] *I have fed / did feed her / them.*

408 **khenònwe's** [k-he-nòn:-we's] *I like her / them* (C-Stem - Trans.)
wa'khenònwene' [wa'-k-he-nòn:-we'-ne'] *I liked her / them;* **khenonhwe'onh** [k-he-non-hwé:-'onh] *I have liked / did like her / them.*

409 **khenoronhkwa'** [k-he-no-rónh-kwa'] *I love her / them* (C-Stem - Trans.)
khenoronhkwahkwe' [k-he-no-rónh-kwah-kwe'] *I loved her / them;*
enkhenoronhkwake' [enk-he-no-rónh-kwa-ke'] *I will love her / them;*
akhenoronhkwake' [ak-he-no-rónh-kwa-ke'] *I would love / for me to love....*

410 **khere ken'en** [khe-re' kén:-'enh] *instead*

411 **kherha'** [k-hér-ha'] *I set something up on* (C-Stem - Subj.)
wàkhren' [wà:-k-hren'] *I set...up on;* **wakhereh** [wàk-he-reh] *I have set / did set...up on.*

412 **kheri'wanontonnis** [k-he-ri'-wa-non-tón:-nis] *I ask her / them* (C-Stem - Trans.) **wa'kheri'wanontonhse'** [wa'-k-he-ri'-wa-nón:-tonh-se'] *I asked her / them;* **kheri'wanontonnih** [k-he-ri'-wa-non-tón:-nih] *I have asked / did ask....*

413 **kherihonnyennis** [k-he-ri-hon-nyén:-nis] *I teach her / them* (C-Stem - Trans.)
wa'kherihonnyen' [wa'-k-he-ri-hón:-nyen'] *I taught her / them;*
kherihonnyennih [k-he-ri-hon-nyén:-nih] *I have taight / did teach her / them.*

414 **kheyateròroks** [khe-ya-te-rò:-roks] *I watch her / them (doing something)* (A-Stem - verb) **wa'kheyateròroke'** [wa'-k-he-ya-te-rò:-ro-ke'] *I watched her / them...;*
kheyateròronh [k-he-ya-te-rò:-ronh] *I have watched / did watch her / them....*

415 **kheyateweyèntons** [k-he-ya-te-we-yèn:-tons] *I take care of her / them* (A-Stem - Trans.) **wa'kheyateweyènton'** [wa'-k-he-ya-te-we-yèn:-ton'] *I took care of her / them;* **kheyateweyèntonh** [k-he-ya-te-we-yèn:-tonh] *I have taken care of / did* take care of her / them.

416 kheyawis [khe-yá:-wis] *I give her / them* (A-Stem - Trans.)
wa'kheyon' [wa'-k-hé:-yon'] *I gave her / them*; **kheyawih** [k-he-yá:-wih] *I have given / did give her / them.*

417 kheyen'a [khe-yén:-ah] *my daughter*
sheyen'a [s-he-yén:-'ah] *your daughter*; **shakoyen'a** [s-ha-ko-yén:-'ah] *his daughter*; **yontatyen'a** [yon-ta-tyén:-'ah] *her daughter*; **yakhiyen'a** [yak-hi-yén:-'ah] *our daughter.*

418 kheyenawa's [k-he-yé:-na-wa's] *I help them* (C-Stem - Trans.)
wa'kheyenawa'se' [wa'-k-he-yé:-na-wa'-se'] *I helped her / them*; **kheyenawàseh** [k-he-ye-na-wà:-seh] *I have helped / did help her / them.*

419 kheyenteri [khe-yen-té:-ri'] *I know her / them* (C-Stem - Trans.)
kheyenterihne' [k-he-yen-te-ríh-ne'] *I knew her / them*; **enkheyenterihake'** [enk-he-yen-te-rí-ha-ke'] *I will know her / them*; **akheyenterihake'** [ak-he-yen-te-rí-ha-ke'] *I would know / for me to know her / them.*

420 khnekirha' [k-hne-kír-ha'] *I drink* (C-Stem - Subj.)
wa'khnekìra' [wa'-k-hne-kì:-ra'] *I drank*; **wakhnekirenh** [wak-hne-kì:-renh] *I have drank / did drink.*

421 khninons [k-hní:-nons] *I buy* (C-Stem - Subj.)
wa'khninon' [wa'-k-hní:-non'] *I bought*; **wakhninonh** [wak-hní:-nonh] *I have bought / did buy.*

422 khnyotakwas [khnyo-tá-kwas] *I take, pull something down* (C-Stem Subj.)
wa'khnyotako' [wa'-k-hnyo-tá:-ko'] *I took, pulled something down*; **wakhnyotakwenh** [wak-hnyo-tá-kwenh] *I have taken, pulled / did take, pull something down.*

423 khnyotha' [k-hnyót-ha'] *I set something upright* (C-Stem - Subj.)
wa'khnyoten' [wa'-k-hnyó:-ten'] *I set...upright*; **wakhnyoteh** [wák-hnyo-teh] *I have set / did set...upright.*

424 khrakwas [k-hrá-kwas] *I take down from s.t.* (C-Stem - Subj.)
wa'khrako' [wa'-k-hrá:-ko'] *I took down...*; **wakhrakwenh** [wak-hrá-kwenh] *I have taken / did take down....*

425 khrenahs [k-hré:-nahs] *I cut (open)* (C-Stem - Subj.)
wa'khrena' [wa'-k-hré:-na'] *I cut...*; **wakhrena'onh** [wak-hre-ná:-'onh] *I have cut / did cut...*

426 khyatonkwas [k-hya-tón:-kwas] *I erase* (C-Stem - Subj.)
wa'khyatonko' [wa'-k-hya-tón:-ko'] *I erased*; **wakhyatonkwenh** [wak-hya-tón-kwenh] *I have erased / did erase.*

427 **khyatons** [k-hyá:-tons] *I write* (C-Stem - Subj.)
wa'kyaton' [wa'-k-hyá:-ton'] *I wrote*; **wakhyatonh** [wak-hyá:-tonh] *I have written / did write*.

428 **kiken'** [kí:-ken'] *this (one)*
ie. **Kiken' nen' ne'e takohs.** [Kí:-ken' nen' né:-'eh ta-kóhs] *This (one) is a cat*;
Kiken' takohs [Kí:-ken' ta-kóhs] *This cat*.

429 **kìteron'** [kì:-te-ron'] *I am sitting / staying (at a place)* (I-Stem - Subj.)
ki'terontahkwe' [ki'-te-ron-táh-kwe'] *I was sitting...*; **enki'terontake'** [en-ki'-te-rón:-ta-ke'] *I will be sitting...*; **aki'terontake'** [a-ki'-te-rón:-ta-ke'] *I would be / for me to be sitting....*

430 **kitskote'** [kíts-ko-te'] *I am sitting down on something* (I-Stem - Subj.)
kitskotehkwe' [kits-kó:-teh-kwe'] *I was sitting down on...*; **enkitskoteke'** [en-kits-kó:-te-ke'] *I will be sitting down on...*; **akitskoteke'** [a0kits-kó:-te-ke'] *I would be / for me to be sitting down on....*

431 **kitskwahere'** [kits-kwá-he-re'] *I am sitting up on something* (I-Stem - Subj.)
kitskwàrehkwe' [kits-kwà:-reh-kwe'] *I was sitting up on...*; **enkitskwàreke'** [en-kits-kwà:-re-ke'] *I will be sitting up on...*; **akitskwàreke'** [a-kits-kwà:-re-ke'] *I would be / for me to be sitting up on....*

432 **kitye's** [kí-tye's] *I fly* (I-Stem - Subj.)
wa'kitye' [wa'-kí-tye'] *I flew*; **wakityeh** [wa-kí-tyeh] *I have fown / did fly*.

433 **kityenontye's** [ki-tye-nón-tye's] *I fly about* (I-Stem - Subj.)
wa'kityenontye' [wa'-ki-tye-nón-tye'] *I flew about*; **wakityenontyeh** [wa-ki-tye-nón-tyeh] *I have flown / did fly*.

434 **kiyaks** [kí:-yaks] *I shoot (with a bow)* (I-Stem - Subj.)
wa'kiyake' [wa'-kí:-ya-ke'] *I shot...*; **wakiyenh** [wa-kí:-yenh] *I have shot / did shoot....*

435 **kohsera'kène** [koh-se-ra'-kè:-neh] *in the winter*
Kohsera'kène eso wàkeren's. [Koh-se-ra'-kè:-ne' é:-soh wà:-ke-ren's] *It snows a lot in the winter*.

436 **konnis** [kón:-nis] *I make / making* (On-Stem - Subj.)
konni' [kón:-ni'] *I am making*; **wa'konni'** [wa'-kón:-ni'] *I made*; **wakonnih** [wa-kón:-nih] *I have made / I did make*.

437 **konnyàtha'** [kon-nyà:-t-ha'] *I make from something* (On-Stem - Subj.)
wa'konnya'te' [wa'-kón-nya'-te'] *I made from something*; **wakonnyàtonh** [wa-kon-nyà:-tonh] *I have made / did make from something*.

438 **kononha** [ro-nón-ha'] *they, them (females)(Free Pronoun)*
Onhka ne'e ne kononha. [Ónh-ka' né:-'eh ne ko-nón-ha'] *Who are they?*

Onkwatenron ne'e ne kononha. [On-kwa-tén:-ronh né:-'eh ne ko-nón-ha'] *They are my friends.* For Emphasis: **Kononha wa'kontikhonni'.** [Ko-nón-ha' wa'-kon-tik-hón:-ni'] *THEY did the cooking.*

439 kononkwe [ko-nón:-kwe'] *female persons; women*
ne kononkwe [ne ko-nón:-kwe'] *the women*; **thiken' kononkwe** [thí:-ken'...] *those women*; **kiken' kononkwe** [kí:-ken'...] *these women*. (see: yakonkwe)

440 kontiksa'okonha [kon-tik-sa'-o-kón-ha'] *female children: girls*
ne kontiksa'okonha [ne kon-tik-sa'-o-kón-ha'] *the girls*; **thiken' kontiksa'okonha** [thí:-ken'...] *those girls*; **kiken' kontiksa'okonha** [kí:-ken'...] *these girls*. (see: yeksa'a)

441 kontiksten'okonha [kon-tik-sten'-o-kón-ha'] *old women*
ne kontiksten'okonha [ne kon-tik-sten'-o-kón-ha'] *the women*; **thiken' kontiksten'okonha** [thí:-ken'...] *those women*; **kiken' kontiksten'okonha** [kí:-ken'...] *these women*. (see: akokstenha)

442 kontirio [kon-tí-ri-o'] *wild animals*
ne kontirio [ne kon-tí-ri-o'] *the wild animals*; **thiken' kontirio** [thí:-ken'...] *those wild animals*; **kiken' kontirio** [kí:-ken'...] *these wild animals*. (see: kario)

443 kowanen [ko-wá:-nenh] *it is big*
Sotsi kowanen. [Só-tsih ko-wá:-nenh] *It is too big*; **Akwah iken' tsi kowanen.** [Kwah í:-ken' tsi ko-wá:-nenh] *It is very big*; **Nikowanen na'a!** [Ni-ko-wá:-nenh ná:-'ah] *It is so big!*; **Yah e'tho tekowanen.** [Yah é-thoh te-ko-wá:-nenh] *It is not big enough.* With nominals: **kanonhsowanen** [ka-nonh-so-wá:-nenh] *a big house*; **kahehtowanen** [ka-heh-to-wá:-nenh] *a big field*; **ka'sere'tsherowanen** [ka'-se-re'ts-he-ro-wá:-nenh] *a big car.* As a verb: **ikkowanen** [ik-ko-wá:-nenh] *I am big*; **rakowanen** [ra-ko-wá:-nenh] *He is big*; **yekowanen** [ye-ko-wá:-nenh] *she is big*; **kakowanen** [ka-ko-wá:-nen] *it is big*: ie. **kakowanen erhar** [...ér-har] *a big dog.* Also: **tewakahsi'towanen.** [Te-wa-kah-si'-to-wá:-nenh] *I have big feet.* **Wake'sere'tsherowanen** [wa-ke'-se-re'ts-he-ro-wá:-nenh] *I have a big car.*

444 ktakehrìta's [k-ta-ke-hrì:-ta's] *I fry something* (C-Stem - Subj.)
wa'ktakehrìta' [wa'-k-ta-ke-hrì:-ta'] *I fried...*; **waktakehrìtenh** [wak-ta-ke-hrì:-tenh] *I have fried / did fry....*

445 ktakwas [k-tá-kwas] *I take out of, remove from* (C-Stem - Subj.)
wa'ktahko' [wa'-k-táh-ko'] *I took out, removed...*; **waktahkwenh** [wak-tá-kwenh] *i have taken out, removed / did take out, remove....*

446 kwa'yenha [kwa'-yén-ha'] *a rabbit; a cottontail*

447 kweskwes [kwés-kwes] *a pig*

448 **kya'tyènen's** [kya'-tyè:-nen's] *I fall from* (C-Stem - Subj.)
wa'kya'tyènenne' [wa'-kya'-tyè:-nen'-ne'] *I fell from*; **wakya'tyehnen'onh** [wak-ya'-tyeh-nén:-'onh] *I have fallen / did fall.*

449 **kyaken's** [kyá:-ken's] *I exit* (C-Stem - Subj.)
wa'kyakenne' [wa'-kyá:-ken'-ne'] *I exited*; **wakyaken'onh** [wak-ya-kén:-'onh] *I have exited / did exit.* (See: **tkyaken's**; **yekyaken's**)

450 **kyatatenonhkwe** [kya-tá-te-nonh-kwe'] *her (female) relative*
(See: yakyatatenonhkwe)

451 **kyàten's** [kyá:-ten's] *I fall* (C-Stem - Subj.)
wa'kyàtenne' [wa'-kyà:-ten'-ne'] *I fell*; **wakya'ten'onh** [wa-kya'-tén:-'onh] *I have fallen / did fall.*

452 **kyenahs** [kyé:-nahs] *I receive, accept; I catch* (C-Stem - Subj.)
wa'kyena' [wa'-kyé:-na'] *I received, accepted, caught*; **wakyena'onh** [wa-kye-ná:-'onh] *I have received / did receive....*

453 **kyenterha's** [kyen-tér-ha's] *I get to know (become acquainted with)* (C-Stem - Subj.)
wa'kyenterhane' [wa'-kyen-tér-ha'-ne'] *I got to know...*; **wakyenterha'onh** [wa-kyen-ter-há:-'onh] *I have gotten to know / did get to know....*

454 **kyenthokwas** [kyent-hó-kwas] *I harvest* (C-Stem - Subj.)
wa'kyenthoko' [wa'-kyent-hó:-ko'] *I harvested*; **wakyenthokwenh** [wak-yent-hó-kwenh] *I have harvested / did harvest*: ie. **kenenhstayenthokwas** [ke-nenhs-ta-yent-hó-kwas] *I harvest corn*; **ikhnenna'tayenthokwas** [ik-hnen-na'-ta-yent-hó-kwas] *I harvest potatoes.*

455 **kyenthos** [kyént-hos] *I plant* (C-Stem - Subj.)
wa'kyentho' [wa'-kyént-ho'] *I planted*; **wakyenthonh** [wak-yént-honh] *I have planted / did plant*: ie. **kenenhstayenthos** [ke-nenhs-ta-yént-hos] *I plant corn*; **ikhnenna'tayenthos** [ik-hnen-na'-ta-yént-hos] *I plant potatoes.*

N

456 **naho'tenhson** [na-ho'-ténh-sonh] *things*
ie. **Akwekon enkatste' ne naho'tenhson wa'ketshenri'.** [A-kwé:-kon én:-kats-te' ne na-ho'-ténh-sonh wa'-kets-hén:-ri'] *I will use all the things I found.*

457 **nahòten** [na-hò:-ten'] *what*
As a statement: **Wa'katkahtho' nahòten wa'thàrihte'.** [Wa'-kat-káh-tho'

na-hò:-ten' wa'-thà:-rih-te'] *I saw what he broke.* With questions: **Wehsàronke' ken nahòten wahenron'.** [Weh-sà:-ron-ke' ken na-hò:-ten' wa-hén:-ron'] *Did you hear what he said?* With negatives: **Yah tewakateryentare nahòten tsiten'.** [Yah te-wa-ka-ter-yén:-ta-re' na-hò:-ten' tsí:-ten'] *I don't know what you mean.* (see: Oh nahòten)

b) **nahòten ok** [na-hò:-ten'k] *something*

ie. **Wa'ehninon' nahòten ok kanoron.** [Wa-eh-ní:-non' na-hò:-tenk ka-nò:-ronh] *She bought something expensive.*

458 ne [néh] *the; the one who / that (creates a sense of specificness)*

ie. **Wakhninonh ne kahyatonhsera.** [Wak-hní:-nonh ne ka-hya-tónh-se-ra'] *I bought the book;* **Riyenteri ne ronkwe.** [Ri-yen-té:-ri' ne rón:-kwe'] *I know the man.*

a) **ne ok ne'e** [nék ne:-'eh] *only...*

ie. **ne ok ne'e kahyatonhsera** [...ka-hya-tónh-se-ra'] *(it is) only the book;* **ne ok ne'e rohtsi'a riyenteri.** [...roh-tsí:-'ah ri-yen-té:-ri'] *(it is) only his older brother that I know.*

b) **ne ok tsi** [nék tsi] *but*

ie. **Yoràse ne ok tsi yah ki' tekenònwe's.** [Yo-rà:-seh nek tsi yah ki' te-ke-nòn:-we's] *It's pretty but I don't like it.*

c) **ne onen** [ne' ó:-nen / né-nenh] *when*

ie. **Yenkataweya'te' ne onen enyokennore'.** [Yen-ka-tá:-we-ya'-te' né-nenh en-yo-kén:-no-re'] *I will go in when it rains.*

d) **ne nahòten** [né: na-hò:-ten'] *the thing that (that which)*

ie. **Wahatkahtho' ne' nahòten wa'kheyon'.** [Wa-hat-káh-tho' ne na-hò:-ten' wa'-khé:-yon'.] *He saw the thing that I gave them.*

e) **ne nen** [né: nen] *when* (see: ne onen)

f) **ne se' ken'en** [né: se' kén:-'enh] *as well*

ie. **Kiken' otsihkwa' wahatshenri' ne se' ken'en.** [Kí:-ken' o-tsíh-kwa' wa-hats-hén:-ri' né: se' kén:-'enh]

459 ne' [né'] *that*

ie. **teyotonhwentsyohon ne' ratorathe's niya'tewenhniserake.** [Te-yo-ton-wen-tsyó-honh ne' ra-to-rát-he's ni-ya'-te-wenh-ni-se-rá:-keh] *It is necessary that he goes hunting every day.*

460 ne'e [né:-'eh] *it is (that) / that's what; (that) it is...*

ie. **Ne'e wahenron'** [Né:-'eh wa-hén:-ron'] *that's what he said;* **Ratorats ne'e.** [Ra-tó:-rats né:-'eh] *he is a hunter.*

a) **ne'e ne** [né:-'eh neh] *(that / who (it) is the...*
   ie. **Wahiken' thiken' ronkwe ne'e ne yah tehohwihstayen'.** [Wa-hí:-ken' ne rón:-kwe' né:-'eh ne yah te-ho-hwíhs-ta-yen'] *I saw that man who is the one without any money.*

b) **ne'e tsi** [né:-eh tsi] *because; as*
   ie. **Rahshakha ne'e tsi tehothonryahseryen'se.** [Rahs-hák-ha' né:-'eh tsi te-hot-hon-ryáh-se-ryen'-se'] *He is coughing because he has a cold.*

461 **nen** [nen] *then*
   ie. **Wahatekhwihsa' nen yahayakenne'.** [Wa-ha-tek-hwíh-sa' nen ya-ha-yá:-ken'-ne'] *He finished his meal (and) then he went out.* (see: onen)

462 **nen' ne'e** [nen' né:-'eh] *(definitely) is*
   ie. **Raonha nen' ne'e nahatyere'.** [Rá-on-ha' nen' né:-'eh na-há-tye-re'] *He (definitely) is the one who did it.*

463 **nène** [nè:-neh] *the one who / that*
   ie. **Riyenteri ne ronkwe nène ratorats.** [Ri-yen-té:-ri' ne rón:-kwe' nè:-ne' ra-tó:-rats] *I know the man who hunts.* (see: ne'e ne)

a) **nène yawet** [nè:-neh yá:-weht] *instead*

464 **netens** [nè:-tens] *or; or else*
   ie. **Tkakonte akerihwihsa' ne kiken' netens yah thayonkkaryakse'.** [T-ká:-kon-teh a-ke-rih-wíh-sa' ne kí:-ken' nè:-tenhs yah tha-yonk-kár-ya'k-se'] *I have to finish this up or (else) I won't get paid for it.*

465 **nihati** [ni-há:-tih] *more than two (male individuals)*
   With nominals: **Wisk nihati rononkwe** [wihsk ni-há:-tih ro-nón:-kwe'] *five men*; **Ahsen nihati ratiksa'okonha** [áh-sen' ni-há:-tih ra-tik-sa'-o-kón-ha'] *three boys.* With verbs: **Oyeri nihati wahatikwatako'.** [O-yé:-rih ni-há:-tih wa-ha-ti-kwa-tá:-ko'] *Ten of them fixed it.* **Kayeri ki' ok nihati wa'khehrori'.** [Ka-yé:-rih kok ni-há:-tih wa'-khe-hró:-ri'] *I told only four of them.* As a question: **To nihati.** [To ni-há:-tih] *How many of them (males):* ie. **To nihati ne ratiksa'okonha wa'kheken'.** [To ni-há:-tih ne ra-tik-sa'-o-kón-ha' wah-s-hé:-ken'] *How many of the boys did you see?*

466 **nikahwihstake** [ni-ka-hwíhs-ta-keh] *...dollars*
   ie. **wisk nikahwihstake** [wihsk ni-ka-hwíhs-ta-keh] *five dollars ($5.00)*; **oyeri nikahwihstake** [o-yé:-rih ni-ka-hwíhs-ta-keh] *ten dollars ($10.00)*; **tewahsen nikahwihstake** [te-wáh-sen' ni-ka-hwíhs-ta-keh] *twenty dollars ($20.00)*;

467 **nikahyonha'ah** [ni-ka-hyon-há:-'ah] *a creek, a stream*
   ie. **Akta tsi nikahyonha'ah thanakerehkwe'.** [Ák-ta' tsi ni-ka-hyon-há:-'ah t-ha-ná-ke-reh-kwe'] *He used to live near the creek.*

468 **nikarihwehsha'** [ni-ka-ri-hwéhs-ha'] *a short time; a short while*
ie. **Nikarihwehsha eh kanatakon yere'skwe'.** [...eh ka-ná:-ta-konh yé:-re's-kwe'] *He was (there) in town for a short while.*

469 **nikatenhsha'** [ni-ka-ténhs-ha'] *it is thin*
ie. **Sotsi nikatenhsha'** [Só-tsih ni-ka-ténhs-ha'] *It's too thin*; **Akwah tsi nikatenhsha'** [A-kwáh tsi ni-ka-ténhs-ha'] *It's quite thin.* With nominals: **nikahswen'karatenhsha'** [ni-kah-swen'-ka-ra-ténhs-ha'] *a thick board*; **niwahsiratenhsha** [ni-wah-si-ra-ténhs-ha'] *a thick blanket.*

470 **nikatyerha'** [ni-ka-tyér-ha'] *I do something*
na'katyere' [na'-ká-tye-re'] *I did something*; **niwakatyerenh** [ni-wa-ka-tyé:-renh] *I have done / I did do something.* With negatives: **Yah tewakatyerenh.** [Yah te-wa-ka-tyé:-renh] *I didn't do / have done something.* As a question: **Oh nihsatyerha'** [Oh nih-sa-tyér-ha'] *What are you doing?* **Wakatshennonni tsi nihatyerha'.** [Wa-kats-hen-nón:-nih tsi ni-ha-tyér-ha'] *I am happy with what he's doing.*

471 **nikhnenyehsha** [nik-hnen-yéhs-ha'] *I am short*
ie. **Nihahnenyehsha'** [ni-hah-nen-yéhs-ha'] *He's short*; **Niyehnenyehsha'** [ni-yeh-nen-yéhs-ha'] *she's short*: ie. **Senha nihahnenyehsha' tsi niyoht ne akaonha.** [Sén-ha' ni-hah-nen-yéhs-ha' tsi ní:-yoht n'a-ká-on-ha'] *He is shorter that she*; **Eh niyehnenyehsha' tsi niyoht ne raonha.** [Eh ni-yeh-nen-yéhs-ha' tsi ní:-yoht ne rá-on-ha'] *She is as short as he.*

472 **nikon** [ní:-kon] *more than two (inanimate things)*
ie. **ahsen nikon** [áh-sen' ní:-konh] *there are three (of them)*; **ahsen nikon ne kahyatonhsera'okon** [...ne ka-hya-tonh-se-ra'-ó:-konh] *three of the books.* As a question: **To nikon.** [To ní:-konh] *How many (are there)?* **To nikon ne ka'sere'tshera'okon** [...ne ka'-se-re'ts-he-ra'-ó:-konh] *How many cars (are there)?*

473 **nikonha** [ni-kón-ha'] *a little bit of*
ie. **Nikonha katsikhètare.** [Ni-kón-ha ka-tsi-khè:-ta-reh] *there's a little bit of sugar in it*; **Ne ok nikonha kanòntare.** [Nek ni-kón-ha ka-nòn:-ta-reh] *There's just a little bit of milk left.*

474 **nikonti** [ni-kón:-tih] *more than two (female / animate individuals)*
With nominals: **Wisk nikonti kononkwe** [wihsk ni-kón:-tih ko-nón:-kwe'] *five women*; **Ahsen nikonti kontiksa'okonha** [áh-sen' ni-kón:-tih kon-tik-sa'-o-kón-ha'] *three girls.* With verbs: **Oyeri nihati wakontikhonni'.** [O-yé:-rih ni-há:-tih wa'-kon-tik-hón:-ni'] *Ten of them cooked.* **Kayeri ki' ok nikonti wa'khehrori'.** [Ka-yé:-rih kok ni-kón:-tih wa'-khe-hró:-ri'] *I told only four of them (females).* As a question: **To nikonti.** [To ni-kón:-tih] *How many of them (females)*: ie. **To nikonti ne kontiksa'okonha wahsheken'.** [To ni-kón:-tih ne

50

kon-tik-sa'-o-kón-ha' wa'-s-hé:-ken'] *How many of the girls did you see?*

475 **nikyerha'** [ni-kyér-ha'] *I do (something) to it*
nàkyere' [nà:-kye-re'] *I did something to it*; **niwakyerenh** [ni-wa-kyé:-renh] *I have done / I did do something to it*. With negatives: **Yah tewakyerenh.** [Yah te-wa-kyé:-renh] *I didn't do / have done anything to it*. As a question: **Oh nihsyerha'** [Oh nih-syér-ha'] *What are you doing to it?* **Oh nahsyere'** [Oh náh-sye-re'] *What did you do to it?* **Wakatshennonni tsi nihayerha'.** [Wa-kats-hen-nón:-nih tsi ni-ha-yér-ha'] *I am happy with what he's doing to it.*

476 **niwa'a** [ni-wá:-'ah] *it is small*
nihra'ah [ni-hrá:-'ah] *he is small*; **niyaka'ah** [ni-ya-ká:-'ah] *she is small*; **niwasa** [ni-wá:-sa'] *small ones*; **nihonnasa** [ni-hon-ná:-sa'] *they (male) are small*; **nikonnasa** [ni-kon-ná:-sa'] *they (female) are small*. When used with nominals: **nikanonhsa'ah** [ni-ka-nonh-sá:-'ah] *a small house*; **nikanahskwa'ah** [ni-ka-nahs-kwá:-'ah] *a small animal*: ie. **nikanahskwa'ah erhar** [ni-ka-nahs-kwá:-'ah ér-har] *a small dog.*

477 **niwahsen** [ni-wáh-senh] *...ty*
ie. **ahsen-niwahsen** [áh-sen' ni-wáh-senh] *thirty*; **wisk-niwahsen-wisk** [wihsk ni-wáh-senh wihsk] *fifty-five*. With nominals: **Kayeri nikatshe'tahsen** [a-yé:-rih ni-kats-he'-táh-senh] *fourty bottles.*

478 **niyawen's** [ni-yá:-wen's] *it happens*
ie. **tsi niyawen's** [tsi ni-yá:-wen's] *with what happens*; **tsi na'awenne'** [tsi na'-á;:-wen'-ne'] *with what happened*; **tsi niyawen'onh** [tsi ni-ya-wén:-'onh] *with what has happened*. As a question: **Oh niyawen's.** [Oh ni-yá:-wen's] *What happens?* **Oh na'awenne'.** [Oh na'-á;:-wen'-ne'] *What happened?* **Oh niyawen'onh.** [Oh ni-ya-wén:-'onh] *What has happened?* With other particles: **tho nayawenne'** [tho na-yá:-wen'-ne'] *in order to / that*; **Eh ne'e na'awenne'.** [Eh -né:-'eh na'-á:-wen'-ne'] *That's what happened.* **Eh ki' nityawen'onh** [Eh ni-tya-wén:-'onh] *It just so happened.*

479 **niyenhsha'** [ni-yénhs-ha'] *it is short*
ie. **Sotsi niyenhsha'.** [só-tsih ni-yénhs-ha'] *It's too short*; **Akwah iken' tsi niyenhsha'** [a-kwah í:-ken' tsi ni-yénhs-ha'] *It's very short*; **Yah eh teyenhsha'** [yah eh te-yénhs-ha'] *It's not short enough*: With nominals: **niwahseriye'tehsha'** [ni-wah-se-ri-ye'-téhs-ha'] *a short rope*; **nikarihwehsha'** [ni-ka-rih-wéhs-ha'] *a short time.*

480 **niyohontehsha** [ni-yo-hon-téhs-ha'] *strawberries*
ie. **Wakekahs ne niyohontehsha.** [Wa-ké:-kahs ne ni-yo-hon-téhs-ha'] *I like strawberries.*

51

481 nok [nok] *and; but*

ie. **Yeksa'a nok raksa'a** [yeh-sá:-'ah nok rak-sá:-'ah] *a girl and a boy*;
onònta nok otsikhèta [o-nòn;_ta' nok o-tsi-khè:-ta'] *milk and sugar*;
kanàtaronk nok owihstohsera [ka-nà:-ta-ronk nok o-wihs-tóh-se-ra'] *bread
and butter*; **tyohyòtsihs nok tyotskara'kowa** [tyo-hyò:-tsihs nok tyots-ka-ra'-
kó:-wah] *salt and pepper*. **Kenònwe's kahnekakon nok yah onònta.** [Ke-
nòn:-we's kah-ne-ká-konh nok yah o-nòn:-ta'] *I like pop but not milk.*

a) **nok are** [nok á:-reh] *and again; but again*

ie. **Wahshakohrori' tohsa nok are sahontyere'.** [Wah-sha-ko-hró:-ri'
tóh-sa' nok á:-reh sa-hón-tye-re'] *He told them not but they did it again.*

b) **nok oni** [nok ó:-ni'] *and also*

ie. **Wakhninon kiken' nok oni thiken atyàtawi'.** [Wak-hní:-nonh kí:-
ken' nok ó:-ni' thí:-ken' a-tyà:-ta-wi'] *I bought this (one) and also that coat.*

482 nonkati [non-ká:-tih] *toward*

ie. **kanonhsakon nonkati** [ka-nónh-sa-konh non-ká:-tih] *toward the house*;
kanatakon nonkati [ka-ná:-ta-konh non-ká:-tih] *toward the town*; **akaonhàke
nonkati** [a-ka-on-hà-keh...] *toward her*; **raonhàke nonkati** [ra-on-hà:-keh...]
toward him. (see: tsi; eh; kenh)

a) **eh nonkati** [eh non-ká:-tih] *(toward) there; over there; (off) that way*
ie. **Eh nonkati niyahare' ne ya'niha'.** [...ni-ya-há:-re' ne ya'-ní-ha']
Your father went off that way.

b) **kenh nonkati** [kenh non-ká:-tih] *toward (here); over here; (over) this way*
ie. **Kenh nonkati nontahsawe.** [...non-táh-sa-we] *Bring it over this way.*

c) **tsi nonkati** [tsi non-ká:-tih] *the direction; the way to*
ie. **Wahiyanenhawe' tsi nonkati niyahare'.** [Wa-hi-ya-nén-ha-we' tsi
non-ká:-tih ni-ya-há:-re'] *I followed his trail in the direction he went.*

483 nonwa [nón:-wa] *now, presently*

ie. **Oh nonwa nisatyerha'.** [Oh nón:-wa' nih-sa-tyér-ha'] *What are you presently
doing?* **Ka' nonwa nonwe wàre'.** [Ka' nón:-wa' nón:-weh wà:-re'] *Where is
he going now?*

484 nonwe [nón:-weh] *at; at / to the place of; located*

Toronto nonwe [To-rón:-toh nón:-weh] *at Toronto / located in Toronto*;
Karhakon nonwe [kar-há:-konh nón:-weh] *It's in the woods / located in the woods.*
(see: tsi; ka'; kenh; ken'; eh)

a) **eh nonwe** [eh nón:-weh] *there; that is where; (to) where*
ie. **Eh nonwe niya'kontiye' ne kahonk.** [...ni-ya'-kon-tí-tye' ne ká-
honk] *That is where the geese flew (to).*

b) **kenh nonwe** [kenh nón:-weh] *here; this is the place*

    ie. **Kenh nonwe tahonnewe'.** [...ta-hón:-ne-we'] *They arrived here.*

c) **tsi nonwe** [tsi nón:-weh] *where; to / at the place (where)*

    ie. **Wahakena'tonhahse' tsi nonwe nihoyo'te'.** [Wa-ha-ke-na'-tón-hah-se' tsi nón:-weh ni-ho-yó-te'] *He showed me where he is working.*

O

485 **o'kenhrakeri** [o'-ken-hrá-ke-rih] *lye; acid*

486 **o'kènra** [o'-kèn:-ra'] *soot, dirt, dust*
o'kenhràke [o'-ken-hrà:-keh] *on the dust, dirt*; **o'kènrakon** [o'-kèn:-ra-konh] *in the dust, dirt*; **o'kenhrakonhson** [o'ken-hra-kónh-sonh] *out in the dust, dirt.* **yo'kènrare** [yo'-kèn:-ra-reh] *it has dirt, dust on it / it's dusty.*

487 **o'nhahte** [ó'-n-hah-teh] *a branch; branches*
With locatives: **o'nhahtàke** [o'-n-hah-tà:-keh] *on the branch...*; **o'nhahtòkon** [o'-n-hah-tò:-konh] *under the branch...*; **tsi tyo'nhahtonte** [tsi tyo'-n-háh-ton-teh] *where there is a branch*; **tsi tyo'nhahtonton** [tsi tyo'-n-hah-tón:-tonh] *where there are branches.* With verbs: **ke'nhahtya'ks** [te'-n-háh-tya'ks] *I cut off a branch*; **teke'nhahtokewas** [te-ke'-n-hah-to-ké:-was] *I strip the branches off.*

488 **o'nhonhsa** [o'n-hónh-sa'] *egg(s)*
With verbs: **ken'nhonhsaks** [ken'-n-hónh-saks] *I eat eggs*; **ken'nhonhsahninons** [ken'-n-honh-sah-ní:-nons] *I buy eggs*; **katen'nhonhsah-ninons** [ka-ten'-n-honh-sah-ní:-nons] *I sell eggs*;

489 **o'nyonhsa** [o'nyónh-sa'] *nose*
ke'nyonhsàke [ke'-nyonh-sà:-keh] *on my nose*; **se'nyonhsàke** [se'-nyonh-sà:-keh] *on your nose*; **ra'nyonhsàke** [ra'-nyonh-sà:-keh] *on his nose*; **ye'nyonhsàke** [ye'-nyonh-sà:-keh] *on her nose*; **ka'nyonhsàke** [ka'-nyonh-sà:-keh] *on its nose.* **wake'nyonhsonte** [wa-ke'-nyónh-son-teh] *I have a nose*; **wake'nyonhsanònwaks** [wa-ke'-nyonh-sa-nòn:-waks] *I have a sore nose*; **Yokwàronte nène ke'nyonhsàke.** [Yo-kwà:-ron-teh nè:-neh ke'-nyonh-sà:-keh] *There's a bump on my nose.*

490 **O'seronni** [O'-se-rón:-ni'] *White people (also Frenchman)*

491 **o'sora** [o-só:-ra'] *a spruce tree*

492 o'tara [o'-tá:-ra'] *clay, chimney (brick); clan*
o'tarahson'a [o'-ta-rah-són:-'ah] *clans.* With locatives: **o'tarakon** [o'-tá:-ra-konh] *in the clay;* **o'taràke** [o'-ta-rà:-keh] *on the clay;* **ken'tarakon** [ken'-tá:-ra-konh] *in the chimney;* **ken'taràke** [ken'-ta-rà:-keh] *on the chimney;* **ken'tarakta'** [ken'-ta-rák-ta'] *near the chimney;* **ken'tarote** [ken'-tá:-ro-teh] *there is / stands a chimney:* ie. **akta tsi ken'tarote** [ák-ta' tsi ken'-tá:-ro-teh] *next to the chimney;* **èneken ahskwàke tken'taraketote.** [è:-ne-kenh ahs-kwà:-keh t-ken'-ta-ra-kè:-to-teh] *up on the roof there is a chimney sticking out.* With verbs: **ken'tararhos** [ki'-ta-rár-hos] *I plaster something;* **ki'tarakarhathos** [ki'-ta-ra-kar-hát-hos] *I plough;* **kate'tarakwètarons** [ka-te'-ta-ra-kwè:-ta-rons] *I plough (a) furrow(s);* **teki'tarotha'** [te-ki'-ta-rót-ha'] *I lay (a) brick(s);* **ki'tarayen'** [ki'-ta-rá:-yen'] *I am a member of a clan;* **niwaki'taròten'** [ni-wa-ki'-ta-rò:-ten'] *I am of ? clan:* ie. **Oh nisen'taròten'** [Oh ni-sen'-ta-rò:-ten'] *What is your clan? / Of what clan are you?* **A'nowara niwaki'taròten'.** [A'-nó:-wa-ra' ni-wa-ki'-ta-rò:-ten'] *I am Turtle clan.*

493 o'tarihenhsera [o'-ta-ri-hénh-se-ra'] *heat; warmth*

494 o'tonwa [o'-tón:-wa'] *a pile*
With locatives: **o'tonwakon** [o'-tón:-wa-konh] *in the pile;* **o'tonhyòkon** [o'-ton-hyò:-konh] *under the pile.* With adjectivals: **yo'tonhyowanen** [yo'-ton-hyo-wá:-nenh] *a big pile;* **niyo'tonwa'ah** [ni-yo'-ton-wá:-'ah] *a small pile.* With verbs: **ki'tonhyotha'** [ki'-ton-hyót-ha'] *I pile something up;* **ki'tonhyonnis** [ki'-ton-hyón:-nis] *I make a pile;* **ki'tonhyonnyanyons** [ki'-ton-hyon-nyá-nyons] *I make piles of something.* (see: yo'tònyote)

495 o'wahràse [o'-wa-hrà:-seh] *fresh meat*

496 o'wàronk [o'-wà:-ronk] *meat*
ie. **ke'wàraks** [ke'-wà:-raks] *I eat meat;* **ke'wahranònwaks** [ke'-wa-hra-nòn:-waks] *I long for some meat (to eat);* **ke'wahrakahstha'** [ke'-wa'hra-káhst-ha'] *I am fond to meat;* **ke'wahrahninons** [ke'-wa-hrah-ní:-nons] *I buy meat / I am a meat buyer;* **kate'wahrahninons** [ka-te'-wa-hrah-ní:-nons] *I sell meat / I am a seller of meat;* **ke'wahrakwètarons** [ke'-wa-hra-kwè:-ta-rons] *I slice off some (a piece of) meat.*

497 o'whahsa [o'-wháh-sa'] *a wrap-around skirt, a dress*
With possessives: **ake'whahsa** [a-ke'-wháh-sa'] *my dress, wrap-around skirt;* **sa'whahsa** [sa'-wháh-sa'] *your dress...;* **akao'whahsa** [a-ka-o'-wháh-sa'] *her dress....* With locatives: **ake'whahsàke** [a-ke'-whah-sà:-keh] *on my dress, wrap-around skirt;* **ake'whahsòkon** [a-ke'-whah-sò:-konh] *under my dress....*

498 oh [oh] *what* Only used with certain verbs to create questions:
ie. **Oh nihsatyerha'.** [Oh nih-sa-tyér-ha'] *What are you doing?;* **Oh niyawen's** [Oh ni-yá:-wen's] *What happens?.*

a) **oh na'kaya'tòten'** [oh na'-ka-ya'-tò:-ten'] *what kind (of thing) is it?*

b) **oh nahòten** [oh na-hò:-ten'] *what is it?; what*
   ie. **Oh nahòten ne sahsenna.** [Oh na-hò:-ten' ne sah-sén:-na'] *What is your name?* **Oh nahòten satkahthonh.** [...sat-káht-honh] *What did you see?* After question: **Sateryentare ken oh nahòten rohninonh.** [Sa-ter-yén:-ta-reh kén oh na-hò:-ten' roh-ní:-nonh] *Do you know what he bought?* After negatives: **Yah tehakhrorih oh nahòten rotkahthonh.** [Yah te-hak-ró:-rih oh na-hò:-ten' rot-káht-honh] *He didn't tell me what he saw.*

c) **oh nikaya'tòten'** [oh ni-ka-ya'-tò:-ten'] *what does it look like?*

d) **oh niyoht** [oh ní:-yoht] *how is it?; how*
   ie. **Oh niyoht ne sa'nihstenha.** [...ne sa'-nih-stén-ha'] *How is your mother;* **Oh niyoht tsi sakwatakwenh.** [...tsi sa-kwa-tá-kwenh] *How did you fix it?*

e) **oh niyotyeren** [oh ni-yo-tyé:-renh] *why is it?; why?*
   ie. **Oh niyotyeren tsi sakwatakwenh.** [...tsi sa-kwa-tá-kwenh] *Why are you fixing it?* **Oh niyotyeren tsi tontayen'.** [...tsi ton-tá:-yen'] *Why did she come back?*

499 **ohaha** [o-há-ha'] *a road, a pathway*
   With locatives: **ohahàke** [o-ha-hà:-keh] *on the road;* **ohaha'kehson** [o-ha-ha'-kéh-sonh] *out on the road;* **ohahakta** [o-ha-hák-ta'] *beside the road;* **ohahaktatye'** [o-ha-hak-tá-tye'] *along the side of the road;* **akta tsi yohatayen'** [ák-ta' tsi yo-há:-ta-yen'] *next to the road;* **èneken tsi yohatayen'** [è:-ne-kenh tsi yo-há:-ta-yen'] *above the road;* **tsi yeyohate** [tsi ye-yo-há:-teh] *at the end of the road, path;* **sha'teyohahihen** [s-ha'-te-yo-ha-hí:-henh] *in the middle of the road.* With verbs: **ikhahahseronnis** [ik-ha-hah-se-rón:-nis] *I fix up a road (make repairs);* **ikhahonnis** [ik-ha-hón:-nis] *I make a road;* **kathahita's** [kat-ha-hí-ta's] *I follow a road, path(way);* **kathaharakwas** [kat-ha-ha-rá-kwas] *I leave the road, path(way);* **kathahatases** [kat-ha-ha-tá:-ses] *I make a detour;* **kathahines** [kat-ha-hí:-nes] *I follow a road, path(way);* **kahahara's** [ka-ha-há:-ra's] *I take the (specific) road, path(way);* **ikhahakweks** [ik-ha-há-kweks] *I blockade a road(way), path(way).*

500 **ohahsa** [o-háh-sa'] *femur; upper part of leg*
   With locatives: **ikhahsàke** [ik-hah-sà:-keh] *on my femur...;* **ihshahsàke** [ihs-hah-sà:keh] *on your femur...;* **rahahsàke** [ra-hah-sà:-keh] *on his femur...;* **yehahsàke** [ye-hah-sà:-keh] *on her femur.* With verbs: **ikhahsakahrewahtha'** [ik-hah-sa-ka-hre-wáht-ha'] *I hurt the upper part of my leg (my femur);* **wakhahsakanònwaks** [wak-hah-sa-nòn:-waks] *the upper part of my leg is sore.*

501 **ohahsera** [o-háh-se-ra'] *a light, lamp*
   ie. **ohahsera'onwe** [o-hah-se-ra'-ón:-weh] *a candle, torch;* **yehahserotahkwa**

[ye-hah-se-ro-táh-kwa'] *a candle stick;* **yehahserenhahstha** [ye-hah-se-ren-háhst-ha'] *a lantern, flashlight:* **ikhahserotha'** [ik-hah-se-rót-ha'] *I turn on a light;* **ikhahswatha'** [ik-hahs-wát-ha'] *I turn out a light;* **kahahserenhawis** [ka-hah-se-ren-há:-wis] *I carry a light (ie. candle, flashlight, lantern, lamp, etc....*

502 **oharennahta** [o-ha-ren-náh-ta'] *purple; black & blue*
ie. **oharennahta niwahsohkòten'** [...ni-wah-soh-kò:-ten'] *it is coloured (dyed) purple;* **oharennahta niwatya'tawi'tsheròten'** [...ni-wa-tya'-ta-wi'ts-he -rò:-ten'] *a purple coat.* With verbs: **wakharennahtare** [wak-ha-ren-náh-ta-reh] *I have a bruise (am black & blue):* ie. **Wakharennahtare nène ikhsinàke.** [...nè:-neh ik-hsi-nà:-keh] *I have bruise on my leg.*

503 **ohkwari'** [oh-kwá:-ri'] *a bear*
wahkwari'takenra [wah-kwa-ri'-ta-kèn:ra'] *a polar bear (a white bear);* **wahkwari'tahòntsi** [wah-kwa-ri'-ta-hòn:-tsih] *a black bear.*

504 **ohnatirontha** [oh-na-ti-rónt-ha'] *rubber, elastic*
ie. **yohnatirontha yonnyàton** [...yon-nyà:-tonh] *it's made of rubber.*

505 **ohnehta** [oh-néh-ta'] *gum; pitch, tar, resin; pine tree*
With locatives: **ohnehtàke** [oh-neh-tà:-keh] *on the gum, pitch...; pine tree;* **ohnehtakta** [oh-neh-ták-ta'] *beside the gum; pitch...; pine tree;* **ohnehtòkon** [oh-neh-tò:-konh] *under the gum; pitch...; pine tree;* With verbs: **yohnehtare** [yoh-néh-ta-reh] *it is gummy, resinous; it has tare on it;* **kahnehtarhon** [kah-neh-tár-honh] *it is cover, smeared with tar, pitch...;* **kenehtarhos** [ke-neh-tár-hos] *I seal, glue something;* **tekenehtya'ks** [te-keh-néh-tya'ks] *I unseal something.*

506 **ohnehta'kowa** [oh-neh-ta'-kó:-wa'] *a pine tree*

507 **ohneka** [oh-né:-ka'] *water, liquid*
With locatives: **ohnekakon** [oh-né:-ka-konh] *in the water;* **ohnekakonhson** [oh-ne-ka-kónh-sonh] *out in the water;* **kahnekòkon** [kah-ne-kò:-konh] *under the water (on the bottom).* With adjectivals: **kahnekiyo** [kah-ne-kí:-yoh] *good water (a good drink);* **kahnekaksen** [kah-ne-kák-senh] *bad water (a poor drink);* **kahneka'shatste** [kah-ne-ka'-s-háts-te'] *a strong drink (whiskey / liquor).* With verbs: **kahnekare** [kah-né:-ka-reh] *it has water in it;* **ikhnekawerons** [ik-hne-ká-we-rons] *I pour water (into it);* **tekhnekontye's** [tek-hne-kón-tye's] *I boil (water or some liquid).* Also **teyohnekontye's** [te-yoh-ne-kón-tye's] *it is boiling (water being trown about).* (see: khnekirha')

508 **ohnekanos** [oh-né:-ka-nos] *drinking water; spring water*

509 **ohnenhsa** [oh-nénh-sa'] *shoulder(s)*
With possessives: **ikhnenhsàke** [ik-hnenh-sà:-keh] *on my shoulder;* **shnenhsàke** [s-hnenh-sà:-keh] *on your shoulder;* **rahnenhsàke** [rah-nenh-sà:-keh] *on his shoulder;* **yehnenhsàke** [yeh-nenh-sà:-keh] *on my shoulder;*

56

onkwahnenhsa'kehson [on-kwah-nenh-sa'-keh-sonh] *on our shoulders*; ratihnensa'kehson [ra-tih-nenh-sa'-kéh-sonh] *on their shoulders*. With verbs: wakhnenhsanònwaks [wak-hnenh-sa-nòn:-waks] *I have a sore shoulder*.

⁵¹⁰ ohnennàta [oh-nen-nà:-ta'] *potatoes*
With verbs: ikhnennàtaks [ik-hnen-nà:-taks] *I eat potatoes*; tekhnenna'tahrihtha' [tek-hnen-na'-ta-hríht-ha'] *I cook potatoes*; ikhnenna'tohares [ik-hnen-na'-tó-ha-res] *I wash / clean off the potatoes*; tekhnenna'tarìta's [tek-hnen-na'-ta-rì:-ta's] *I fry potatoes*; ikhnennàtohs [ik-hnen-nà:-tohs] *I boil potatoes*; ikhnenna'takènserons [ik-hnen-na'-ta-kèn:-se-rons] *I peal potatoes*; ikhnenna'tarahwihstothsyons [ik-hnen-na'-ta-ra-hwihs-tót-hsyons] *i peel potatoes*; tekhnenna'tyàkhons [tek-hnen-na'-tyà:-k-hons] *I cut up potatoes*; ikhnenna'tanònwaks [ik-hnen-na'-ta-nòn:-waks] *I long for (some) potatoes*; ikhnenna'takahstha' [ik-hnen-na'-ta-káhst-ha'] *I am a big eater of potatoes*; ikhnenna'tayenthos [ik-hnen-na'-ta-yént-hos] *I plant potatoes*; ikhnenna'tayenthokwas [ik-hnen-na'-ta-yent-hó-kwas] *I harvest the potatoes*; ikhnenna'tohkwats [ik-hnen-na'-tóh-kwats] *I dig potatoes*; kathenna'tòkta's [kat-hnen-na'-tò:-k-ta's] *I run out of potatoes*; kathnenna'tahninons [kat-hnen-na'-tah-ní:-nons] *I sell potatoes*; ikhnenna'tahninons [ik-hnen-na'-tah-ní:-nons] *I buy potatoes*.

⁵¹¹ ohnyàsa [oh-nyà:-sa'] *throat (inside the neck)*
ikhnyàsakon [ik-hnyà:-sa-konh] *in my throat*; shnyàsakonh [s-hnyà:-sa-konh] *in your throat*; rahnyàsakonh [rah-nyà:-sa-konh] *in his throat*; yehnyàsakonh [yeh-nyà:-sa-konh] *in her throat*. With verbs: wakenyahranònwaks [wa-ke-nya-hra-nòn:-waks] *I have a sore neck*; With verbs: wakhnya'sanònwaks [wak-hnya'-sa-nòn:-waks] *I have a sore throat*; wakathnyàso [wa-kat-hnyà:-soh] *I have a swollen throat*; khehnyàsas [k-heh-nyà:-sas] *I have my arms around someone's neck*; khehnya'sawakon [k-heh-nya'-sa-wá:-konh] *I have hold of someone by the neck*. Related words: khnya'sotha' [k-hnya'-sót-ha'] *I raise my head*; khnya'sotatye's [k-hnya'-so-tá-tye's] *I have my head above water*.

⁵¹² ohohkwa [o-hóh-kwa'] *cheek(s); buttock(s)*
khohkwàke [k-hoh-kwà:-keh] *on my cheek...*; shohkwàke [s-hoh-kwà:-keh] *on your cheek...*; rahohkwàke [ra-hoh-kwà:-keh] *on his cheek...*; yehohkwàke [ye-hoh-kwà:-keh] *on her cheek...*; onkwahohkwa'kehson [on-kwa-hoh-kwa'-kéh-sonh] *on our cheeks...*; ratihohkwa'kehson [ra-ti-hoh-kwa'-kéh-sonh] *on their cheek....* With verbs: wakhohkwanònwaks [wak-hoh-kwa-nòn:-waks] *I have a sore cheek...*;

⁵¹³ ohohsera [o-hó-hse-ra'] *a basswood tree*

⁵¹⁴ ohonhsa [o-hónh-sa'] *ear (inner ear); hearing*
kahonhsakon [ka-hónh-sa-konh] *in my ear*; sahonhsakon [sa-hónh-sa-konh]

in your ear;   **rahonhsakon** [ra-hónh-sa-konh] *in his ear*;   **yonhonhsakon** [yon-hónh-sa-konh] *in her ear*;   **onkwahonhsakonhson** [on-kwa-honh-sa-kónh-sonh] *in our ears*;   **ronahonhsakonhson** [ro-na-honh-sa-kónh-sonh] *in their ears.*   With verbs: **kahonhsiyo** [ka-honh-sí:-yoh] *I have good hearing*;   **kahonhsaksen** [ka-honh-sák-senh] *I have poor hearing*;   **wakahonhsanònwaks** [wa-ka-honh-sa-nòn:-waks] *I have an earache.*   Related words: **katahonhsatats** [ka-ta-hónh-sa-tats] *I listen*;   **katahonhsiyohstha'** [ka-ta-honh-si-yóhst-ha'] *I pay attention to*;   **wakatahonhsoryes** [wa-ka-ta-honh-sór-yes] *I over-hear / eavesdrop.*   **tekatahonhsaneraks** [te-ka-ta-honh-sa-né-raks] *I miss-interpret / have a poor grasp of what is said.*

515 **ohonhta** [o-hónh-ta'] *ear (outer ear)*

kahonhtàke [ka-honh-tà:-keh] *on my ear*;   **sahonhtàke** [s-honh-tà:-keh] *on your ear*;   **rahonhtàke** [ra-honh-tà:-keh] *on his ear*;   **yonhonhtàke** [yon-honh-tà:-keh] *on her ear*;   **onkwahonhta'kehson** [on-kwa-honh-ta'-kéh-sonh] *on our ears*;   **ronahonhta'kehson** [ra-ti-honh-ta'-kéh-sonh] *on their ears.*   With verbs: **wakahonhtanònwaks** [wa-ka-honh-ta-nòn:-waks] *I have a sore ear*;   **tekatahonhtakweks** [te-ka-ta-honh-tá-kweks] *I lose my hearing*;   **tekahonhtakahre** [te-ka-honh-tá:-ka-hre'] *My ears are ringing*;   **tekahonhtakwekon** [te-ka-honh-ta-kwé:-konh] *I am deaf*;   **wakahonhtaronhkwane** [wa-ka-honh-ta-rónh-kwa-neh] *I have an itchy ear*;   **kheyatahonhtarha'** [k-he-ya-ta-honh-tár-ha'] *I speak into someone's.*

516 **ohonrota** [o-hon-ró:-ta'] *a pipe*

With locatives: **ohonrotakon** [o-hon-ró:-ta-konh] *in the pipe*;   **ohonrotàke** [o-hon-ro-tà:-keh] *on the pipe.*

517 **ohonte** [ó-hon-teh] *green; grass (herbs); weeds*

ie. **ohonte niwahsohkòten'** [...ni-wah-soh-kò:-ten'] *it is coloured / dyed green*;   **ohonte niwatya'tawi'tsheròten'** [...ni-wa-tya'-ta-wi'ts-he-rò:-ten'] *a green shirt, coat, dress.*   With locatives: **ohontàke** [o-hon-tà:-keh] *on the grass*;   **ohontakon** [o-hón:-ta-konh] *in the grass*;   **ohontakonhson** [o-hon-ta-kónh-sonh] *out in the grass.*   With adjectivals: **kahontiyo** [ka-hon-tí:-yoh] *good grasses, herbs*;   **kahontaksen** [ka-hon-ták-senh] *weeds*;   **kahontahòntsi** [ka-hon-ta-hòn:-tsih] *dark green*;   **kahontakenra** [ka-hon-ta-kén:-ra'] *light green.*   With verbs: **yohontare** [yo-hón:-ta-reh] *it has grass in it / it is weedy*;   **yohontaratye'** [yo-hon-ta-rá-tye'] *it is getting weedy*;   **ikhontaks** [ik-hón:-taks] *I eat grass, herbs*;   **ikhontya'ks** [ik-hón-tya'ks] *I cut the grass / mow the lawn*;   **khontakwas** [k-hon-tá-kwas] *I pull weeds*;   **khontakarenyes** [k-hon-ta-ka-ré-nyes] *I draw in hay.*   Related words: **kahontakon** [ka-hon-tá-konh] *sweetgrass*;   **yehontohseràtha** [ye-hon-toh-se-rà:-t-ha'] *salad dressing*;   **kahontya'ks** [ka-hón-tya'ks] *a lawn mower*;   **niyohontehsha** [ni-yo-hon-téhs-ha'] *strawberries.*

518 ohsa [óh-sa'] *mouth, lip(s); spout*

ikhsakon [ík-hsa-konh] *in my mouth*; **ithsakon** [ít-hsa-konh] *in your mouth*; **rahsakon** [ráh-sa-konh] *in his mouth*; **yehsakon** [yéh-sa-konh] *in her mouth*; **kahsakon** [káh-sa-konh] *in its mouth*; **onkwahsakonhson** [on-kwah-sa-kónh-sonh] *in our mouth's*; **ratihsakonhson** [ra-tih-sa-kónh-sonh] *in their mouth's.* With verbs: **kathsohs** [kát-hsohs] *I put a liquid to my mouth*; **kathskweks** [káths-kweks] *I shut my mouth*; **kathskwekhsyons** [kaths-kwék-hsyons] *I open my mouth*; **ikhsakàronte** [ik-hsa-kà:-ron-teh] *I have my mouth open*; **kathsohares** [kat-hsó-ha-res] *I rinse my mouth*; **wakhsanònwaks** [wak-hsa-nòn:-waks] *I have a sore mouth / sore lip.* Related words: **kahsa** [káh-sa'] *a cork*; **yonthsokewàtha** [yont-hso-ke-wà:-t-ha'] *a serviette*; **kathsokwas** [kat-hsó-kwas] *I smoke*; **kathsotsireks** [kat-hso-tsí:-reks] *I suck on my lip.*

519 ohsahèta [oh-sa-hè:-ta'] *beans*

With verbs: **ikhsahètaks** [ik-sa-hè:-taks] *I eat beans*; **ikhsahe'tayenthos** [ik-hsa-he'-ta-yént-hos] *I plant beans*; **ikhsahe'tayenthokwas** [ik-hsa-he'-ta-yent-hó-kwas] *I harvest the beans*; **ikhsahe'takwas** [ik-hsa-he'-tá-kwas] *I pick beans*; **ikhsahètohs** [ik-hsa-hè:-tohs] *I boil beans*; **kathsahe'tontha'** [kat-hsa-he'-tónt-ha'] *I bake beans.*

520 ohsakàra [oh-sa-kà:-ra'] *mouth*

ikhsakàrakon [ík-hsa-kà:-ra-konh] *in my mouth*; **ithsakàrakon** [it-hsa-kà:-ra-konh] *in your mouth*; **rahsakàrakon** [rah-sa-kà:-ra-konh] *in his mouth*; **yehsakàrakon** [yeh-sa-kà:-ra-konh] *in her mouth*; **kahsakàrakon** [kah-sa-kà:-ra-konh] *in its mouth*; **onkwahsakahrakonhson** [on-kwah-sa-ka-hra-kónh-sonh] *in our mouth's*; **ratihsakahrakonhson** [ra-tih-sa-ka-hra-kónh-sonh] *in their mouth's.* With verbs: **wakhsakahranònwaks** [wak-hsa-ka-hra-nòn:-waks] *I have sore mouth.*

521 ohshehs [óhs-hehs] *syrup, honey*

ie. **wahtha ohshehs** [wáht-ha' óhs-hehs] *maple syrup*; **ikhshehstonnis** [ik-hshehs-tón:-nis] *I make syrup, honey*; **ikhshehstanònwaks** [ik-hshehs-ta-nòn:-waks] *I long for some honey, syrup*; **ikhshehstakahstha'** [ik-hshehs-ta-káhst-ha'] *I use too much syrup, honey.* Related words: **kontihshehstonnis** [kon-tih-sehs-tón:-nis] *honey bees.*

522 ohsherha [ohs-hér-ha'] *dough*

ie. **kahsherhakon** [kahs-hér-ha-konh] *in the dough*; **ikhsherhonnis** [ikhs-her-hón:-nis] *I mix dough.* Related words: **kahsherhonni** [kahs-her-hón:-ni'] *doughnuts*; **yohsherhatken** [yohs-her-hát-ken'] *yeast.*

523 ohshonwa [ohs-hón:-wa'] *a hole*

ie. **yohshonwehs** [yohs-hón:-wehs] *it is deep / a deep hole*; **niyohshonwehsha** [ni-yohs-hon-wéhs-ha'] *a shallow hole*; **kahshonyonnis** [kahs-hon-yón:-nis] *I* *make a hole in something.*

524 ohsina [oh-síː-na'] *leg(s)*

ikhsinàke [ik-hsi-nàː-keh] *on my leg*; **ithsinàke** [it-hsi-nàː-keh] *on your leg*; **rahsinàke** [rah-si-nàː-keh] *on his leg*; **yehsinàke** [yeh-si-nàː-keh] *on her leg*; **onkwahsina'kehson** [on-kwah-si-na'-kéh-sonh] *on our legs*; **ratihsina'kehson** [ra-tih-si-na'-kéh-sonh] *on their legs*. With verbs: **wakhsinanònwaks** [wa-kh-si-na-nòn:-waks] *I have a sore leg*; **ikhsinakahrewàtha'** [ik-hsi-na-ka-hre-wàː-t-ha'] *I hurt my leg*; **kathsinanikons** [kat-hsi-na-níː-konhs] *I sprain my leg*; **kathsino'katha'** [kat-hsi-no'-kát-ha'] *I limp*; **yekathsinakwarihsyons** [ye-kat-hsi-na-kwa-ríh-syons] *I straighten out my legs*; **kathsinakwìtha'** [kat-hsi-na-kwìː-t-ha'] *I move my legs aside*; **kathsinon'neks** [kat-hsi-nón'-neks] *I move my legs out of the way*. Related words: **athsinha** [at-hsín-ha'] *a garter(s)*; **athsinòron** [at-hsi-nòː-ronh] *a leggin(s)*.

525 ohsinekòta [oh-si-ne-kòː-ta'] *ankle(s)*

ikhsineko'tàke [ik-hsi-ne-ko'-tàː-keh] *on my ankle(s)*; **ithsineko'tàke** [it-hsi-ne-ko'-tàː-keh] *on your ankle(s)*; **rahsineko'tàke** [rah-si-ne-ko'-tàː-keh] *on his ankle(s)*; **yehsineko'tàke** [yeh-si-ne-ko'-tàː-keh] *on her ankle(s)*; **onkwahsineko'ta'kehson** [on-kwah-si-ne-ko'-ta'-kéh-sonh] *on our ankles*; **ratihsineko'ta'kehson** [ra-tih-si-ne-ko'-ta'-kéh-sonh] *on their ankles*. With verbs: **wakhsineko'tanònwaks** [wa-kh-si-ne-ko'-ta-nòn:-waks] *I have a sore ankle(s)*; **ikhsineko'takahrewàtha'** [ik-hsi-ne-ko'-ta-ka-hre-wàː-t-ha'] *I hurt my ankle(s)*; **kathsineko'tanikons** [kat-hsi-ne-ko'-ta-níː-konhs] *I sprain my ankle(s)*.

526 ohsìta [oh-sìː-ta'] *foot; feet*

kahsi'tàke [kah-si'-tàː-keh] *on my foot*; **sahsi'tàke** [sah-si'-tàː-keh] *on your foot*; **rahsi'tàke** [rah-si'-tàː-keh] *on his foot*; **yonhsi'tàke** [yonh-si'-tàː-keh] *on her foot*; **onkwahsi'ta'kehson** [on-kwah-si'-ta'-kéh-sonh] *on our feet*; **ronhsi'ta'kehson** [ronh-si'-ta'-kéh-sonh] *on their feet*. This form is also used: **kahsìke** [kah-si'-tàː-keh] *on my...*; **sahsìke** [sah-si'-tàː-keh] *on your...*; **rahsìke** [rah-si'-tàː-keh] *on his...*; **yonhsìke** [yonh-si'-tàː-keh] *on her...*; **onkwahsi'kehson** [on-kwah-si'-kéh-sonh] *on our...*; **ronhsi'kehson** [ronh-si'-ta'-kéh-sonh] *on their...*. With verbs: **wakahsi'tanònwaks** [wa-kah-si'-ta-nòn:-waks] *I have a sore foot / feet*; **tewakahsi'taronhkwane** [te-wa-kah-si'-ta-rónh-kwa-ne'] *I have itchy feet*; **tewakahsi'tananawenhstha'** [te-wa-kah-si'-ta-na-na-wénhst-ha'] *I get my weet wet*; **kerasi'ton'neks** [ke-rah-si'-tón'-neks] *I move my feet out of the way*; tekahsi'tasihara's [te-kah-si'-ta-síː-ha-ra's] *I get my foor caught*; **wakahsi'ton'onh** [wa-kah-si'tón:'-onh] *My foot is asleep*.

527 ohskawiyak [ohs-ka-wíː-yak] *a bass (fish)*

528 ohskennonton [ohs-ken-nón:-tonh] *a deer*

529 **ohsnonhsa** [oh-snónh-sa'] *hand(s); finger(s)*

ikhsnonhsàke [kahsnonh-sà:-keh] *on my foot*; **ithsnonhsàke** [sahsnonh-sà:-keh] *on your foot*; **rahsnonhsàke** [rahsnonh-sà:-keh] *on his foot*; **yehsnonhsàke** [yonhsnonh-sà:-keh] *on her foot*; **onkwahsnonhsa'kehson** [on-kwahsnonh-sa'-kéh-sonh] *on our feet*; **ratihsnonhsa'kehson** [ronhsnonh-sa'-kéh-sonh] *on their feet*. This form is also used: **kehsnònke** [keh-snòn:-keh] *on my...*; **sahsnònke** [sah-snòn:-keh] *on your...*; **rahsnònke** [rah-snòn:-keh] *on his...*; **yehsnònke** [yeh-snòn:-keh] *on her...*; **onkwahsnon'kehson** [on-kwah-snon'-kéh-sonh] *on our...*; **ratihsi'kehson** [ra-tih-snon'-kéh-sonh] *on their....* With verbs: **wakehsnonhsanònwaks** [wa-keh-snonh-sa-nòn:-waks] *My hand is sore*; **wakehsnonhsakahrewàtha'** [wa-keh-snonh-sa-ka-hre-wà:-t-ha'] *I hurt my hand*; **wakehsnonhsaronhkwane** [wa-keh-snonh-sa-rónh-kwa-ne'] *My hand is itchy*; **kennihsnonhsohs** [ken-nih-snónh-sohs] *I put my hands in water*; **kennihsnonhsòroks** [ken-nih-snonh-sò:-roks] *I poke my finger into something*; **kennihsnonhson'neks** [ken-nih-snonh-són'-neks] *I move my hand out of the way.*

530 **ohsohkwa** [oh-sóh-kwa'] *dye; colour(ing)*

ie. **Oh niwahsohkòten'** [Oh ni-wah-soh-kò:-ten'] *What colour is it / what kind of dye is it?* **Onekwenhtara niwahsohkòten'** [O-ne-kwénh-ta-ra' ni-wah-soh-kò:-ten'] *it is dyed / coloured red.* Related words: **kahsohs** [káh-sohs] *I dye something.*

531 **ohsòkwa** [oh-sò:-kwa'] *a nut; nuts*

ie. **ohso'kwahson'a** [oh-so'-kwahh-són:-'ah] *nuts (different kinds)*; With verbs: **ikhso'kwaròroks** [ik-hso'-kwa-rò:-roks] *I gather nuts*; **kathso'kwaweyentons** [kat-hso'-kwa-we-yén:-tons] *I store nuts*; **ikhsòkwaks** [ik-hsò:-kwaks] *I eat nuts.*

532 **ohson'karàke** [oh-son'-ka-rà:-keh] *on the floor*

ie. **Ohson'karàke kayen'.** [Oh-son'-ka-rà:-keh ká:-yen'] *it is laying on the floor.*

533 **ohstonha** [oh-stón-ha'] *a little; a bit*

ie. **Ohstonha wakhwihstayen'.** [Oh-stón-ha' wak-hwíhs-ta-yen'] *I have a little bit of money.*

534 **ohstyen'** [óhs-tyen'] *a bone*

With locatives: **ohstyèntakon** [ohs-tyèn:-ta-konh] *in the bone*; **ohstyen'tàke** [ohs-tyen'-tà:-keh] *on the bone*. With verbs: **ikhstyòkanons** [ikhs-tyò:-ka-nons] *I gnaw on a bone*; **wakhstyen's** [wákhs-tyen's] *I have a bone in my throat.* Related words: **ohstyen'tohskon** [ohs-tyen'-tóhs-konh] *boney (nothing but bones)*; **ohstyen'takonha** [ohs-tyen'-ta-kón-ha'] *marrow*; **kahstyen'toton** [kahs-tyen'-tó:-tonh] *a skeleton*; **ohstyen'takèron** [ohs-tyen'-ka-kè:-ronh] *an accumulation of bones.*

535 ohswa [óh-swa'] *back*

With possessives: **ikhswàke** [ik-hswà:-keh] *on my back*; **ithswàke** [it-hswà:-keh] *on your back*; **rahswàke** [rah-swà:-keh] *on his back*; **yehswàke** [yeh-swà:-keh] *on her back*; **onkwahswa'kehson** [on-kwah-swa'-kéh-sonh] *on our backs*; **ratihswa'kehson** [ra-tih-swa'-kéh-sonh] *on their backs*. Also: **ithsònne'** [it-hsòn:-ne'] *at my back; behind me*; **rahsònne'** [rah-sòn:-ne'] *at his back...*; **yehsònne'** [yeh-sòn:-ne'] *at her back...*; **onkwahsonhnehson** [on-kwah-sonh-néh-sonh] *at our backs...*; **ratihsonhnehson** [ra-tih-sonh-néh-sonh] *at their backs....* With verbs: **wakhswanònwaks** [wak-hswa-nòn:-waks] *I have sore back*; **kathswakahrewahtha'** [kat-hswa-ka-hre-wáht-ha'] *I hurt my back*; **tekathswanàkhons** [te-kat-hswa-nà:-k-hons] *I scratch my back (against something)*; **kathswatenyes** [kat-hswa-té-nyes] *I back up*; **khehswatenyàtha'** [k-heh-swa-te-nyà:-t-ha'] *I make someone back up*. Related words: **ohswakaront** [oh-swá:-ka-ront] *a whale.*

536 ohswènkare [oh-swèn:-ka-reh] *a board, plank*

With locatives: **ohswen'karàke** [oh-swen'-ka-rà:-keh] *on the board... (related to the phrase: ohson'karàke on the floor)*; **ohswen'karòkon** [oh-swen'-ka-rò:-konh] *under the board....* With adjectivals: **kahswen'karatenhs** [kah-swen'-ka-rá:-tenhs] *a thick board...*; **nikahswen'karatenhsha** [ni-kah-swen'-ka-ra-ténhs-ha'] *a thin board*; **kahswen'kariyo** [kah-swen'-ka-rí:-yoh] *a good board....* Related words: **yohswen'karohare** [yoh-swen'-ka-ró-ha-reh] *a shelf*; **Tsi yohswen'karènton** [tsi yoh-swen'-ka-rèn:-tonh] *a hotel, tavern*; **tekhswen'kariya'ks** [tek-hswen'-ka-rí:-ya'ks] *I cross the floor*; **ikhswen'karohares** [ik-hswen'-ka-ró-ha-res] *I wash the floor.*

537 ohsyehònta [oh-sye-hòn:-ta'] *stomach*

With possessves: **ikhsyehon'tàke** [ik-hsye-hon'-tà:-keh *on my stomach*; **ithsyehon'tàke** [it-hsye-hon'-tà:-keh *on your stomach*; **rahsyehon'tàke** [rah-sye-hon'-tà:-keh *on his stomach*; **yehsyehon'tàke** [yeh-sye-hon'-tà:-keh *on her stomach*. With verbs: **wakhsyehon'tanònwaks** [wak-hsye-hon'-ta-nòn:-waks] *I have a stomachache.*

538 ohtera [oh-té:-ra'] *roots*

With locatives: **ohterakonhson** [oh-te-ra-kónh-sonh] *amongst the roots*; **ohtera'kehson** [oh-te-ra'-kéh-sonh] *on the roots*; **ohtero'konhson** [oh-te-ro'-kónh-sonh] *under the roots*. With adjectivals: **yohterehs** [yóh-te-rehs] *long roots*; **yohterowanen** [yoh-te-ro-wá:-nenh] *a large, thick root*; **niyohtera'ah** [ni-yoh-te-rá:-'ah] *small, fine roots*. With verbs: **yohteronte** [yóh-te-ron-teh] *it has roots; there are roots on it*; **yohteronta's** [yoh-te-rón:-ta's] *it takes root*; **kehteraks** [kéh-te-raks] *I eat roots*; **kahterya'ks** [kah-tér-ya'ks] *I cut off at the root*; **kehterothsyons** [keh-te-rót-hsyons] *I pull out by the roots.*

539 ohwihsta [o-hwíhs-ta'] *money*

With verbs: **wakhwihstayen'** [wak-hwíhs-ta-yen'] *I have money*; **wakhwihstakate** [wak-hwihs-ta-ká:-teh] *i have lots of money*; **wakhwihstayenta's** [wak-hwihs-ta-yén:-ta's] *I get some money / come by some money*; **wakhwihstontye's** [wak-hwihs-tón-tye's] *I lose money*; **ikhwihstaniha's** [ik-hwihs-ta-ní-ha's] *I lend money*; **kathwihstaniha's** [kat-hwihs-ta-ní-ha's] *I borrow money*; **ikhwihstakwas** [ik-hwihs-tá-kwas] *I earn money*; **ikhwihstanenhskwas** [ik-hwihs-ta-nénhs-kwas] *I steal money*; **ikhwihstenhawe** [ik-hwihs-tén-ha-we'] *I carry money with me*; **tekathwihstakhahsyons** [te-kat-hwihs-tak-há-hsyons] *I budget my money*; **khehwihstotakwas** [k-he-hwihs-to-tá-kwas] *I take money away from someone.* Related words: **skahwihstat** [ska-hwíhs-tat] *one dollar*; **tekahwihstake** [te-ka-hwíhs-ta-keh] *two dollars*; **wisk nikahwihstake** [wihsk ni-ka-hwíhs-ta-keh] *five dollars*; **yehwihstarahkwa** [ye-hwihs-ta-ráh-kwa'] *a wallet*; **ohwihstanoron** [o-hwihs-ta-nó:-ronh] *gold*; **ohwihstanoronhson'a** [o-wihs-ta-no-ronh-són:-'ah] *jewellery.*

540 ohwihstakenra [o-hwis-ta-kén:-ra'] *silver*

541 ohwihstanoron [o-hwihs-ta-nó:-ronh] *gold*

542 ohyakwira [o-hya-kwí:-ra'] *toe(s)*

With possessives: **ikhyakwiràke** [ik-hya-kwi-rà:-keh] *on my toe*; **shyakwiràke** [shya-kwi-rà:-keh] *on your toe*; **rahyakwiràke** [ra-hya-kwi-rà:-keh] *on his toe*; **yehyakwiràke** [ye-hya-kwi-rà:-keh] *on her toe.* **Wakhyakwiranònwaks** [wak-hya-kwi-rà-nòn:-waks] *I have a sore toe*; **ikhyakwirakahrewahtha'** [ik-hya-kwi-ra-ka-hre-wáht-ha'] *I hurt my toe.*

543 Ohyariha [O-hya-rí-ha'] *June*

544 Ohyarihkowa [O-hya-rih-kó:-wa'] *July*

545 ohyohsa [o-hyóh-sa'] *elbow; corner*

With possessives: **ikhyohsàke** [ik-hyoh-sà:-keh] *on my elbow*; **ihshyohsàke** [ihs-hyoh-sà:-keh] *on your elbow*; **rahyohsàke** [ra-hyoh-sà:-keh] *on his elbow*; **yehyohsàke** [ye-hyoh-sà:-keh] *on her elbow.* With verbs: **wakhyohsanònwaks** [wak-hyoh-sa-nòn:-waks] *I have a sore elbow*; **tewakhyohsanònwaks** [te-wak-hyoh-sa-nòn:-waks] *I have sore elbows (both of my elbows are sore)*; **ikhyohsakahrewahtha'** [ik-hyoh-sa-ka-hre-wáht-ha'] *I hurt my chin*; **tewakhyohsyonkwas** [te-wak-hyoh-syón:-kwas] *I bump my elbow*; **tekathyohsaherha'** [te-kat-hyoh-sa-hér-ha'] *I rest my elbows on something*; **kheyathyohskons** [k-he-yat-hyóhs-kons] *I poke someone with my elbow.* Related words: **teyothyohsate** [te-yot-hyóh-sa-teh] *it makes an angle, corner*; **tsi teyothyohsate** [tsi te-yot-hyóh-sa-teh] *at the corner.*

546 ohyotsha [o-hyóts-ha'] *chin*
   With possessives: **ikhyotshàke** [ik-hyots-hà:-keh] *on my chin*; **ihshyotshàke** [ihs-hyots-hà:-keh] *on your chin*; **rahyotshàke** [ra-hyots-hà:-keh] *on his chin*; **yehyotshàke** [ye-hyots-hà:-keh] *on her chin*. With verbs: **wakhyotshanònwaks** [wak-hyots-ha-nòn:-waks] *I have a sore chin*; **ikhyotshakahrewahtha'** [ik-hyohts-ha-ka-hre-wáht-ha'] *I hurt my chin*.

547 ok [ok] *only; just*
   ie. **Raonha ok sahoyo'tensha'.** [Ra-on-há: ok sa-ho-yo'-téns-ha'] *Only he went back to work.*

   a) **ok nahòten** [ok na-hò:-ten'] *something*
      ie. **Ok nahòten wahakon' ne akeke'.** [Ok na-hò:-ten' wa-há:-kon' ne' á:-ke-ke'] *He gave me something to eat.*

548 okahkwènta [o-kah-kwèn:-ta'] *a wheel, tire; a circle*
   With locatives: **okahkwen'tàke** [o-kah-kwen'-tà:-keh] *on the tire, wheel*; **okahkwèntakon** [o-kah-kwèn:-ta-konh] *in the circle*. With verbs: **yokahkwèntonte** [yo-kah-kwèn:-ton-teh] *it has a wheel, tire attched*; **ikkahkwen'tontha'** [ik-kah-kwen'tónt-ha'] *I attach a wheel, tire*; **tekkahkwen'tatenyes** [tek-kah-kwen'-ta-té-nyes] *I change a tire, wheel*; **ikkahkwen'tonnis** [ik-kah-kwen'-tón:-nis] *I make circle(s)*; Related words: **tekakahkwèntonte** [te-ka-kah-kwèn:-ton-teh] *a bicycle.*

549 okahrehta [o-ka-hréh-ta'] *eyelash(es)*
   With possessives: **ikkahrehtàke** [ik-ka-hreh-tà:-keh] *on my eyelash(es)*; **skahrehtàke** [ska-hreh-tà:-keh] *on your eyelash(es)*; **rakahrehtàke** [ra-ka-hreh-tà:-keh] *on his eyelash(es)*; **yekahrehtàke** [ye-ka-hreh-tà:-keh] *on her eyelash(es)*; **onkwakahrehta'kehson** [on-kwa-ka-hreh-ta'-kéh-sonh] *on our eyelashes*; **ratikahrehta'kehson** [ra-ti-ka-hreh-ta'-kéh-sonh] *on their eyelashes.*

550 okahrìtshera [o-ka-hrì:ts-he-ra'] *toy; game*
   ie. **okahritsherahson'a** [o-ka-hrits-he-rah-són:-'ah] *toys, games*; **wakatkahritsheronni'** [wa-kat-ka-hrits-he-rón:-ni'] *I am playing with a game/toy.*

551 okàra [o-kà:-ra'] *eye(s); eyesight*
   ikkàrakon [ik-kà:-ra-konh] *in my eye(s)*; **ihskàrakon** [ihs-kà:-ra-konh] *in your eye(s)*; **rakàrakon** [ra-kà:-ra-konh] *in his eye(s)*; **yekàrakon** [ye-kà:-ra-konh] *in her eye(s)*; **onkwakahrakonhson** [on-kwa-ka-hra-kónh-sonh] *in our eye(s)*; **ratikahrakonhson** [ra-ti-ka-hra-kónh-son'] *in their eyes*. With adjectivals: **ikkahriyo** [ik-ka-hrí:-yoh] *I have good vision*; **ikkahraksen** [ik-ka-hrák-senh] *I have poor eyesight*. With verbs: **wakkahranònwaks** [wak-ka-hra-nòn:-waks] *I have sore eye(s)*; **wakkahrisen** [wak-ka-hrí:-senh] *I have something in my eye(s)*; **ikkahratakwas** [ik-ka-hra-tá-kwas] *I take something out of my eye*; **katkahratiha's** [kat-ka-hra-tí-ha's] *I aim at*; **katkahrotha'** [kat-ka-hrót-ha'] *I*

stare at; **katkahrokeriks** [kat-ka-hró:-ke-riks] *I wink at*; **tekkahrake'totha'** [tek-ka-hra-ke'-tót-ha'] *I peek out from under something*; **khekahraya'ks** [k-he-ka-hrá:-ya'ks] *I give someone a blackeye / I hit someone in the eye.*

552 **okonhsa** [o-kónh-sa'] *face*

With possessives: **ikkonkhsne'** [ik-kónk-hsne'] *on my face*; **skonkhsne'** [skónk-hsne'] *on your face*; **rakonkhsne'** [ra-kónk-hsne'] *on his face*; **yekonkhsne'** [ye-kónk-hsne'] *on her face*; **kakonkhsne'** [ka-kónk-hsne'] *on its face*; **onkwakonkhsnehson** [on-kwa-konk-hsnéh-sonh] *on our faces*; **ratikonkhsnehson** [ra-ti-konk-hsnéh-sonh] *on their faces*. With verbs: **ikkonhsakahrewahtha'** [ik-konh-sa-ka-hre-wáht-ha'] *I hurt my face*; **wakkonhsanònwaks** [wak-konh-sa-nòn:-waks] *My face is sore*; **ikkonhsanennyo'kwanenhstha'** [ik-konh-sa-nen-nyo'-kwa-nénhst-ha'] *I freeze my face*; **katkonhsohares** [kat-konh-só-ha-res] *I wash my face*; **katkonhsanewarons** [kat-konh-sa-ne-wá:-rons] *My face gets red; I flush, get embarrassed*; **tekatkonhsayeronnyons** [te-kat-konh-sa-ye-rón-nyons] *I make a face (at)*; **ikkonhsahserohen** [ik-konh-sah-se-ró-henh] *I have a mean face / I'm serious*; **wakatkonhskeron** [wa-kat-kónh-ske-ronh] *I have a wrinkled face*. Related words: **kakonhsa** [ka-kónh-sa'] *mask*; **yekonhsohare'tahkwa** [ye-konh-so-ha-re'-táh-kwa'] *facecloth*; **yontkonhsokewahtha** [yont-konh-so-ke-wáht-ha'] *a (face) towel.*

553 **okonkwara** [o-kón:-kwa-ra'] *forehead*

With possessives: **ikkonkwaràke** [ik-kon-kwa-rà:-keh] *on my forehead*; **skonkwaràke** [skon-kwa-rà:-keh] *on your forehead*; **rakonkwaràke** [ra-kon-kwa-rà:-keh] *on his forehead*; **yekonkwaràke** [ye-kon-kwa-rà:-keh] *on her forehead*; **onkwakonkwara'kehson** [on-kwa-kon-kwa-ra'-kéh-sonh] *on our foreheads*; **ratikonkwara'kehson** [ra-ti-kon-kwa-ra'-kéh-sonh] *on their foreheads*. With verbs: **ikkonkwarakahrewahtha'** [ik-kon-kwa-ra-ka-hre-wáht-ha'] *I hurt my forehead.*

554 **okontstara** [o-kónts-ta-ra'] *forehead*

With possessives: **ikkontstaràke** [ik-kont-sta-rà:-keh] *on my forehead*; **skontstaràke** [skont-sta-rà:-keh] *on your forehead*; **rakontstaràke** [ra-kont-sta-rà:-keh] *on his forehead*; **yekontstaràke** [ye-kont-sta-rà:-keh] *on her forehead*; **onkwakontstara'kehson** [on-kwa-kont-sta-ra'-kéh-sonh] *on our foreheads*; **ratikontstara'kehson** [ra-ti-kont-sta-ra'-kéh-sonh] *on their foreheads*. With verbs: **ikkontstarakahrewahtha'** [ik-kont-sta-ra-ka-hre-wáht-ha'] *I hurt my forehead.*

555 **okònwara** [o-kòn:-wa-ra'] *a face*

With possessives: **ikkonhwaràke** [ik-kon-hwa-rà:-keh] *on my forehead*; **skonhwaràke** [skon-hwa-rà:-keh] *on your forehead*; **rakonhwaràke** [ra-kon-hwa-rà:-keh] *on his forehead*; **yekonhwaràke** [ye-kon-hwa-rà:-keh] *on her* *forehead*; **onkwakonhwara'kehson** [on-kwa-kon-hwa-ra'-kéh-sonh] *on our foreheads*; **ratikonhwara'kehson** [ra-ti-kon-hwa-ra'-kéh-sonh] *on their foreheads.* With verbs: **wakkonhwaranònwaks** [wak-kon-hwa-ra-nòn:-waks] *My face is sore*; **ikkonhwarakahrewahtha'** [ik-kon-hwa-ra-ka-hre-wáht-ha'] *I hurt my forehead.*

556 **oksa** [ók-sa'] *quick; fast*
   ie. **Oksa sasahtenti!** [ók-sa' sa-sah-tén:-ti] *Go home, quick!*

   a) **oksa ok** [ók-sak] *quickly*
      ie. **Oksa ok sahahtenti'.** [...sa-hah-tén:-ti'] *He quickly went home.* (see: akwah oksa ok)

557 **okwaho** [o-kwá-hoh] *a wolf*

558 **okwire** [ó-kwi-reh] *a bush, bushes*
   With locatives: **okwiraktatye'** [o-kwi-rak-tá-tye'] *along the bushes (bushline, hedge)*; **okwirakonhson** [o-kwi-ra-kónh-sonh] *out in the bushes.* With verbs: **ikkwirya'ks** [ik-kwír-ya'ks] *I cut brush, cut a bush*; **ikkwirotha'** [ik-kwi-rót-ha'] *I plant a bush, shrub.*

559 **okwitsha** [o-kwíts-ha'] *knee*
   With possessives: **ikkwitshàke** [ik-kwits-hà:-keh] *on my knee*; **skwitshàke** [skwits-hà:-keh] *on your knee*; **rakwitshàke** [ra-kwits-hà:-keh] *on his knee*; **yekwitshàke** [ye-kwits-hà:-keh] *on her knees*; **onkwakwitsha'kehson** [on-kwa-kwits-ha'-kéh-sonh] *on their knees.* With verbs: **wakkwitshanònwaks** [wak-kwits-ha-nòn:-waks] *I have a sore knee*; **ikkwitshakahrewahtha'** [ik-kwits-ha-ka-hre-wáht-ha'] *I hurt my knee.*

560 **onahsakenra** [o-nah-sa-kén:-ra'] *a goose*

561 **onake** [ó:-na-keh] *canoe (birch-bark canoe)*

562 **onatsha** [o-náts-ha'] *buttocks; ass*
   With possessives: **kenatshàke** [ke-nats-hà:-keh] *on my buttocks*; **senatshàke** [se-nats-shà:-keh] *on your buttocks*; **ranatshàke** [ra-nats-hà:-keh] *on his buttocks*; **yenatshàke** ye-nats-hà:-keh] *on her buttocks*; **onkwanatsha'kehson** [on-kwa-nats-ha'-kéh-sonh] *on our buttocks*; **ratinatsha'kehson** [ra-ti-nats-ha'-kéh-sonh] *on their buttocks.*

563 **onawatsta** [o-na-wáts-ta'] *mud*
   With locatives: **onawatstàke** [o-na-wats-tà:-keh] *in the mud*; **onawatsta'kehson** [o-na-wats-ta'-kéh-sonh] *out in the mud*; **kanawatstakèron** [ka-na-wats-ta-kè:-ronh] *there's mud about*; **kanawatstayen'tatye's** [ka-na-wats-ta-yen'-tá-tye's] *there's mud laying about*; **yonawatstare** [yo-na-wats-tó-ha-reh] *there's mud on it / it's muddy*; **yonawatstohskon** [yo-na-wats-tóhs-konh] *it all*

muddy / covered with mud. With verbs: **kenawatstonnis** [ke-na-wats-tón:-nis] *I play in the mud*; **kenawastokewas** [ke-na-wats-to-ké:-was] *I wipe off the mud*; **wakenawatstohskon** [wa-ke-na-wats-tóhs-konh] *I am covered with mud.*

564 **onawira** [o-na-wí:-ra'] *teeth; a tooth*
With possessives: **kenawiràke** [ke-na-wi-rà:-keh] *on my teeth (tooth)*; **senawiràke** [se-na-wi-rà:-keh] *on your teeth...*; **ranawiràke** [ra-na-wi-rà:-keh] *on his teeth...*; **yenawiràke** [ye-na-wi-rà:-keh] *on her teeth*; **onkwanawira'kehson** [on-kwa-na-wi-ra'-kéh-sonh] *on our teeth*; **ratinawira'kehson** [ra-ti-na-wi-ra'-kéh-sonh] *on their teeth.* With verbs: **wakenawiranònwaks** [wa-ke-na-wi-ra-nòn:-waks] *I have a toothache*; **tewakenawirya'kse** [te-wa-ke-na-wír-ya'k-se'] *I break a tooth.*

565 **onekwa** [o-né-kwa'] *peas*
ie. **kenekwaks** [ke-né-kwaks] *I eat peas*; **kenekwanònwaks** [ke-ne-kwa-nòn:-waks] *I am fond of peas.*

566 **onekwenhsa** [o-ne-kwénh-sa'] *blood*
ie. **yonekwenhsare** [yo-ne-kwénh-sa-reh] *it is covered with blood*; **kanekwenhsohskon** [ka-ne-kwenh-sóhs-konh] *it all bloody*; **yonekhwa'onh** [yo-nek-hwá:-'onh] *it is bleeding*; **kenekhwas** [ke-nék-hwas] *I bleed*; **wakenekhwa'onh** [wa-ke-nek-hwá:-'onh] *I am bleeding.* Related words: **tekanekwenhsatsikhètare** te-ka-ne-kwenh-sa-tsi-k-hè:-ta-reh] *diabetes*; **yewatenekwenhsa'ahtha** [ye-wa-te-ne-kwenh-sa'-áht-ha'] *lukemia.*

567 **onekwenhtara** [o-ne-kwénh-ta-ra'] *red*
ie. **onekwenhtara niwahsohkòten'** [...ni-wah-soh-kò:-ten'] *it is coloured (dyed) red*; **onekwenhtara niwatya'tawi'tsheròten'** [...ni-wa-tya'-ta-wi'ts-he-rò:-ten'] *a red coat, dress, shirt.* Related words: **kanekwenhtararaken** [ka-ne-kwenh-ta-ra-rá:-kenh] *light red*; **kanekwenhtarahòntsi** [ka-ne-kwenh-ta-ra-hòn:-tsih] *dark red*; **onekwenhtarahtane** [o-ne-kwenh-ta-rah-tà:-ne'] *scarlet fever.*

568 **onekwènta** [o-ne-kwèn:-ta'] *stomach*
With possessives: **kenekwen'tàke** [ke-ne-kwen'-tà:-keh] *on my stomach*; **senekwen'tàke** [se-ne-kwen'-tà:-keh] *on your stomach*; **ranekwen'tàke** [ra-ne-kwen'-tà:-keh] *on his stomach*; **yenekwen'tàke** [ye-ne-kwen'-tà:-keh] *on her stomach*; **onkwanekwen'ta'kehson** [on-kwa-ne-kwen'-ta'-kéh-sonh] *on our stomachs*; **ratinekwen'ta'kehson** [ra-ti-ne-kwen'-ta'-kéh-sonh] *on their stomachs.* With verbs: **wakenekwen'tanònwaks** [wa-ke-ne-kwen'-ta-nòn:-waks] *I have a sore stomach.*

569 **onen** [ó:-nen] *now; already*
ie. **Onen tsi sàkewe', onen rohtentyonh.** [Ó-nen tsi sà:-ke-we', ó:-nen roh-tén-tyonh] *Now when I arrived, he was already gone.*

a) **onen thoha** [o-nen thó-ha'] *pretty soon*
   ie. **Onen thoha enyakoweyennenta'onh.** [O-nen thó-ha' en-ya-ko-we-yen-nen-tá:-'onh] *she will be ready pretty soon.*

570 **onen'ta'onwe** [o-nen'-ta'-ón:-weh] *a hemlock tree*

571 **onen'takeri** [o-nen'-tá-ke-ri'] *beer*

572 **onen'takwenhton** [o-nen'-ta-kwénh-tonh] *a red cedar tree*

573 **onenha** [o-nén-ha'] *corn seed*

574 **onenharatase** [o-nen-ha-ra-tá:-seh] *a grape, grapes*

575 **onenhste** [ó:-nenhs-teh] *corn*
   With adjectivals: **yonenhstathen** [yo-nenhs-tát-henh] *dried corn*; **yonenhstase** [yo-nénhs-ta-seh] *fresh corn / green corn.* With verbs: **kenenhstaks** ke-nénhs-taks] *I eat corn*; **kenenhstahninons** [ke-nenhs-tah-ní:-nons] *I buy corn*; **kenenhstohares** [ke-nenhs-tó-ha-res] *I lye corn*; **kenenhstoharakwas** [ke-nenhs-to-ha-rá-kwas] *I remove corn (from the cob)*; **kenenhstanònwaks** [ke-nenhs-ta-nòn:-waks] *I am fond of corn*; **katenenhstòkta's** [ka-te-nenhs-tò:-k-ta's] *I run out of corn.*

576 **onenhsto** [o-nénh-stoh] *corn soup*

577 **onènta** [o-nèn:-ta'] *evergreen(s)*

578 **onentsha** [o-nénts-ha'] *arm(s)*
   With possessives: **kenentshàke** [ke-nents-hà:-keh] *on my arm(s)*; **senentshàke** [se-nents-hà:-keh] *on your arm(s)*; **ranentshàke** [ra-nents-hà:-keh] *on his arm(s)*; **yenentshàke** [ye-nents-hà:-keh] *on her arm(s)*; **onkwanentsha'kehson** [on-kwa-nents-ha'-kéh-sonh] *on our arms*; **ratinentsha'kehson** [ra-ti-nents-ha'-kéh-sonh] *on their arms.* With verbs: **tewakenentshonton** [te-wa-ke-nents-hón:-tonh] *I have (both) arms*; **tewakenentshanònwaks** [te-wa-ke-nents-ha-nòn:-waks] *my arms are sore*; **katenentshanikons** [ka-te-nents-ha-ní:-kons] *I sprain my arm*; **tekatenentshya'ks** [te-ka-te-nents-hya'ks] *I break my arm*; **tekatenentsha'serha'** [te-ka-te-nents-ha'-sér-ha'] *I cross my arms.*

579 **onentshawìtha** [o-nents-ha-wì:t-ha'] *wrist*
   With lossessives: **kenentshawi'tàke** [ke-nents-ha-wi'-tà:-keh] *on my wrist*; **senentshawi'tàke** [se-nents-ha-wi'-tà:-keh] *on your wrist*; **ranentshawi'tàke** [ra-nents-ha-wi'-tà:-keh] *on his writs*; **yenentshawi'tàke** [ye-nents-ha-wi'-tà:-keh] *on her wrist.* With verbs: **katenentshawi'tanikons** [te-ka-te-nents-ha-wi'-ta-ní:-kons] *I sprain my wrist*; **tekatenentshawìtyaks** [te-ka-te-nents-ha-wì:-tya'ks] *I break my wrist*; **Wakenentshawi'tanònwaks** [wa-ke-nents-ha-wi'-ta-nòn:-waks] *I have a sore wrist*; **katenentshawi'takahrewahtha'** [ka-te-nents-ha-wi'-ta-ka-hre-wáht-ha'] *I hurt my wrist.*

580 **onenya** [o-nén:-ya'] *a stone; stones*
    With locatives: **onenyòkon** [o-nen-yò:-konh] *under the stone;* **onenyo'konhson** [o-nen-yo'-kónh-sonh] *under the stones;* **onenyàke** [o-nen-yà:-keh] *on the stone;* **onenyakta** [o-nen-yák-ta'] *beside the stone.* Related words: **onenyohskon** [o-nen-yóhs-koh] *it's stoney, full of stones;* **atenenyarhon** [a-te-nen-yár-honh] *a stone giant;* **kanenyat** [ka-nén:-yat] *it is loaded.*

581 **Onenyotehàka** [O-nen-yo-te-hà:-kah] *the Oneida nation*

582 **onerahtakate** [o-ne-rah-ta-ká:-teh] *lettuce*

583 **onerahte** [ó:-ne-rah-teh] *a leaf; leaves*
    ie. **yonerahtakate** [yo-ne-rah-ta-ká:-teh] *it is leafy;* **yonerahtohskon** [yo-ne-rah-tóhs-konh] *it is all leaves (nothing but leaves);* **yotenerahtohon** [yo-te-ne-rah-tó-honh] *it is leafy / the folliage is dense;* **yonerahten'onhatye'** [yo-ne-rah-ten'-on-há-tye'] *the leaves are falling (right along).*

584 **Onerahtokha** [O-ne-rah-tók-ha'] *April*

585 **Onerahtokkowa** [O-ne-rah-tok-kó:-wa'] *May*

586 **onhka** [ónh-ka'] *who*
    ie. **Onhka wa'ehninon'.** [ónh-ka' wa'-eh-ní:-non'] *Who bought it?*
    a) **onhka ok** [ónh-kak] *someone, somebody*
        ie. **Onhka ok wa'ehninon'.** [Ónh-kak wa'-eh-ní:-non'] *Someone bought it.*
    b) **onhka ki' ok** [onh-ka kók] *whoever; whosoever*
        ie. **Onhka ki' ok yenònwe's, tkakonte enyekarya'ke'.** [Ónh-ka kók ye-nòn:-we's, tká:-kon-teh en-ye-kár-ya'-ke'] *Whoever likes it will have to pay for it.*

587 **onhkare'okon** [onh-ka-re'-ó:-konh] *who all*
    ie. **Onhkare'okon eh yehonne'skwe' shiyòkarahs.** [Onh-ka-re'-ó:-konh eh ye-hón:-ne's-kwe' shi-yò:-ka-rahs] *Who all was there last night.*

588 **onhte** [ónh-teh] *perhaps, probably*
    ie. **Raonha onhte wahanowenhte'.** [Rá-on-ha' ónh-teh wa-ha-nó:-wenh-te'] *Perhaps he (is the one who) lied about it;* **Wahanowenhte' onhte.** [Wa-ha-nó:-wenh-te' ónh-teh] *He probably lied about it.*

589 **onhwentsya** [on-hwén-tsya'] *earth, land, soil*
    With locative: **onhwentsyàke** [on-hwen-tsyà:-keh] *on the ground;* **onhwentsyòkon** [on-hwen-tsyò:-konh] *under the ground / in the cellar, basement;* **sha'teyonhwentsihen** [sha'-te-yon-hwen-tsí:-henh] *in the middle of the earth;* **kenh tsi yonhwentsyate** [kenh -tsi yon-hwen-tsyá:-teh] *here on earth.* Related words: **sewenhwentsyat** [se-wen-hwén-tsyat] *one mile;*

yonhwentsiraronnyon [yon-hwen-tsi-ra-rón-nyonh] *map(s) / geography*; tsyonhwentsyote [tsyo-hwén-tsyo-teh] *a province*; yotonhwentsyotonnyon [yo-ton-hwen-tsyo-tón-nyonh] *coast to coast*.

590 **oni** [ó:-ni'] *also; too*
ie. **Akaonha oni wa'onkyenawa'se'.** [A-ká-on-ha' ó:-ni' wa'-on-kyé:-na-wa'-se'] *She also helped me*; **Kenonwe's oni kiken'.** [Ke-nòn:-we's ó:-ni' kí:-ken'] *I like this one too.*

591 **onkwa'nihstenha** [on-kwa'-nihs-tén-ha'] *our mother* (See: ake'nihstenha)

592 **onkwahsotha** [on-kwah-sót-ha'] *our grandmother* (See: akhsotha)

593 **onkwahtsi'a** [on-kwah-tsí:-'ah] *our older sister* (See: aktsi'a)

594 **onkwe** [ón:-kwe'] *a person*
With pronominals: **ronkwe** [rón:-kwe'] *he is a person: a man*; **yakonkwe** [ya-kón:-kwe'] *she is a person: a woman*; **tehnonkwe** [teh-nón:-kwe'] *they (two males) are persons: two males*; **tekenonkwe** [te-ke-nón:-kwe'] *they (two females) are persons: two women*; **rononkwe** [ro-nón:-kwe'] *they (males) are people: men*; **kononkwe** [ko-nón:-kwe'] *they (females) are persons: women*; **ononkwe** [o-nón:-kwe'] *they (generic) are persons: people*. Related words: **onkwehokon** [on-kwe-hó:-konh] *people [generic, non-specific)*; **onkwehokonhson** [on-kwe-ho-kónh-sonh] *out amongst the people.*

595 **onkwehonwe** [on-kwe-hón:-weh] *native, aboriginal people*
Also: **onkwehonwetsherakonhson** [on-kwe-hon-wets-he-ra-kónh-sonh] *out in the native community.*

596 **onkwehonwehneha** [on-kwe-hon-weh-né-ha'] *native, aboriginal way of doing*

597 **onkwehonwène'** [on-kwe-hon-wè:-neh] *on the reserve / in the native territory*
Also: **onkwehonwehnehson** [on-kwe-hon-weh-néh-sonh] *on the reserves / in the native territories.*

598 **onon'onhsera** [o-non'-ónh-se-ra'] *squash*
Related words: **kanon'onhsero** [ka-non'-ónh-se-roh] *boiled squash*; **watenon'onhseronte** [wa-te-non'ónh-se-ron-teh] *baked squash*; **onon'onhserakahte** [o-non'-onh-se-ra-káh-teh] *watermelon*; **onon'onhsera'kowa** [o-non'-onh-se-ra'-kó:-wah] *a pumpkin*; **onon'onhseràri** [o-non'-onh-se-rà:-rih] *cooked squash*; **onon'onhserathen** [o-non'-onh-se-rát-henh] *dried squash*; **kanon'onhserakerahs** [ka-non'-onh-se-rá-ke-rahs] *cucumber(s).*

599 **ononhkwa'** [o-nónh-kwa'] *medicine, remedy, cure*
With adjectivals: **kanonhkwatsheriyo** [ka-nonh-kwats-he-rí:-yoh] *good medicine (a good remedy)*; **kanonhkwatsheraksen** [ka-nonh-kwats-he-rák-senh] *a poor remedy / drugs, dope.* With verbs: **wakenonhkwatsherayen'** [wa-ke-nonh-

70

kwats-he-rá:-yen'] *I have some medicine*; **kenonhkwatshenryes** [ke-nonh-kwats-hénr-yes] *I find / locate a cure, some medicine*; **kenonhkwisaks** [ke-nonh-kwí:-saks] *I look for a cure, some medicine*. Related words: **ononhkwahson'a** [o-nonh-kwah-són:-'ah] *remedies, drugs, medicines*.

600 **ononhkwise** [o-nónh-kwi-seh] *hair*
With possessives: **kenonhkwiseràke** [ke-nonh-kwi-se-rà:-keh] *in my hair*; **senonhkwiseràke** [se-nonh-kwi-se-rà:-keh] *in your hair*; **ranonhkwiseràke** [ra-nonh-kwi-se-rà:-keh] *in his hair*; **yenonhkwiseràke** [ye-nonh-kwi-se-rà:-keh] *in her hair*. With verbs: **wakenonhkwiserehs** [wa-ke-nonh-kwí-se-rehs] *I have long hair*; **niwakenonhkwiserehsha'** [ni-wa-ke-nonh-kwi-se-réhs-ha'] *I have short hair*; **Wakenonhkwiserahòntsi** [wa-ke-nonh-kwi-se-ra-hòn:-tsih] *I have black hair*. Related words: **tewakenonhkeri** [te-wa-ke-nónh-ke-ri'] *I have curley hair*; **wakenhraten** [wa-ken-hrá-tenh] *I have white hair / fair hair*.

601 **Ononhsatokenhti** [O-nonh-sa-to-kénh-tih] *a church*

602 **ononkwe** [o-ón:-kwe'] *persons, people (non-specific)* (See: onkwe)

603 **ononta** [o-nón:-ta'] *a hill*
With locatives: **onontàke** [o-non-tà:-keh] *on the hill*; **onontoharake** [o-non-to-ha-rá:-keh] *at the top of the hill (summit, peak)*; **akta tsi yonontote** [ák-ta' tsi yo-nón:-to-teh] *near, next to the hill*; **onontakon** [o-nón:-ta-konh] *the base of the hill*; **yonontakarenre** [yo-non-ta-ka-rèn:-reh *the slope of the hill*. With verbs: **kenontàra's** ke-non-tà:-ra's] *I climb a hill*; **kenontawènrats** [ke-non-ta-wèn:-rats] *I cross over a hill*; **kenontathsnenhtha'** [ke-non-tat-hsnénht-ha'] *I descend a hill*.

604 **onònta** [o-nòn:-ta'] *milk*
With adjectivals: **kanon'tiyo** [ka-non'-tí:-yoh] *good milk*; **kanon'taksen** [ka-non'-ták-senh] *bad milk, spoiled*; **yonon'tatken** [yo-non'-tát-kenh] *sour milk*. With verbs: **wakenòntayen'** [wa-ke-nòn:-ta-yen'] *I have milk (to drink)*; **kenon'tawèrons** [ke-non'-tá-we-rons] *I pour some milk*; **kenon'tahninons** [ke-non'-tah-ní:-nons] *I buy milk*. Related words: **kanòntat** [ka-nòn:-tat] *a milk cow*; **onon'tahson'a** [o-non'-tah-són:-'ah] *diary products*; **kanon'tihsa** [ka-non'-tíh-sa'] *buttermilk*; **onon'takeri** [o-non'-tá-ke-rih] *breast milk*; **onòntara** [o-nòn:-ta-ra'] *soup*.

605 **Ononta'kehàka** [O-non-ta'-ke-hà:-kah] *the Onondaga nation*

606 **onontsi** [o-nón:-tsi] *head*
kenontsihstàke [ke-nya'-tà:-keh] *on my head*; **senontsihstàke** [se-nya'-tà:-keh] *on your head*; **ranontsihstàke** [ra-nya'-tà:-keh] *on his head*; **yenontsihstàke** [ye-nya'-tà:-keh] *on her head*; **onkwanontsihsta'kehson** [on-kwa-nya'-ta'-kéh-sonh] *on our heads*; **ratinontsihsta'kehson** [ra-ti-nya'-ta'-

kéh-sonh] *on their heads*. This form is also used: **kenontsìne'** [ke-non-tsì:-ne'] *on my...*; **senontsìne'**[se-non-tsì:-ne'] *on your...*; **ranontsìne'** [ra-non-tsì:-ne'] *on his...*; **onkwanontsihnehson** [on-kwa-non-tsih-nénh-sonh] *on our...*; **ratinontsihnehson** [ra-ti-non-tsih-néh-sonh] *on their....* With verbs: **wakenontsihstanònwaks** [wa-ke-nya'-ta-nòn:-waks] *I have a sore head / a headache*; **kenontsihstonte** [ke-non-tsíhs-ton-teh] *I have a head (attached)*; **katenontsihstohares** [ka-te-non-tsihs-tó-ha-res] *I wash my head*; **katenontsihston'neks** [ka-te-non-tsihs-tón'-neks] *I move my head out of the way*; **tewakatenontsihstawe'ehstha'** [te-wa-ka-te-non-tsihs-ta-we'-éhst-ha'] *I have a pain in my head (a migraine)*; **wakenontsihstaronhkwane** [wa-ke-non-tsihs-ta-rónh-kwa-neh] *I have an itchy head*; **yekenontsihstota's** [ye-ke-non-tsihs-tó:-ta's] *I land on my head*; **khenontsihstayeks** [k-he-non-tsihs-tá:-yeks] *I hit her / them on the head*.

⁶⁰⁷ **onònwara** [o-nòn:-wa-ra'] *brain (head)*

With verbs: **kennonhwaròroks** [ken-non-hwa-rò:-roks] *I cover my head (put on a hat)*; **kennonhwarohrokhsyons** [ken-non-hwa-ro-hrók-hsyons] *I uncover my head (take off my hat)*; **kenonhwarya'ks** [ke-non-hwár-ya'ks] *I rack my brain*: also: **teyononhwarya'kte** [te-yo-non-hwár-ya'k-teh] *it's brain-racking*.

⁶⁰⁸ **onowen'** [o-nó:-wen'] *a lie*

ie. **katenowenhtha'** [ka-te-no-wenht-ha'] *I lie about*; **kennowenhtonnis** [ken-no-wenh-tón:-nis] *I make up lies*; **kennowenhtha'** [ken-no-wénht-ha'] *I tell a lie*; **khenowenhtha'** [k-he-no-wénht-ha'] *I lie to her/them*.

⁶⁰⁹ **onwa** [ón:-wa'] *presently; now*

a) **onwa kenh wente** [ón:-wa' kenh wén:-teh] *today*

ie. **Katke ok onwa kenh wente tkakonte kanatakon yahake'.** [Kát-kek on-wa' kenh wén:-teh t-ká:-kon-teh ka-ná:-ta-kon ya-há:-ke'] *Sometime today I have to go to town.*

⁶¹⁰ **onwahtsi ok** [(on)-wáh-tsyok] *later on; in a while*

ie. **Onwahtsi ok enkonyenawa'se' entenikwatako'.** [...en-kon-yé:-na-wa'-se' en-te-ni-kwa-tá:-ko'] *later on I will help you fix it.*

⁶¹¹ **onyàra** [o-nyà:-ra'] *neck; back of the neck*

kenyahràke [ke-nya-hrà:-keh] *on my neck*; **senyahràke** [se-nya-hrà:-keh] *on your neck*; **ranyahràke** [ra-nya-hrà:-keh] *on his neck*; **yenyahràke** [ye-nya-hrà:-keh] *on her neck*; **onkwanyahra'kehson** [on-kwa-nya-hra'-kéh-sonh] *on our necks*; **ratinyahra'kehson** [ra-ti-nya-hra'-kéh-sonh] *on their necks*. With verbs: **wakenyahranònwaks** [wa-ke-nya-hra-nòn:-waks] *I have a sore neck*; **tekatenyahrawe'ehstha'** [te-ka-te-nya-hra-we'-éhst-ha'] *I have a pain in my neck*; **tekatenyahrahonhterakwas** [te-ka-te-nya-hra-honh-te-rá-kwas] *I break my neck*.

612 **onyare** [ó-nya-reh] *a snake*

613 **onyàta** [o-nyà:-ta'] *throat (front of the neck)*
kenya'tàke [ke-nya'-tà:-keh] *on my throat*; **senya'tàke** [se-nya'-tà:-keh] *on your throat*; **ranya'tàke** [ra-nya'-tà:-keh] *on his throat*; **yenya'tàke** [ye-nya'-tà:-keh] *on her throat*; **onkwanya'ta'kehson** [on-kwa-nya'-ta'-kéh-sonh] *on our throats*; **ratinya'ta'kehson** [ra-ti-nya'-ta'-kéh-sonh] *on their throats*. With verbs: **wakenya'tanònwaks** [wa-ke-nya'-ta-nòn:-waks] *I have a sore throat*; **wakenya'tathenhs** [wa-ke-nya'-tát-henhs] *my throat is dry (I'm thirsty)*.

614 **orenhsa** [o-rénh-sa'] *the tibia (the leg from knee to ankle)*

615 **orhen'kehtsi** [or-hen'-kéh-tsih] *early (in the morning)*
ie. **Orhen'kehtsi niya'tewenhniserake ikye'skwe'.** [Or-hen'-kéh-tsih ni-ya'-te-wenh-ni-se-rá:-keh í-kye's-kwe'] *I used to get up early every morning.*

616 **orhen'kène** [or-hen'-kè:-neh] *in the morning*
ie. **Orhen'kène tahontahsawen' wahontenonhsonni'.** [...ta-hon-táh-sa-wen' wa-hon-te-nonh-són:-ni'] *They atarted building the house in the morning.*

617 **orhotsheri** [or-hóts-he-ri'] *string beans*

618 **orhyoken** [or-hyó:-ken'] *a chipmunk*

619 **orònya** [o-ròn:-ya'] *blue*
ie. **Orònya niwahsohkòten'.** O-ròn:-ya' ni-wah-soh-kò:-ten'' *it is coloured (dyed) blue*; **Orònya niwatya'tawi'tsheròten'** [O-ròn:-ya' ni-wa-tya'-ta-wi'ts-he-rò:-ten'] *a blue coat, shirt, dress.*

620 **othenen** [o-thé:-nenh] *anything; any*
ie. **Othenen ken sayen'.** [O-t-hé-nen kén sá:-yen'] *Do you have anything?* Also: **Othenen ken sahwihstayen'.** [O-t-hé-nenh kén sa-hwíhs-ta-yen'] *Do you have any money?*

621 **othèsera** [ot-hè:-se-ra'] *flour*

622 **othsyana** [ot-hsyá:-na'] *a handful*
With verbs: **tekathsyanahkwa'** [te-kat-hsya-náh-kwa'] *I pick up a handful*; **wakathsyanontye's** [wa-kat-hsya-nón-tye's] *I throw a handful.*

623 **oti** [o-tí:] *tea*
With verbs: **iktitsherahnekirha'** [ik-tits-he-rah-ne-kír-ha'] *I drink tea*; **iktitsheronnis** [ik-tits-he-rón:-nis] *I make tea*. Related words: **yetitsherarahkwa** [ye-tits-he-ra-ráh-kwa'] *a tea pot.*

624 **otokenha** [o-to-kén-ha'] *a white oak*

625 **otsi'era** [o-tsi'-é:-ra'] *nail(s) (ie. finger nails; toe nails)*

626 otsi'nohyohsa [o-tsi-no-hyóh-sa'] *back*

With possessives: **iktsi'nohyohsàke** [ik-tsi'-no-hyoh-sà:-keh] *on my back*; **ihstsi'nohyohsàke** [ihs-tsi'-no-hyoh-sà:-keh] *on your back*; **ratsi'nohyohsàke** [ra-tsi'-no-hyoh-sà:-keh] *on his back*; **yetsi'nohyohsàke** [ye-tsi'-no-hyoh-sà:-keh] *on her back*; **katsi'nohyohsàke** [ka-tsi'-no-hyoh-sà:-keh] *on its back*; **onkwatsi'nohyohsa'kehson** [on-kwa-hyoh-sa'-kéh-sonh] *on our backs*; **ratitsi'nohyohsa'kehson** [ra-ti-tsi'-no-hyoh-sa'-kéh-sonh] *on their backs*. With verbs: **waktsi'nohyohsanònwaks** [wak-tsi'-no-hyoh-sa-nòn:-waks] *I have a backache*; **iktsi'nohyohsakahrewahtha'** [ik-tsi'-no-hyoh-sa-ka-hre-wáht-ha'] *I hurt my back*.

627 otsi'nowa [o-tsi'-nó:-wa'] *an insect; a bug*

ie. **otsi'nowahson'a** [o-tsi-no-wah-són:-'ah] *insects, bugs*. Related words: **katsi'nonhtaks** [ka-tsi'-nónh-taks] *monkey*; **katsi'nowakerahs** [ka-tsi'-no-wá-ke-rahs] *a bedbug*. With verbs: **iktsi'nowaks** [ik-tsi'-nó:-waks] *I eat insects, bugs*.

628 otsihkwa [o-tsíh-kwa'] *a button; a fist; a club*

ie. **otsihkwahson'a** [o-tsih-kwah-són:-'ah] *vegetables (root crops)*. With verbs: **iktsihkotha'** [ik-tsih-kót-ha'] *I button up (do up the buttons)*; **iktsihkotakwas** [ik-tsih-ko-tá-kwas] *I unbutton*; **waktsihkwakwe'nonni'** [wak-tsih-kwa-kwe'-nón:-ni'] *I make a fist*; **khetsihkwatatis** [k-he-tsih-kwa-tá:-tis] *I shake my fist at someone*; **tekattsihkwa'eks** [te-kat-tsih-kwá:-'eks] *I play lacrosse*. Realated words: **otsihkwa'kowa** [o-tsih-kwa'-kó:-wah] *a turnip*; **yotsihkwatskàra** [o-tsih-kwats-kà:-ra'] *a radish*; **otsinekwar nikatsihkòten'** [o-tsí:-ne-kwar ni-ka-tsih-kò:-ten'] *carrot(s)*; **onekwenhtara nikatsihkòten'** [o-ne-kwénh-ta-ra' ni-ka-tsih-kò;_ten'] *beet(s)*; **attsihkwa'e** [at-tsih-kwá:-'eh] *a lacrosse game*; **yetsihkotahkwa** [ye-tsih-ko-táh-kwa'] *a button*; **yotsihkote** [yo-tsíh-ko-teh] *there is a knot on it*.

629 otsihkwa ohtera [o-tsíh-kwa' oh-té:-ra'] *turnips*

630 otsikhèta [o-tsi-khè:-ta'] *sugar; candy*

ie. **katsikhètare** [ka-tsik-hè:-ta-reh] *it has sugar on it / in it*; **katsikhètayen'** [ka-tsik-hè:-ta-yen'] *there is sugar on it*; **teyottsikhètare** [te-yot-tsik-hè:-ta-reh] *it is sweet*; **iktsikhètaks** [ik-tsi-k-hè:-taks] *I eat sugar, candy*; **iktsikhe'takahstha'** [ik-tsi-k-he'-ta-káhst-ha'] *I am a heavy user of sugar*; **kattsikhe'tòkta's** [kat-tsi-k-he'-tò:-k-ta's] *I run out of sugar*; **tekattsikhe'tarhos** [te-kat-tsi-k-he'-tár-hos] *I sweeten something*. Related words: **katsikhe'tonni** [ka-tsi-k-he'-tón:-ni'] *a honey bee*; **katsikhe'takenra** [ka-tsi-k-he'-ta-kén:-ra'] *white sugar*; **katsikhe'tahòntsi** [ka-tsi-k-he'-ta-hòn:-tsih] *brown sugar*.

631 **otsinekwar** [o-tsí-ne-kwar] *yellow; bile*

ie. **otsinekwar niwahsohkòten'** [o-tsí:-ne-kwar ni-wah-soh-kò:-ten'] *it's yellow (coloured / dyed)*; **otsinekwar niwatya'tawi'tsheròten'** [o-tsí:-ne-kwar ni-wa-tya'-ta-wi'ts-he-rò:-ten'] *a yellow shirt, dress.*

632 **otsinekwar ohtera** [o-tsí-ne-kwar oh-té:-ra'] *carrots*

633 **otsisera** [o-tsí-se-ra'] *window pane*

With locatives: **otsiseràke** [o-tsi-se-rà:-keh] *on the window pane*; **otsiserakon** [o-tsi-se-rà:-konh] *on the window pane.* With verbs: **tektsiserahrihtha'** [tek-tsi-se-ra-hríht-ha'] *I break a window pane.*

634 **otsìtsya** [o-tsì:-tsya'] *flower(s), blossom(s)*

ie. **katsìtsyare** [ka-tsì:-tsya-reh] *it has a flower / blossom on it*; **yotsìtsyonte** [yo-tsì:-tsyon-teh] *it is flowering, blossoming.* Related words: **yotsi'tsyatken** [yo-tsi'-tsyát-kenh] *vinegar*; **yetsi'tsyarahkwa** [ye-tsi'-tsya-ráh-kwa'] *a flower vase, pot*; **katsi'tsyayenthon** [ka-tsi'-tsya-yént-honh] *a flower bed, garden*; **katsi'tsyakerahs** [ka-tsi'-tsyá-ke-rahs] *beer*; **iktsi'tsyahnekirha'** [ik-tsi'-tsyah-ne-kír-ha'] *I drink beer.*

635 **otstènra** [ots-tèn:-ra'] *a rock; rocks*

With locatives: **otstenhràke** [ots-ten-hrà:-keh] *on the stone*; **otstenhròkon** [ots-ten-hrò:-konh] *under the stone.* With verbs: **yotstenhrakètote** [yots-ten-hra-kè:-to-teh] *a (piece of) stone sticking up*; **teyotstenhròren** [te-yots-ten-hrò:-renh] *a crevasse in the stone, rock*; **teyotstenhroken** [te-yots-ten-hró:-kenh] *between two (pieces of) stone*; **kitstenhrotha'** [kits-ten-hrót-ha'] *I put up a stone wall*; **kitstenhrarihsyons** [kits-ten-hra-ríh-syonhs] *I demolish a stone wall*; **khetstenhroya'ks** [khets-ten-hró:-ya'ks] *I throw a stone at someone.* Related words: **yotstenhrakàronte** [yots-ten-hra-kà:-ron-teh] *a cave, cavern*; **tehentstenhrotha'** [te-hents-ten-hrót-ha'] *a stone mason.*

636 **otya'ke** [ó-tya'-keh] *the other; others*

ie. **otya'ke ne kahyatonhsera'okon** [...ne ka-hya-tonh-se-ra'-ó:-konh] *the other books.*

637 **otyarènta** [o-tya-rèn:-ta'] *orange; squash blossom*

ie. **otyarènta niwahsohkòten'** [...ni-wah-soh-kò:-ten'] *it is orange coloured (dyed)*; **otyarènta niwatya'tawitsheròten'** [...ni-wa-tya'-ta-wi'ts-he-rò:-ten'] *an orange (coloured) coat, dress, shirt.* Related words: **otyaren'ta'a** [o-tya-ren'-tá:-'ah] *a canary.*

638 **otyohkwa** [o-tyóh-kwa'] *a group; a collection, set*

With numericals: **skentyohkwat** [sken-tyóh-kwat] *one group*; **tekentyohkwake** [te-ken-tyóh-kwa-keh] *two groups*; **ahsen nikentyohkwake** [áh-sen' ni-ken-tyóh-kwa-keh] *three groups.* Related words: **tyotityohkwa** [tyo-ti-tyóh-kwa'] *a set, collection of.* ie. **ahsen nityotityohkwake ne kaksahson'a** [...ne kak-sah-són:-'ah] *three sets of dishes;* **kontityohkowanen** [kon-ti-tyoh-ko-wá:-nenh] *a (large) herd, flock, gathering.*

639 **owenna** [o-wén:-na'] *voice, word; speech*
With possessives: **akewenna** [a-ke-wén:-na'] *my voice, word;* **sawenna** [sa-wén:-na'] *your voice, word;* **raowenna** [ra-o-wén:-na'] *his voice, word;* **akaowenna** [a-ka-o-wén:-na'] *her voice, word;* **onkwawennahson'a** [on-kwa-wen-nah-són:-'ah] *our voices, words;* **raotiwennahson'a** [ra-o-ti-wen-nah-són:-'ah] *their voices, words;* With verbs: **kewennahsnore** [ke-wen-nah-snó:-reh] *I speak quickly;* **kewennahserohen** [ke-wen-nah-se-ró-henh] *I speak harshly;* **kewennènta's** [ke-wen-nèn:-ta's] *I finish speaking;* **kewenninekenhs** [ke-wen-ní-ne-kenhs] *I speak about something;* **kewennahnotha'** [ke-wen-nah-nót-ha'] *I read;* **katewennarahkwa'** [ka-te-wen-na-ráh-kwa'] *I am obedient (do what I'm told);* **tekewennatenyes** [te-ke-wen-na-té-nyes] *I translate;* **tewakewennayeronnyonh** [te-wa-ke-wen-na-ye-rón-nyonh] *I mumble / am mumbling;* **wakewennayo'thiye** [wa-ke-wen-na-yo'-t-hí:-yeh] *I am shrewd;* **wakatewennatyeni** [wa-ka-te-wen-na-tyé:-ni'] *I am talkative.* Related words: **yontewennata'ahstha** [yon-te-wen-na-ta'-áhst-ha'] *a telephone;* **kawennokwas** [ka-wen-nó-kwas] *a radio;* **yewennahnotahkwa** [ye-wen-nah-no-táh-kwa'] *reading material;* **kawennowanahtha** [ka-wen-no-wa-náht-ha'] *a microphone.*

640 **oweyonhkara** [o-we-yónh-ka-ra'] *thumb*
With possessives: **keweyonhkaràke** [ke-we-yonh-ka-rà:-keh] *on my thumb;* **seweyonhkaràke** [se-we-yonh-ka-rà:-keh] *on your thumb;* **raweyonhkaràke** [ra-we-yonh-ka-rà:-keh] *on his thumb;* **yeweyonhkaràke** [ye-we-yonh-ka-rà:-keh] *on her thumb.* With verbs: **-keweyonhkarakahrewahtha'** [ke-we-yonh-ka-ra-ka-hre-wáht-ha'] *I hurt my thumb;* **Wakeweyonhkaranònwaks** [wa-ke-we-yonh-ka-ra-nòn:-waks] *I hurt my thumb.*

641 **owihstohsera** [o-wihs-tóh-se-ra'] *butter*
ie. **kewihstohserarhos** [ke-wihs-toh-se-rár-hos] *I spread butter on something;* **katewihstohseròkta's** [ka-te-wihs-toh-se-rò:-k-ta's] *I run out of butter;* **kewihstohserahninons** [ke-wihs-toh-se-rah-ní:-nons] *I buy butter;* **kewihstohserata's** [ke-wihs-toh-se-rá-ta's] *I put butter into something.*

642 **owira** [o-wí:-ra'] *a baby*
With verbs: **katewiranonnha'** [ka-te-wi-ra-nónn-ha'] *I baby-sit;* **katewirarakwas** [ka-te-wi-ra-rá-kwas] *I adopt a baby, child;* **wakewirayenta's** [wa-ke-wi-ra-yén:-ta's] *I have a child, baby;* **wakewirakate** [wa-ke-wi-ra-ká:-teh] *I have many babies, children;* **wakewiriyos** [wa-ke-wi-rí:-yohs] *I have well-behaved children;* **wakewiraksens** [wa-ke-wi-rák-sens] *I have misbehaved children;* **wakewirontyes** [wa-ke-wi-rón-tye's] *I abandon my baby;* **kewirinekenhs** [ke-

wi-rí-ne-kenhs] *I get an abortion.*

643 owira'a [o-wi-rá:-'ah] *a baby (person)*

644 owise [ó:-wi-seh] *a glass; ice*
With locatives: **owisàke** [o-wi-sà:-keh] *on the ice*; **owisòkon** [o-wi-sò:-konh] *under the ice*; **kawisakon** [ka-wí:-sa-konh] *in the glass.* With adjectivals: **yowisiyo** [yo-wi-sí:-yoh] *pretty / clear glass*; **yowisahniron** [yo-wi-sah-ní:-ronh] *strong ice*; **kawisowanen** [ka-wi-so-wá:-nenh] *a large glass*; **kawisatenhs** [ka-wi-sá:-tenhs] *thick ice*; **nikawisatenhsha** [ni-ka-wi-sa-ténhs-ha'] *thin ice*; **teyowisahstarathe'** [te-yo-wi-sahs-ta-rát-he'] *the ice is sparkling*; **tekawisàris** [te-ka-wi-sà:-ris] *the ice is breaking up*; **kawisokwas** [ka-wi-só-kwas] *the ice is moving out*; **yowisayenton** [yo-wi-sa-yén:-tonh] *there are patches of ice*; **yowisake'toton** [yo-wi-sa-ke'-tó:-tonh] *there are patches of ice sticking out (through the snow)*; **teyotewisonte** [te-yo-te-wí:-son-teh] *the ice is attached (to it); ie. an icicle.* With verbs: **tekewisahrihtha'** [te-ka-wi-sa-hríht-ha'] *I break a glass*; **tewakatewisonte** [te-wa-ka-te-wí:-son-teh] *I am wearing glasses*; **tewakatewisya'ks** [te-wa-ka-te-wí:-sya'ks] *the ice breaks under me*; **tewakewisohse** [te-wa-ke-wí:-soh-se'] *I am dazzled / blinded by the ice / snow.'*

645 oya [ó:-ya'] *another*
ie. **Oya wakhninonh.** [Ó:-ya' wak-hní:-nonh] *I bought another (one).*

646 oyana [o-yá:-na'] *a pair; a track*
With numericals: **tsyoyanat** [tsyo-yá:-nat] *one pair*; **teyoyanake** [te-yo-yá:-na-keh] *two pair*; **ahsen niyoyanake** [áh-sen' ni-yo-yá-na-keh] *three pair.* With verbs: **tekyanàkhon'** [te-kya-nà:-k-hon'] *I follow a path (in the woods)*; **kheyanìseres** [k-he-ya-nì:-se-res] *I follow someone's track*; **kheyanenhawis** [k-he-ya-nen-há:-wis] *I follow / walk in someone else's track.* Related words: **tekayanonni'** [te-ka-ya-nón:-ni'] *a footprint*; **kheyanenhawe'** [k-he-ya-nén-ha-we'] *I follow someone.*

647 oyàta [o-yà:-ta'] *body, self, person*
With locatives: **oyàtakon** [o-yà:-ta-konh] *inside the body*; **oya'tàke** [o-ya'-tà:-keh] *on the body.* With possessives: **kya'tàke** [kya'-tà:-keh] *on me (on my person, body)*; **sya'tàke** [sya'-tà:-keh] *on you...*; **raya'tàke** [ra-ya'-tà:-keh] *on him...*; **yeya'tàke** [ye-ya'-tà:-keh] *on her...*; **onkwaya'ta'kehson** [on-kwa-ya'-ta'-kéh-sonh] *on us...*; **ratiya'ta'kehson** [ra-ti-ya'-ta'-kéh-sonh] *on them....* With verbs: **kyàtonte** [kyà:-ton-teh] *I have a body*; **thikyàtate** [t-hi-kyà:-ta-teh] *I am the other (person)*; **wakya'tanònwaks** [wa-kya'-ta-nòn:-waks] *I have a sore body / I ache all over.* Related words: **oya'takonha** [o-ya'-ta-kón-ha'] *tallow, fat*; **nikyàtawen's** [ni-kyà:-ta-wen's] *something happens to me*; **tewakya'tonkohtha'** [te-wa-kya'-ton-kóht-ha'] *I am relaxed, at ease*; **wakya'tanekaron** [wa-kya'-ta-ne-ká:-ronh] *I am active, lively*; **tewakya'tahkariyo** [te-wa-kya'-tah-ka-rí:-yoh]

I am agile; **katyàtarons** [ka-tyà:-ta-rons] *I join a club, organization.*

648 oyen'kwahonwe [o-yen'-kwa'-hón:-weh] *Indian tobacco*

649 oyenhèta [o-yen-hè-ta'] *a perch (fish)*

650 oyènkwa [o-yèn:-kwa'] *tobacco*
With adjectivals: **kayen'kwiyo** [ka-yen'-kwí:-yoh] *good tobacco*; **yoyen'kwàte** [yo-yen'-kwà:-teh] *strong tobacco*; **oyen'kwa'onwe** [o-yen'-kwa'-ón:-weh] *traditional tobacco (Indian tobacco)*. With verbs: **kyen'kwanònwaks** [kyen'-kwa-nòn:-waks] *I crave tobacco*; **kyen'kwakahstha'** [kyen'-kwa-káhst-ha'] *I am a heavy smoker*; **kyen'kwakerahs** [kyen'-kwá-ke-rahs] *I smell of tobacco*; **katyen'kwanhontha'** [ka-tyen'-kwan-hónt-ha'] *I chew tobacco.*

651 oyènkwara [o-yèn:-kwa-ra'] *smoke*
ie. **watyen'kwaronnis** [wa-tyen'-kwa-rón:-nis] *it smokes (ie. wood, stove)*; **kayen'kwarakerahs** [ka-yen'-kwa-rá-ke-rahs] *it smells of smoke*; **kayen'kwarowanen** [ka-yen'-kwa-ro-wá:-nenh] *a great deal of smoke*; **thitkayen'kwarahere** [t-hit-ka-yen'-kwa-rá-he-reh] *it is full of smoke / there's lots of smoke.*

652 oyente [ó:-yen-teh] *wood; firewood*
With locatives: **kayentàke** [ka-yen-tà:-keh] *on the firewood*; **kayentakta** [ka-yen-ták-ta'] *beside the firewood*; **kayentòkon** [ka-yen-tò:-konh] *under the firewood*. With adjectivals: **kayentiyo** [ka-yen-tí:-yoh] *good firewood*; **kayentaksen** [ka-yen-ták-senh] *poor firewood*; **yoyentase** [yo-yen-tá:-seh] *green wood*; **yoyentathen** [yo-yen-tát-henh] *dry firewood*; **yoyentatken** [yo-yent-kenh] *rotten wood*; **yoyenta'tonyote** [yo-yen-ta'-tón:-yo-teh] *a pile of firewood*; With verbs: **kyenta'tonhyotha'** [kyen-ta'-ton-hyót-ha'] *I pile up firewood*; **kyentya'ks** [kyén-tya'ks] *I cut (some) firewood*; **kyentakohe's** [kyen-ta-kó-he's] *I go and get firewood*; **kyentakwas** [kyen-tá-kwas] *I gather firewood*; **tekyentòrens** [te-kyen-tò:-rens] *I split firewood*; **kyentakarenyes** [kyen-ta-ka-ré-nyes] *I draw firewood*; **katyentathsa'ahtha'** [ka-tyen-tat-hsa'-áht-ha'] *I burn wood for heat.*

653 oyeri [o-yé:-rih] *ten*
ie. **oyeri nikon** [...ní:-konh] *(there's) ten of them (onjects)*; **oyeri nikonti** [...ni-kón:-tih] *(there's) ten of them (female / animal)*; **oyeri nihati** [...ni-há:-tih] *(there's) ten of them (male)*. **oyeri nikatshètake** [...ni-kats-hè:-ta-keh] *ten bottles*; **oyeri niwakyen'** [...ni-wák-yen'] *I have ten*; **oyeri niwaketshètayen'** [...ni-wa-kets-hè:-ta-yen'] *I have ten bottles.*

654 oyerònta [o-ye-ròn:-ta'] *a body, carcass*
With locatives: **kayeron'tàke** [ka-ye-ron'-tà:-keh] *on the body, carcass*; **kayeròntakon** [ka-ye-ròn:-ta-konh] *inside the body, carcass.*

78

R

655 rake'niha [ra-ke'-ní-ha'] *my father*
See also: **ya'niha** [ya'-ní-ha'] *your father*; **ro'niha** [ro'-ní-ha'] *his father*; **ronwa'niha** [ron-wa'-ní-ha'] *her father*; **shonkwa'niha** [shon-kwa'-ní-ha'] *our father*.

656 rakenoha'a [ra-ke-no-há:-'ah] *my uncle*
See also: **yanoha'a** [ya-no-há:-'ah] *your uncle*; **ronoha'a** [ro-no-há:-'ah] *his uncle*; **ronwanoha'a** [ron-wa-no-há:-'ah] *her uncle*; **shonkwanoha'a** [shon-kwa-no-há:-'ah] *our uncle*.

657 rakhsotha [rak-hsót-ha'] *my grandfather*
See also: **yahsotha** [yah-sót-ha'] *your gandfather*; **rohsotha** [roh-sót-ha'] *his gandfather*; **ronwahsotha** [ron-wah-sót-ha'] *her gandfather*; **shonkwahsotha** [shon-kwah-sót-ha'] *our gandfather*.

658 raksa'a [rak-sá:-'ah] *a male child; a boy*
ie. **ne raksa'a** [ne rak-sá:-'ah] *the boy*; **thiken' raksa'a** [thí:-ken'...] *that boy*; **kiken' raksa'a** [kí:-ken'...] *this boy*. With numericals: **shayàtat raksa'a** [s-ha-yà:-tat rak-sá:-'ah] *one boy*; **tehniyahsen tehniksa'a** [teh-ni-yáh-senh teh-nik-sá:-'ah] *two boys*; **ahsen nihati ratiksa'okonha** [áh-sen' nihá:-tih ra-tik-sa'-o-kón-ha'] *three boys*. With adjectivals: **nihra'a raksa'a** [ni-hrá:-'ah rak-sá:-'ah] *a small boy*; **raksa'towanen** [rak-sa'-to-wá:-nenh] *a large boy*; **raksa'tiyo** [rak-sa'-tí:-yoh] *a good boy*; **raksa'taksen** [rak-sa'-ták-senh] *a bad boy*. **ratiksa'okonha** [ra-tik-sa'-o-kón-ha'] *boys*.

659 raktsi'a [rak-tsí:-'ah] *my older brother*
See also: **yahtsi'a** [yah-tsí:-'ah] *your older brother*; **rohtsi'a** [roh-tsí:-'ah] *his older brother*; **ronwahtsi'a** [ron-wah-tsí:-'ah] *her older brother*; **shonkwahtsi'a** [shon-kwah-tsí:-'ah] *our older brother*.

660 ranekenhteron [ra-ne-kénh-te-ronh] *a young man; a male*
ne ranekenhteron [ne ra-ne-kénh-te-ronh] *the young man*; **thiken' ranekenhteron** [thí:-ken'...] *that young man*; **kiken' ranekenhteron** [kí:-ken'...] *this young man*. With numericals: **shayàtat ranekenhteron** [s-ha-yà:-tat ra-ne-kénh-te-ronh] *one young man*; **tehniyahsen tehninekonteronh** [teh-ni-yáh-senh teh-ni-ne-kénh-teronh] *two young men*; **ahsen nihati ratinekenhteron** [áh-sen' nihá:-tih ra-ti-ne-kénh-te-ronh] *three young men*. With adjectivals: **rahnenyehs ranekenhteron** [rah-nén:-yehs...] *a tall young man*; **nihahnenyehsha ranekenhteron** [ni-hah-nen-yéhs-ha'] *a short young man*; **roya'tahkariyo ranekenhteron** [ro-ya'tak-ka-rí:-yo'...] *an agile young man*. (see: ratinekenhteron)

661   **raonha** [rá-on-ha'] *he, him (Free Pronoun)*
   Onhka ne'e ne raonha. [Ónh-ka' né:-'eh neh rá-on-ha'] *Who is he?*   **Raonha
   ne'e ne raktsi'a.** [Rá-on-ha' né:-'eh neh rak-tsí:-'ah] *He is my older brother.*
   For Emphasis: **Raonha rotorathonhne'.** *HE (is the one who) went hunting (but is
   not returned).*

662   **ratiksa'okonha** [ra-tik-sa'-o-kón-ha'] *children; male children: boys*
   ne ratiksa'okonha [ne ra-tik-sa'-o-kón-ha'] *the boys*;   **thiken' ratiksa'okonha**
   [thí:-ken'...] *those boys*;   **kiken' ratiksa'okonha** [kí:-ken'...] *these boys.*
   Ronatkahritsheronni' ne ratiksa'okonha. [Ro-nat-ka-hrits-he-rón:-ni' ne
   ra-tik-sa'-o-kón-ha'] *The boys are playing.*

663   **ratinekenhteron** [ra-ti-ne-kénh-te-ronh] *young men; males*
   ne ratinekenhteron [ne ra-ti-ne-kénh-te-ronh] *the young men*;   **thiken'
   ratinekenhteron** [thí:-ken'...] *those young men*;   **kiken' ratinekenhteron** [kí:-
   ken'...] *these young men.* (see: ranekenhteron)

664   **Ratirhakonha** [Ra-tir-ha-kón-ha'] *the Cree*

665   **ratitsyenhayens** [ra-ti-tsyén-ha-yens] *councillors (males)*
   ne ratitsyenhayens [ne ra-ti-tsyén-ha-yens] *the councillors*;   **thiken'
   ratitsyenhayens** [thí:-ken'...] *those councillors*;   **kiken' ratitsyenhayens** [kí:-
   ken'...] *these councillors.*   **Ronatkennihson ken ne ratitsyenhayens.** [Ro-nat-
   ken-níh-sonh kén ne ra-ti-tsyén-ha-yens] *Are the councillors are having a meeting?*
   (see: ratsyenhayens)

666   **ratorats** [ra-tó:-rats] *a hunter*
   ne ratorats [ne ra-tó:-rats] *the hunter*;   **thiken' ratorats** [thí:-ken'...] *that
   hunter*;   **kiken' ratorats** [kí:-ken'...] *this hunter.*   With numericals: **shayàtat
   ratorats** [s-ha-yà:-tat ra-tó:-rats] *one hunter*;   **tehniyahsen tehyatorats** [teh-ni-
   yáh-senh te-hya-tó:-rats] *two hunters*;   **ahsen nihati rontorats** [áh-sen' nihá:-
   tih ron-tó-rats] *three hunters.*   **Ratorats nen' ne'e.** [Ra-tó:-rats nen' né:-'eh] *He
   is a hunter*;   **Ratoratsheriyo nen' ne'e.** [Ra-to-rats-he-rí:-yoh nen' né:-'eh] *He
   is a good hunter*;   **Ratoratsheraksen nen' ne'e.** [Ra-to-rats-he-rák-senh nen'
   né:-'eh] *He is a poor hunter*;

667   **ratsyenhayens** [ra-tsyén-ha-yens] *a councillor (male)*
   ne ratsyenhayens [ne ra-tsyén-ha-yens] *the councillor*;   **thiken' ratsyenhayens**
   [thí:-ken'...] *that councillor*;   **kiken' ratsyenhayens** [kí:-ken'...] *this councillor.*

668   **Rawenniyo** [Ra-wen-ní:-yoh] *God*

669   **ri'kenha** [ri'-kén-ha'] *my younger brother*
   etshe'kenha [ets-he'-kén-ha'] *your younger brother*;   **ro'kenha** [ro'-kén-ha'] *his
   younger brother*;   **shako'kenha** [s-ha-ko'-kén-ha'] *her younger brother*;
   etshitewa'kenha [ets-hi-te-wa'-kén-ha'] *our younger brother.*

670 **riyen'a** [ri-yén:-ah] *my son*
etshyen'a [ets-hyén:-'ah] *your son*; **ronwayen'a** [ron-wa-yén:-'ah] *her son*;
etshitewayen'a [ets-hi-te-wa-yén:-'ah] *our son.*

671 **ro'kenha** [ro'-kén-ha'] *his younger brother* (see: ri'kenha)

672 **ro'niha** [ro'-ní-ha'] *his father* (See: rake'niha)

673 **ro'nihstenha** [ro'-nihs-tén-ha'] *his mother* (See: ake'nihstenha)

674 **rohskenhrakehte** [rohs-ken-hra-kéh-teh] *a warrior; a male*
ie. **ne rohskenhrakehte** [ne rohs-ken-hra-kéh-teh] *the warrior*; **thiken'**
rohskenhrakehte [thí:-ken'...] *that warrior*; **kiken rohskenhrakehte** [kí:-
ken'...] *this warrior.* With numericals: **shayàtat rohskenhrakehte** [s-ha-yà:-
tat rohs-ken-hra-kéh-teh] *one warrior*; **tehniyahsen tehniksa'a** [teh-ni-yáh-
senh te-ho-tihs-ken-hra-kéh-teh] *two warriors*; **ahsen nihati**
rotihskenhrakehte [áh-sen' nihá:-tih ro-tihs-ken-hra-kéh-teh] *three warriors.*
rotihskenhrakehte [ro-tihs-ken-hra-kéh-teh] *warriors.* **Ro'nikonhratshanit**
kiken' rohskenhrakehte. [Ro'-ni-kon-hrats-há:-niht...] *This warrior is brave.*

675 **rohsotha** [roh-hsót-ha'] *his grandfather / his grandmother* (See: rakhsotha)

676 **rohtsi'a** [roh-tsí:-'ah] *his older brother / his older sister* (See: raktsi'a)

677 **rokstenha** [rok-stén-ha'] *an old man*
ie. **ne rokstenha** [ne roks-tén-ha'] *the old man*; **thiken' rokstenha** [thí:-
ken'...] *that old man*; **kiken' rokstenha** [kí:-ken'...] *this old man*;
rotiksten'okonha [ro-tiks-ten'-o-kón-ha'] *old men.* With numericals:
shayàtat rokstenha [s-ha-yà:-tat rok-stén-ha'] *one old man*; **tehniyahsen**
tehnikstenha [teh-ni-yáh-senh teh-nik-stén-ha'] *two old men*; **ahsen nihati**
rotiksten'okonha [áh-sen' nihá:-tih ro-tik-sten'-o-kón-ha'] *three old men.*
Onhka nen' ne'e thiken' rokstenha. [Ónh-ka' nen' né:-'eh thí:-ken' roks-
tén-ha'] *Who is that old man?* **Rakhsotha nen' ne'e thiken' rokstenha.** [Rak-
hsót-ha' nen' né:-'eh thí:-ken' roks-tén-ha'] *That old man is my grandfather.*

678 **ronara'se'a** [ro-na-ra'-sé:-'ah] *his/her (male/female) cousin* (See: onkyara'se'a)

679 **ronatenron** [ro-na-tén:-ronh] *his / her (male/female) friend* (see: onkyatenron)

680 **rone** [ró:-neh] *spouse: her husband / his wife*

681 **ronkwe** [rón:-kwe'] *a male person; a man*
ie. **ne ronkwe** [ne rón:-kwe'] *the man*; **thiken' ronkwe** [thí:-ken'...] *that man*;
kiken' ronkwe [kí:-ken'...] *this man*; **rononkwe** [ro-nón:-kwe'] *men.* With
numericals: **shayàtat ronkwe** [s-ha-yà:-tat rón:-kwe'] *one boy*; **tehniyahsen**
tehnonkwe [teh-ni-yáh-senh teh-nón:-kwe'] *two men*; **ahsen nihati rononkwe**
[áh-sen' nihá:-tih ro-nón:-kwe'] *three men.*

682 **ronoha'a** [ro-no-há:-'ah] *his uncle* (See: rakenoha'a)

683 **rononha** [ro-nón-ha'] *they, them (males)(Free Pronoun)*
ie. **Onhka ne'e ne rononha.** [Ónh-ka' né:-'eh ne ro-nón:-ha'] *Who are they?*
Onkwatenroh ne'e ne rononha [On-kwa-tén:-ronh né:-'eh ne ro-nón:-ha']
They are my friends. For Emphasis: **Rononha rontorathonhne'** *THEY (are the ones who) went hunting (but are now returned).*

684 **rononkwe** [ro-nón:-kwe] *male persons; men*
ie. **ne rononkwe** [ne ro-nón:-kwe'] *the men;* **thiken' rononkwe** [thí:-ken'...]
those man; **kiken' rononkwe** [kí:-ken'...] *these man;* **ronkwe** [ro-nón:-kwe']
man.

685 **ronwa'kenha** [ron-wa'-kén-ha'] *her younger brother* (See: ri'kenha)

686 **ronwayen'a** [ron-wa-yén:-ah] *her son* (See: riyen'a)

687 **ronwayen'a** [ron-wa-yén:-ah] *his parents* (See: yonkyen'a)

688 **rotihskenhrakehte** [ro-tihs-ken-hra-kéh-teh] *warriors; males*
ie. **ne rotihskenhrakehte** [ne ro-tihs-ken-hra-kéh-teh] *the warriors;* **thiken'**
rotihskenhrakehte [thí:-ken'...] *those warriors;* **kiken' rotihskenhrakehte**
[kí:-ken'...] *these warriors.* (see: rohskenhrakehte)

689 **rotiksten'okonha** [ro-tik-sten'-o-kón-ha'] *old men; old people (males & females)*
ie. **ne rotiksten'okonha** [ne ro-tiks-ten'-o-kón-ha'] *the old men;* **thiken';**
rotiksten'okonha [thí:-ken'...] *those old men;* **kiken' rotiksten'okonha** [kí:-
ken'...] *these old men.* (see: rokstenha)

690 **Rotinonhsyonni** [Ro-ti-nonh-syón:-nih] *the Iroquois Confederacy*

691 **royen'a** [ro-yén:-ah] *his son* (See: riyen'a)

S

692 **sa'nihstenha** [sa'-nihs-tén-ha'] *your mother* (See: ake'nihstenha)

693 **sahsotha** [sah-sót-ha'] *your grandmother* (See: akhsotha)

694 **sahtsi'a** [sah-tsí:-'ah] *your older sister* (See: aktsi'a)

695 **se'** [se'] *indeed; definitely*
ie. **Raonha se' nahayere'.** [Rá-on-ha' se' na-há-ye-re'] *He definitely did it.*

a) **se' ok** [sók] *so then*

ie. **se' ok wahenron',** [sok wa-hén:-ron'] *so then he said,*

696 · **Sehske'kowa** [Sehs-ke'-kó:-wa'] *September*

697 **Sehskeha** [Sehs-ké-ha'] *August*

698 **sewahyowane** [se-wa-hyó:-wa-neh] *an apple*

ie. **Sewahyowane wakàyayen'** [Se-wa-hyó:-wa-ne' wa-kà:-ya-yen'] *I have (an) apple(s).* **sewahyowane tekahswàne** [...te-kah-swà:-ne'] *apple pie.*

699 **sewatyeren** [se-wa-tyé:-renh] *sometimes*

ie. **Sewatyeren ahsonhtakwekon enwakye'onh.** [...ah-son-ta-kwé:-konh en-wa-kyé:-'onh] *Sometimes I will be awake all night.*

700 **sha'tekon** [sha'-té:-konh] *eight*

ie. **sha'tekon nikon** [...ní:-konh] *(there's) eight of them (onjects)*; **sha'tekon nikonti** [...ni-kón:-tih] *(there's) eight of them (female / animal)*; **sha'tekon nihati** [...ni-há:-tih] *(there's) eight of them (male).* **sha'tekon-yawenre** [...-ya-wén:-reh] *eighteen*; **sha'tekon-niwahsen** [...-ni-wáh-senh] *eighty.* **sha'tekon nikatshètake** [...ni-kats-hè:-ta-keh] *eight bottles*; **sha'tekon niwakyen'** [...ni-wák-yen'] *I have eight*; **sha'tekon niwaketshètayen'** [...ni-wa-kets-hè:-ta-yen'] *I have eight bottles.*

701 **shako'kenha** [sha-ko'-kén-ha'] *his younger sister* (See: khe'kenha)

702 **shako'niha** [sha-ko'-ní-ha'] *her father* (See: rake'niha)

703 **shakohsotha** [sha-koh-sót-ha'] *her grandfather* (See: rakhsotha)

704 **shakohtsi'a** [sha-koh-tsí:-'ah] *her older brother* (See: raktsi'a)

705 **shakonoha'a** [sha-ko-no-há:-'ah] *her uncle* (See: rakenoha'a)

706 **shakoyen'a** [sha-ko-yén:-ah] *his daughter* (See: kheyen'a)

707 **shayàtat** [sha-yà:-tat] *one (male individual)*

ie. **shayàtat ronkwe** [s-ha-yà:-tat rón:-kwe'] *one man*; **shayàtat raksa'a** [s-ha-yà:-tat rak-sá:-'ah] *one boy.* **shayàtat ne rononkwe** [s-ha-yà:-tat ro-nón:-kwe'] *one of the men*; **shayàtat ne ratiksa'okonha** [s-ha-yà:-tat ne ra-tik-sa'-o-kón-ha'] *one of the boys.* **Shayàtat wahatoratha'.** [...wa-ha-to-rát-ha'] *one (of them) went hunting.*

708 **she'kenha** [she'-kén-ha'] *your younger sister* (See: khe'kenha)

709 **shekon** [shé:-konh] *still*

ie. **Shekon yokennoren'.** [Shé:-konh yo-ken-nó:-ren'] *It's still raining.*

a) **shekon are** [she-konh á:-reh] *yet again; still again*

    ie. **Shekon are tenthahtenti'.** [She-konh á:-reh tent-hah-tén:-ti'] *He will still come back again.*

b) **shekon oya** [she-konh ó:-ya'] *somemore*

    ie. **Shekon oya' sakhninon'** [She-kon ó:-ya' sak-hní:-non'] *I bought somemore.*

710 **sheyen'a** [she-yén:-ah] *your daughter* (See: kheyen'a)

711 **shiyòkarahs** [shi-yó:-ka-rahs] *last night*

    ie. **Shiyòkarahs tontakewe'.** [Shi-yò:-ka-rahs ton-tà:-ke-we'] *I returned last night.* Also: **oya' shityòkarahs** [ó:-ya' shi-tyò:-ka-rahs] *the night before last.*

712 **shonkwa'niha** [shon-kwa'-ní-ha'] *our father* (See: rake'niha)

713 **shonkwahsotha** [shon-kwah-sót-ha'] *our grandfather* (See: rakenoha'a)

714 **shonkwahtsi'a** [shon-kwah-tsí:-'ah] *our older brother* (See: raktsi'a)

715 **shonkwanoha'a** [shon-kwa-no-há:-'ah] *our uncle* (See: rakenoha'a)

716 **Shonkwaya'tihson** [Shon-kwa-ya'-tíh-sonh] *the Creator*

717 **Shotinontowane'hàka** [Sho-ti-non-to-wa-ne'-hà:-kah] *the Seneca nation*

718 **siksik** [sík-sik] *a sheep*

    ie. **aketshenen siksik** [a-kets-hé:-nen...] *my sheep.* **Siksik wakenahskwayen'.** [...wa-ke-náhs-kwa-yen'] *I have (some) sheep.*

719 **ska'nyonhsa** [ska'-nyónh-sa'] *a moose*

720 **skahwihstat** [ska-hwíhs-tat] *one dollar*

    Also: **tekahwihstake** [te-ka-hwíhs-ta-keh] *two dollars*; **ahsen nikahwihstake** [áh-sen' ni-ka-hwíhs-ta-keh] *three dollars.* **Skahwihstathson** [ska-hwihs-táth-hsonh] *each dollar*; **niya'tekahwihstake** [ni-ya'-te-ka-hwíhs-ta-keh] *every dollar.*

721 **skakahraksen** [ska-ka-hrák-senh] *a pickerel (fish)*

722 **skanekwenhtarati** [ska-ne-kwenh-ta-rá:-tih] *raspberries*

723 **skawerowane** [ska-we-ró:-wa-ne'] *a turkey*

724 **skayàtat** [ska-yà:-tat] *one (animate individual)*

    ie. **akwah ne ok ne'e shayàtat erhar** [kwah-nék né: ska-yà:-tat ér-har] *just only the one dog*; **skayàtat ki' ok erhar** [ska-yà:-tat kok ér-har] *only one dog*; **skayàtat erhar** [ska-yà:-tat ér-har] *one dog*; **skayàtat ne erharhokonha** [...ne er-har-ho-kón-ha'] *one of the dogs*; **skayàtat ne aketshenen'okonha erhar** [...ne a-kets-he-nen'-ó-konh ér-har] *one of my dogs.* **Skayàtat wakenahskwayen'.** [...wa-ke-náhs-kwa-yen'] *I have one (animal).*

725 skennen [skén-nenh] *peace; tranquillity*

ie. **Skennen kenhak!** [Skén:-nenh kén-hak] *Let there be peace!*

726 skennenha [sken-nén-ha'] *quiet; peaceful*

ie. **Skennenha tsi ratatis.** [Sken-nén-ha' tsi ra-tá:-tis] *He is a quiet speaker.*

727 skennenhahson'a [ske-nen-hah-són:-'ah] *softly; quietly; speacefully*

ie. **Skennenhahson'a tsi ire'.** [Sken-nen-hah-són:-'ah tsi í:-re'] *He walks softly, quietly.*

728 sorak [só:-rak] *a duck*

ie. **kakowanen sorak** [ka-ko-wá:-nenh...] *a large duck*; **niwa'ah sorak** [ni-wá:-'ah...] *a small duck*; **aketshenen sorak** [a-kets-hé:-nenh...] *my (pet) duck*; **Sorak wakenahskwayen'** [...wa-ke-náhs-kwa-yen'] *I have (some / a) duck(s)*. **yotityohkowanen sorak** [yo-ti-tyoh-ko-wá:-nenh só:-rak] *a flock of ducks (on the ground)*; **yotityohkwaratye' sorak** [yo-ti-tyoh-ko-wá:-nenh só:-rak] *a flock of ducks (in the air)*.

T

729 tahnon [táh-non'] *and; besides*

ie. **Raonha tahnon ne i'i** [Rá-on-ha' táh-non' ní:-'ih] *He and I*; **onònta tahnon otsikhèta** [o-nòn:-ta' tah-non' o-tsi-k-hè:-ta'] *milk and (besides) sugar*. (See: nok)

730 take' [tá:-ke'] *I am coming* (E-Stem - Subj.)

ie. **tiwakenonh** [ti-wa-ké:-nonh] *I have come / did come*; **tonkenonhatye** [ton-ke-non-há-tye'] *I was coming*.

731 takohs [ta-kóhs] *a cat*

ie. **kakowanen takohs** [ka-ko-wá:-nenh...] *(it's a) a big cat*; **niwa'ah takohs** [ni-wá:-'ah...] *(it's) a small cat*; **owira takohs** [o-wí:-ra' ta-kóhs] *a kitten*. **aketshenen takohs** [a-kets-hé:-nenh...] *my cat*; **Takohs wakenahskwayen'.** [Ta-kóhs wa-ke-náhs-kwa-yen'] *I have a cat*.

732 taonhtaneken [ta-onh-ta-né:-ken'] *a rabbit; a jack rabbit*

733 taraktarak [ta-rák-ta-rak] *a cricket*

734 tawine [ta-wí:-neh] *an otter*

735 tehniksa'a [teh-nik-sá:-'ah] *two children (male & female); two boys* (See: raksa'a)

736 **tehnikstenha** [teh-nik-stén-ha'] *two old men; two old people (male & female)* (See: rokstenha)

737 **tehnìteron** [teh-nì:-te-ron'] *his spouse / her spouse* (See: teyakenìteron)

738 **tehniyahsen** [teh-ni-yáh-senh] *two (male individuals)* (See: tekeni)

739 **tekahshenthos** [te-kahs-hént-hos] *I cry / am crying* (A-Stem - Subj.) **wa'tkahshentho'** [wa'-t-kahs-hént-ho'] *I cried;* **tewakahshenthonh** [te-wa-kahs-hént-honh] *I did cry / have cried.* ie. **Tohsa tehsahshentho** [Tóh-sa te-sahs-hént-ho] *Don't cry!* **Wa'tyonhshentho' ne takhenonke'.** [Wa'-tyonhs-hént-ho' ne tak-hé:-non-ke'] *She cried to be fed.*

740 **tekahstya'ks** [te-káhs-tya'ks] *a parrot*

741 **tekahwihstake** [te-ka-hwíhs-ta-keh] *a two dollar bill* (See: skahwihstat)

742 **tekanyen'kwatase** [te-ka-nyen'-kwa-tá:-seh] *there is a snowstorm*

743 **tekarihstoraraks** [te-ka-rihs-tò:-ra-raks] *typewriter*

744 **tekatawenryehs** [te-ka-ta-wén-ryehs] *I travel (about)* (A-Stem - Subj.) **wa'tkatawenrye'** [wa'-t-ka-ta-wén-rye'] *I travelled;* **tewakatawenrye'onh** [te-wa-ka-ta-wen-ryé-honh] *I have travelled / did travel.*

745 **tekatens** [te-ká:-tenhs] *airplane*

746 **tekatèntsha's** [te-ka-tèn:-ts-ha's] *I score (a goal); I profit from* (A-Stem - - Subj.) **wa'tkatèntsha'** [wa't-ka-tèn:-ts-ha'] *I scored...;* **tewakatèntshonh** [te-wa-ka-tèn:-ts-honh] *I have scored / did score....*

747 **tekatkaryas** [te-kat-kár-yas] *I run out of; I am in need of* (A-Stem - - Subj.) **wa'tkatkari'** [wa't-kat-ká:-ri'] *I ran out of...;* **wakatkaryenh** [wa-kat-kár-yenh] *I have run / did run out of....*

748 **tekato'tsinehtha'** [te-ka-to'-tsi-néht-ha'] *I skate* (A-Stem - Subj.) **wa'tkato'tsinehte'** [wa't-ka-to'-tsí:-neh-te'] *I skated;* **tewakato'tsinehtonh** [te-wa-ka-to'-tsi-néh-tonh] *I have skated / did skate.*

749 **tekatskàhonhs** [te-kats-kà:-honhs] *I eat a meal* (A-Stem - Subj.) **wa'tkatskàhon'** [wa'-t-kats-kà:-hon'] *I ate a meal;* **Tewakatskàhonh** [te-wa-kats-kà:-honh] *I have eaten / did eat; I am eating.*

750 **tekawenryehs** [te-ka-wén-ryehs] *I stir something (about)* (A-Stem - Subj.) **wa'tkawenrye'** [wa'-t-ka-wén-rye'] *I stirred something...;* **tewakawenryehonh** [te-wa-ka-wen-ryé-honh] *i have stirred / did stir....*

751 **tekaweratase** [te-ka-we-ra-tá:-seh] *there is a tornado*

752 **tekehkwa'** [te-kéh-kwa'] *I pick something up* (E-Stem - Subj.)

wàtkehkwe' [wà:-t-keh-kwe'] *I picked something up*; **tewakehkwenh** [te-wa-kéh-kwenh] *i have picked something up.*

753 **tekehtahkwa'** [te-keh-táh-kwa'] *I believe* (E-Stem - Subj.)
takehtahkwe' [ta-kéh-tah-kwe'] *I believed*; **tiwakehtahkwenh** [ti-wa-keh-táh-kwenh] *I have believed / did believe.*

754 **tekenera'ks** [te-ke-né-ra'ks] *I mistake s.t. (one for another)* (C-Stem - Subj.)
wa'tkenerya'ke' [wa'-t-ke-né-ra'-ke'] *I mistook something...*; **tewakenerenh** [te-wa-ke-né-renh] *I have mistaken / did mistake....* With nominals:
tekenhniseranera'ks [te-kenh-ni-se-ra-né-raks] *I mistake the date*;
tekhyatonhseraneraks [tek-hya-tonh-se-ra-né-raks] *I mistake the book.*

755 **tekeni** [té-ke-nih] *two*
With nominals: **tekatshètake** [te-kats-hè:-ta-keh] *two bottles*; **teyohserake** [te-yoh-se-rá:-keh] *two years*; **tewahtahkwake** [te-wah-tah-kwá:-keh] *two (pair of) shoes.* See also: **tekeniyahsen** [te-ke-ni-yáh-sen'] *two (female / animals)*: ie. **tekeniyahsen tekenonkwe** [...te-ke-nón:-kwe'] *two women*; **tekeniyahsen erhar** [...ér-har] *two dogs.* **tehniyahsen** [teh-ni-yáh-sen'] *two (males)*: ie. **tehniyahsen tehniksa'a** [...teh-nik-sá:-'ah] *two boys.*

756 **Tekenihatont** [Te-ke-ní-ha-tont] *Tuesday*
shiTekenihaton'kenha [shi-te-ke-ni-ha-ton'-kén-ha'] *last Tuesday.*

757 **tekeniksa'a** [te-ke-nik-sá:-'ah] *two female children; two girls* (See: yeksa'a)

758 **tekenikstenha** [te-ke-nik-stén-ha'] *two old women* See: akokstenha)

759 **tekeniyahsen** [te-ke-ni-yáh-senh] *two (female / animate individuals)* (See: tekeni)

760 **tekenni'tsyonhkwahkwa'** [te-ken-ni'-tsyonh-kwáh-kwa'] *I jump* (En-Stem - Subj.) **wa'thenni'tsyonhkwahkwe'** [wa'-t-hen-ni'-tsyónh-kwah-kwe'] *I jumped*; **tewakenni'tsyonhkwahkwenh** [te-wa-ken-ni'tsyonh-kwáh-kwenh] *I did jump / have jumped*; **tewakenni'tsyonhkwahkwenhatye'** [te-wa-ken-ni'-tsyonh-kwah-kwenh-há-tye'] *I am jumping (right along).*

761 **tekenonnyahkwa'** [te-ke-non-nyáh-kwa'] *I dance* (C-Stem - Subj.)
wa'tkenonnyahkwe' [wa'-t-ke-nón:-nyah-kwe'] *I danced*;
tewakenonnyahkwenh [te-wa-ke-non-nyáh-kwenh] *I did dance / have danced; I am dancing.*

762 **tekhna'neta's** [tek-hna'-né-ta's] *I copy, duplicate* (C-Stem - Subj.)
wa'tekhna'neta' [Wa'-tek-hna'-né-ta'] *I copied...*; **tewakhna'netenh** [te-wak-hna'-né-tenh] *I have copied / did copy....*

763 **tekhrihtha'** [tek-hríht-ha'] *I break s.t.* (C-Stem - Subj.)
wa'tekhrihte' [wa'-ték-hrih-te'] *I broke*; **tewakhrihtonh** [te-wak-hríh-tonh] *I did break / have broken*; Also: **tekhrihtanyons** [tek-hrih-tá-nyons] *I break*

87

something up.

764 **tekhwihshenheyes** [tek-hwihs-hén-he-yes] *I become tired* (C-Stem - verb)
wa'tekhwihshenheye' [wa'-tek-hwihs-hén-he-ye'] *I became tired;*
tewakhwihshenheyonh [te-wak-hwihs-hen-hé:-yonh] *I have become tired / I am tired.*

765 **tekkanere'** [tek-ká-ne-re'] *I am looking at s.t.* (C-Stem - Subj.)
wa'tekkanere' [wa'-tek-ká-ne-re'] *I looked at...;* **tewakkanereh** [te-wak-ká-ne-reh] *I did look at / have looked at....*

766 **tekta's** [ték-ta's] *I stand up / stop* (C-Stem - Subj.)
wa'tektane' [wa'-ték-ta'-ne'] *I stood up / stopped;* **tewakta'onh** [te-wak-tá:-'onh] *I have stood up / did stand up; have stopped / did stop; I am standing.*

767 **tektenyes** [tek-té-nyes] *I change* (C-Stem - Subj.)
wa'tekteni' [wa'-tek-té:-ni'] *I changed;* **tewaktenyonh** [te-wak-té-nyonh] *I have changed / did change;* Also: **tekattenyes** [te-kat-té-nyes] *I become changed.*

768 **tekya'ks** [té-kya'ks] *I cut in half / break in two* (C-Stem - Subj.)
wa'tekya'ke' [wa'-té-kya'-ke'] *I cut in two / broke in half;* **tewakyàkonh** [te-wa-kyà:-konh] *I have / did cut in two; I have broken / did break in half.*

769 **tekyens** [té-kyens] *I gamble / play card* (C-Stem - Subj.)
wa'tekyen' [wa'-té-kyen'] *I gambled / played cards;* **tewakyenh** [te-wák-yen'] *I have gambled / did gamble; have played / did play cards.*

770 **tesenìteron** [teh-se-nì:-te-ron'] *your spouse, partner*

771 **tewahsen** [te-wáh-senh] *twenty*
ie. **tewahsen-enhskat** [te-wáh-senh - énhs-kat] *twenty-one;* **tewahsen-tekeni** [...- té-ke-nih] *twenty-two;* **tewahsen-ahsen** [...- áh-sen'] *twenty-three;* **tewahsen-kayeri** [...- ka-yé:-rih] *twenty-four;* **tewahsen-wisk** [...- wíhsk] *twenty-five;* **tewahsen-yayak** [...- yá:-yak] *twenty-six;* **tewahsen-tsyatak** [...-tsyá:-tak] *twenty-seven;* **tewahsen-sha'tekon** [...- sha'-té:-konh] *twenty-eight;* **tewahsen-tyohton** [...- tyóh-tonh] *twenty-nine.*

772 **tewakatonhwentsyoni** [te-wa-ka-ton-hwen-tsyó:-nih] *I want / need* (C-Stem - Obj.) **tewakatonhwentsyonihne'** [te-wa-ka-ton-hwen-tsyo-níh-ne'] *I wanted...;* **tenwakatonhwentsyonihake'** [ten-wa-ka-ton-hwen-tsyo-ní-ha-ke'] *I will be wanting...;* **taonkwatonhwenstyonihake'** [ta-on-kwa-ton-hwen-tsyo-ní-ha-ke'] *I would be / for me to be wanting....*

773 **tewakeka** [te-wa-ké:-kah] *I am a fast runner* (C-Stem - Obj.)
tewakekahkwe' [te-wa-ké:-kah-kwe'] *I was a fast runner;* **tenwakekahake'** [ten-wa-ke-ká-ha-ke'] *i will be a fast runner;* **taonkekahake'** [ta-on-ke-ká-ha-ke'] *I would be . for me to be a fast runner.*

774 **tewakhsterihenhs** [te-wak-hste-rí-henhs] *I hurry* (C-Stem - Obj.)
wa'tewakhsterihen' [wa'-te-wak-hste-rí-hen'] *I hurried*; **tewakhsterihen'onh**
[te-wak-hste-ri-hén:-'onh] *I have hurried / did hurry.*

775 **tewakhsterihenh** [te-wak-hste-rí-henh] *I am in a hurry* (C-Stem - Obj.)
tewakhsterihenhne' [te-wak-hste-ri-hénh-ne'] *I was in a hurry*;
tenwakhsterihenh [ten-wak-hste-rí-henh] *I will be in a hurry*; **taonkhsterihenh**
[ta-onk-hste-rí-henh] *I have been in a hurry / for me to have been in a hurry.*

776 **tewakhwihshenheyon** [te-wak-hwihs-hen-hé:-yonh] *I am tired* (C-Stem -
Obj.) **tewakhwihshenheyonhne'** [te-wak-hwihs-hen-he-yónh-ne'] *I was tired*;
tenwakhwihshenheyonh [ten-wak-hwihs-hen-hé:-yonh] *I will be tired*;
taonkhwihshenheyonh [ta-onk-hwihs-hen-hé:-yonh] *I would be tired / for me to
be tired.*

777 **tewaki'tsyonkha'** [te-wa-ki'-tsyónk-ha'] *I sneeze* (I-Stem - Obj.)
wa'tewaki'tsyonke' [wa'-te-wa-kí'-tsyon-ke'] *I sneezed*; **tewaki'tsyonkenh**
[te-wa-ki'tsyón:-kenh] *I have sneezed / did sneeze.*

778 **tewen'nyawe'ehseron** [te-wen'nya-we'-éh-se-ronh] *thousand*
ie. **enhskat-tewen'nyawe'ehseron** [énhs-kat -...] *one thousand*; **tekeni-**
tewen'nyawe'ehseron [té-ke-nih -...] *two thousand*; **ahsen-**
tewen'nyawe'ehseron [áh-sen' -...] *three thousand.*

779 **tewen'nyawer** [te-wen'-nyá-wer] *hundred*
ie. **enhskat-tewen'nyawer** [énhs-kat -...] *one hundred*; **tekeni-tewen'nyawer**
[té-ke-nih -...] *two hundred*; **ahsen-tewen'nyawer** [áh-sen' -...] *three hundred.*

780 **tewennine'karahwanyon's** [te-wen-ni-ne'-ka-rah-wá-nyons] *it lightnings*

781 **teyekhahstha** [te-yek-háhst-ha'] *glue*

782 **teyo'seretsheràka** [te-yo'-se-re'ts-he-rà:-kah] *train*

783 **teyohiyòtsihs** [te-yo-hyó:-tsihs] *it is salty*

784 **teyohsahe'tahnekonnyàtha** [te-yoh-sa-he'-tah-ne-kon-nyà:t-ha'] *coffee*

785 **teyohstarathe'** [te-yoh-sta-rát-he'] *it is shiney*
teyohstarathehkwe' [te-yohs-ta-rát-heh-kwe'] *it was shiney.*

786 **teyohswathe'** [te-yoh-swát-he'] *it is bright*
teyohswathehkwe' [te-yoh-swát-heh-kwe'] *it was bright.*

787 **teyontenyàteren'** [te-yon-te-nyà:-te-ren'] *a scarf; a necktie*

788 **teyoteryen'thara** [te-yo-ter-yen'-thá:-ra'] *it is dangerous*
ie. **Sotsi teyoteryen'thara ne' eh yahonne'.** [Só-tsih te-yo-ter-yen'-thá:-ra'
ne' éh yáh-se'] *It is too dangerous for you to go there.*

789 **teyotonhwentsyohon** [te-yo-ton-hwen-tsyó-honh] *it is necessary*
    ie. **Teyotonhwentsyohon ne aonkyo'tensha'** [te-yo-ton-hwen-tsyó-honh na-on-kyo'-téns-ha'] *It is necessary for me to go to work.*

790 **teyotshàkton** [te-yots-hà:-k-tonh] *it is crooked; curved*

791 **teyottsikhètare** [te-yot-tsi-khè:-ta-reh] *it is sweet*
    ie. **Sotsi teyottsikhètare** [Só-tsih te-yot-tsi-khè:-ta-reh] *it too is sweet*; **Yah e'tho tha'teyottsikhètare** [Yah é'-t-ho tha'-te-yot-tsi-khè:-ta-reh] *it is not sweet enough.*

792 **thetenre** [the-tén:-reh] *yesterday*
    ie. **Thetenre wakyo'tenshonhne'** [the-tén:-reh wa-kyo'tens-hónh-ne'] *Yesterday I went to work.*

793 **thiken'** [thí:-ken'] *that (one)*
    ie. **Thiken ne'e ne érhar.** [thí;-ken' né:-'eh ne ér-har] *That (one) is a dog;* **Thiken' erhar** [thí:-ken' ér-har] *That dog.*

794 **Thiyaweronhatye'** [thi-ya-we-ron-há-tye'] *it doesn't matter; Never mind!*
    (See: yaweronhatye')

795 **tho ok nikon** [tho'k ní:-konh] *a few of...*
    ie. **tho ok nikon nikahyatonhserake** [thok ní:-konh ni-ka-hya-tonh-se-rá:-keh] *a few books;* **tho ok nikon ne kahyatonhseraokon** [thok ní:-konh ne ka-hya-tonh-se-ra'-ó:-konh] *a few of the books;*

796 **thoha** [thó-ha'] *nearly*
    ie. **Thoha wisk niyohwihsta'e.** [Thó-ha' wíhsk ni-yo-hwihs-tá:-'eh] *It's nearly five o'clock.*

797 **tkakonte** [tká:-kon-teh] *have to*
    ie. **Tkakonte aonkyo'tensha'** [...a-on-kyo'-téns-ha'] *I have to go to work;* **Tkakonte onkyo'tensha'** [...on-kyo'-téns-ha'] *I had to go to work;* **Tkakonte enwakyo'tensha'** [...en-wa-kyo'-téns-ha'] *I will have to go to work.*

798 **tkataweyàtha'** [t-ka-ta-we-yà:-t-ha'] *I come in* (A-Stem - Subj.) **takataweya'te** [ta-ka-tá:-we-ya'-te] *I came in;* **tewakataweyàtonh** [ti-wa-ka-ta-we-yà:-tonh] *I have come / did come in; I am inside.* (see: yekataweyàtha')

799 **tkathsnenhtha'** [t-kat-hsnenht-ha'] *I come down (from there to here)* (A-Stem - Subj.) **takathsnenhte'** [ta-káths-nenh-te'] *I came down;* **tiwakathsnenhtonh** [ti-wa-kaths-nénh-tonh] *I have / did come down; I am down.*

800 **tkatirontha'** [t-ka-ti-rónt-ha'] *I pull (on something)* (A-Stem - Subj.) **takatironten'** [ta-ka-ti-rón:-ten'] *I pulled...;* **tiwakatironteh** [ti-wa-ka-tí:-ron-teh] *I have pulled / did pull....*

801 tkayeri [t-ka-yé:-rih] *it is right, proper*

802 tkennonhtons [t-ken-nónh-tons] *I control / have control of s.t.*
takennonhton' [ta-ken-nónh-ton'] *I controlled / had control...*;
tiwakennonhtonh [ti-wa-ken-nónh-tonh] *I have controlled / did control.*

803 tkerathenhs [t-ke-rát-henhs] *I climb up (from there to here)*
takerathen' [ta-ke-rát-hen'] *I climbed up*; **tiwakerathen'onh** [ti-wa-ke-rat-hén:-'onh] *I have climbed / did climb up....*

804 tkherihwa'serakwas [t-k-he-ri-hwa'-se-rá-kwas] *I answer her / them*
takherihwa'serako' [tak-he-rih-wa'-se-rá:-ko'] *I answered her / them*;
tikherihwa'serakwenh [tik-he-rih-wa'-se-rá-kwenh] *I have asnwered/ did answer her / them.*

805 tkyaken's [t-kyá:-ken's] *I go in*
takyakenne' [ta-kyá:-ken'-ne'] *I went in*; **tiwakyaken'onh** [ti-wak-ya-kén:-'onh] *I have gone in / did go in; I am inside.*

806 to [to] *how*
ie. **To nitisayen'** [To ni-ti-sá:-yen'] *How old are you?* **To nisayen'** [To ni-sá:-yen'] *How many do you have?*

a) **to nikarìwehs** [to ni-ka-rì:-wehs] *how long (does it take)?*
ie. **To nikarìwehs tsi sahtahkonnis.** [...tsi sah-tah-kón:-nis] *How long does it take to make moccasins?*

b) **to nikon** [to ní:-konh] *how many?*
ie. **To nikon sahninonh.** [...sah-ní:-nonh] *How many did you buy?*

c) **to niyenhs** [to ní:-yenhs] *how long is it?*
ie. **To niyenhs ne ahseriye' ratstha'.** [...ne ah-se-rí:-ye' rátst-ha'] *How long is the rope he's using?*

d) **to niyoht** [to ní:-yoht] *how is it?*
ie. **To niyoht tsi nahatyere'.** [...tsi na-há-tye-re'] *How did he do it?*

e) **to niyore** [to ni-yó:-reh] *how far is it?*
ie. **To niyore tesatawenrye'onhne'.** [...te-sa-ta-wen-rye'-ónh-ne'] *How far did you travel?*

807 tohka [tóh-ka'] *several*
ie. **tohka nikahyatonhserake** [...ni-ka-hya-tonh-se-rá:-keh] *several books.*

808 tokat [tó-kat'] *if; perhaps*
ie. **Yenkataweya'te' tokat enyokennore'.** [Yen-ka-tá:-we-ya'-te' tó-ka' en-yo-kén:-no-re'] *I will go inside if it rains.*

a) **tokat nonwa** [to-kat-nón:-wa'] *maybe; perhaps now*

ie. **Tokat nonwa yenkataweya'te' tokat ayokennore'.** [To-ka' nón:-wa' yen-ka-tá:-we-ya'-te' tó-ka' a-yo-kén:-no-re'] *Maybe I will go in if it rains (should rain).*

809 **tokenhske'** [tó:-kenh-ske'] *truly*

ie. **Tokenhske tsi nihronkwe'tiyo.** [...tsi ni-hron-kwe'-tí:-yoh] *He is truly a nice man.*

810 **tsi** [tsi] *at, to; when; where; that*

ie. **tsi kanhokàronte** [tsi kan-ho-kà:-ron-teh] *doorway; at the door,* **Akta tsi kanhokàronte ithrate'.** [Ák-ta' tsi kan-ho-kà:-ron-teh ít-hra-te'] *He is standing beside the doorway.*

a) **tsi kanonhsiyo** [tsi ka-nonh-sí:-yoh] *livingroom; in the livingroom*

b) **tsi kenhyenahninons** [tsi ken-hye-nah-ní:-nons] *gas station*

c) **tsi nahe** [tsi ná-heh] *since; ago*

ie. **Wisk niyohserake tsi nahe wa'thyaterane'.** [Wihsk ni-yoh-se-rá:-keh tsi ná-heh wa'-t-hyá-te-ra'-ne'] *I met him five years ago.*

d) **tsi nahòten** [tsi na-hò:-ten'] *with what; by what*

ie. **Wake'nikonhrahseriyo tsi nahòten wahakhrori'.** [Wa-ke'-ni-kon-hrah-se-rí:-yoh tsi na-hò:-ten' wa-hak-hró:-ri'] *I pleased with what he told me.*

e) **tsi nen nahe** [tsi nen ná-heh] *since; ago*

ie. **Eso niyohserake tsi nen nahe tkhekenhne'.** [É:-soh ni-yoh-se-rá:-keh tsi nen ná-heh t-khe-kénh-ne'] *It's been many years since I (last) saw her.*

f) **tsi nikarìwehs** [tsi ni-ka-rì:-wehs] *during the time (that)*

ie. **Wa'keksoharenyon' tsi nikarìwehs yehoyaken'onh.** [Wa'-kek-so-ha-ré-nyon' tsi ni-ka-rì:wehs ye-ho-ya'-kén:-'onh] *I washed dishes during the time he was out.*

g) **tsi nikayen'** [tsi ni-ká:-yen'] *the one (who)*

h) **tsi niwahsontehs** [tsi ni-wah-són:-tehs] *during the night*

ie. **Tsi niwahsontehs kanatakon thoyo'tenhs.** [...ka-ná:-ta-konh t-ho-yó'-tenhs] *He works in town during the night.*

i) **tsi niwenhniserehs** [tsi ni-wenh-ní:-se-reh] *during the day*

ie. **Ranònwe's ne ahotahwe' tsi niwenhniserehs.** [Ra-nòn:-we's na-hó:-tah-we' tsi ni-wenh-ní:-se-rehs] *He likes to sleep during the day.*

j) **tsi niwenhnìtehs** [tsi ni-wenh-nì:-tehs] *during the month*

k) **tsi niyohserehs** [tsi ni-yóh-se-rehs] *during the year*

l) **tsi niyohsnore tsi** [tsi ni-yoh-snó:-reh tsi] *as fast as*

ie. **Wa'tharahtate' tsi niyohsnore tsi wahakweni'.** [Wa'-t-ha-ráh-ta-te' tsi ni-yohs-nó:-reh tsi wa-ha-kwé:-ni'] *He ran as fast as he was able to.*

m) **tsi niyoht ne** [tsi ní:-yoht ne] *than*
   ie. **Senha yekowanen tsi niyoht ne raonha.** [Sén-ha' ye-ko-wá:-nenh tsi ní:-yoht ne rá-on-ha'] *She is bigger than he.*

n) **tsi niyoht tsi** [tsi ní:-yoht tsi] *as; with the way that*
   ie. **Wakenehrakwas tsi niyoht tsi nahatyere'.** [Wa-ke-ne-hrá-kwas tsi ní:-yoht tsi na-há-tye-re'] *I am surprised with the way he did it / went about it.*

o) **tsi niyore tsi** [tsi ni-yó:-reh tsi] *as far as*
   ie. **Wa'tyakyareron' tsi niyore tsi tkeritote.** [Wa'-tya-ka-ré:-ron' tsi ni-yó:-reh tsi-t ker-hí:-to-teh] *We raced as far as the tree (standing there).*

p) **tsi niyore** [tsi ni-yó:-reh] *until*
   ie. **Enwakyo'tenhseke' tsi niyore enyokennore.** [En-wa-kyo'-ténh-se-ke' tsi ni-yó:-reh en-yo-kén:-no-reh] *I will work until it rains.*

q) **tsi nonwe** [tsi nón:-weh] *where; at the place of / where*
   ie. **Wahakhrori tsi nonwe nihoyo'te'.** [Wa-hak-hró:-ri' tsi nón:-weh ni-ho-yó'-te'] *He told me where he is working.*

r) **tsi ok nahòten** [tsyok na-hò:-ten'] *with something*
   ie. **Wahakwatako' tsi ok nahòten ratstha' wahahninon'.** [Wa-ha-kwa-tá:-ko' tsyok na-hò:-ten' rátst-ha' wa-hah-ní:-non'] *He fixed it using something he bought / with something he bought.*

s) **tsi ok niyore** [tsyok ni-yó:-reh] *just until*
   ie. **Wa'thontawenrye' tsi ok niyore wahontonhkarya'ke'.** [Wa'-t-hon-ta-wén-rye' tsyok ni-yó:-reh wa-hon-tonh-kár-ya'-ke'] *They travelled just until they got hungry.*

t) **tsi ok niyore tsi** [tsyok ni-yó:-reh tsi] *just / only as far as*
   ie. **Wa'tyakyareron' tsi ok niyore tsi tkeritote.** [Wa'-tya-ka-ré:-ron' tsyok ni-yó:-reh tsi-t ker-hí:-to-teh] *We raced only / just as far as the tree (standing there).*

u) **tsi ok nonwe** [tsyok nón:-weh] *somewhere; someplace; sometime*
   ie. **Kanatakon tsi ok nonwe yahahninon'.** [Ka-ná:-ta-kon tsyok nón:-weh ya-hah-ní:-non'] *He bought in town someplace;* **Tsi ok nonwe thetenre yehohninonronhne'.** [...the-tén:-reh ye-hoh-ni-non-rónh-ne'] *He went shopping somethime yesterday.*

v) **tsi tetkanonnyahkwa** [tsi tet-ka-non-nyáh-kwa'] *at the dance*
   ie. **Tsi tetkanonnyahkwa wa'tyakyaterane' kiken' tsyakothonwisen.** [...wa'-tya-kyá-te-ra'-ne' kí:-ken' tsya-kot-hon-wí:-senh] *I met this young woman at the dance.*

w) **tsi teyonto'tsinehtahkwa** [tsi yon-to'-tsi-neh-táh-kwa'] *hockey rink; arena*

x) **tsi teyontska'honhkwa** [tsi te-yont-ska'-hónh-kwa'] *restaurant*

y) **tsi teyontskàhons** [tsi te-yonts-kà:-hons] *diningroom; in the diningroom*

z) **tsi teyothyohsate** [tsi te-yot-hyóh-sa-teh] *at the corner*
   ie. **Tsi teyothyohsate ithrate' ne ranekenhteron.** [...ít-hra-te' ne ra-ne-kénh-te-ron'] *The young man is standing at the corner.*

aa) **tsi yakoheyon'tayentahkwa** [tsi ya-ko-he-yon'-ta-yen-táh-kwa'] *the hospital*

bb) **tsi yekhonnyàtha** [tsi yek-hon-nyà:-tha'] *kitchen; in the kitchen*

cc) **tsi yekhwahninons** [tsi yek-hwah-ní:-nons] *grocery store*

dd) **tsi yeksayentahkwa** [tsi -yek-sa-yen-táh-kwa'] *a cupboard; in the cupbroad*
   ie. **Tsi yeksayentahkwa tkaksahronnyon'.** [...t-kak-sa-hrón-nyon'] *The dishes are sitting up in the cupboard.*

ee) **Tsi yenaktohares** [Tsi Ye-nak-tó-ha-rehs] *Saturday*
   ie. **shiYenaktohare'kenha** [Shi-ye-nak-to-ha-re'-kén-ha'] *last Saturday.*

ff) **tsi yetskwa'ehstha** [tsi yets-kwa'-éhst-ha'] *barn*

gg) **tsi yohnawate** [tsi yoh-ná:-wa-teh] *a well; a spring*

hh) **tsi yohsonhtakàronte** [tsi yoh-sonh-ta-kà:-ron-teh] *window; at the window*
   ie. **akta tsi yohsonhtakàronte** [ák-ta' tsi...] *next to the window;* **tsi yohsonhtakahronton** [tsi yoh-sonh-ta-ka-hrón:-tonh] *at the windows.* **Tsi yohsonhtakàronte ithrate'.** [...ít-hra-te'] *He is standing at the window.*

ii) **tsi yonnonhwetstha** [tsi yon-non-hwéts-tha'] *bedroom; in the bedroom*

jj) **tsi yontenhninontha** [tsi yon-tenh-ni-nónt-ha'] *store*

kk) **tsi yotahshetahkwen** [tsi yo-tahs-he-táh-kwenh] *bathroom; in the bathroom*

811 **tsi'tenha** [tsi'-tén-ha'] *a bird*
   ie. **ne tsi'tenha** [ne tsi'-tén-ha'] *the bird;* **thiken' tsi'tenha** [thí:-ken'...] *that bird;* **kiken' tsi'tenha** [kí:-ken'...] *this bird;* **tsi'ten'okonha** [tsi'-ten'-o-kón:-ha'] *birds (of a similar kind);* **tsi'tenhson'a** [tsi-tenh-són:-'ah] *birds (different kinds).* **Oh nikatsi'tenhseròten'.** [Oh ni-ka-tsi'-tenh-se-rò:-ten'] *What kind of bird is it?* **katsi'tenhserahòntsi** [ka-tsi'-tenh-se-ra-hòn:-tsih] *a black bird;* **katsi'tenhserowanen** [ka-tsi'-tenh-se-ro-wá:-nenh] *a large bird;* **nikatsi'tenhsera'ah** [ni-ka-tsi'-tenh-se-rá:-'ah] *a small bird.*

812 **tsihskoko** [tsihs-kó:-koh] *a robin*

813 **tsihstarare** [tsihs-tá:-ra-reh] *a grasshopper*

814 **tsihstekeri** [tsihs-té-ke-rih] *an owl*

815 **tsikeren'tanhnyaks** [tsi-ke-ren'-táh-nyaks] *a frog*

816 **tsikhnennàtaks** [tsik-hnen-nà:-taks] *a toad*

817 **tsikonhses** [tsi-kónhs-ses] *a pike (fish)*

818 **tsiks** [tsí:ks] *a fly*

819 **tsiktsinonnawen** [tsik-tsi-nón:-na-wen'] *a butterfly*

820 **tsinowen** [tsi-no':-wen'] *a mouse*
ie. **ne tsinowen** [ne tsi-nó:-wen'] *the mouse*; **thiken' tsinowen** [thí:-ken'...]
that mouse; **kiken' tsinowen** [kí:-ken'...] *this mouse*; **tsinowen'okonha** [tsi-no-wen'-o-kón:-ha'] *mice.*

821 **tsitsho** [tsíts-hoh] *a fox*

822 **tsyakothonwisen** [tsya-kot-hon-wí:-senh] *a young woman; a female*
ie. **ne tsyakothonwisen** [ne tsya-kothon-wí:-senh] *the young woman*; **thiken'
tsyakothonwisen** [thí:-ken'...] *that young woman*; **kiken' tsyakothonwisen**
[kí:-ken'...] *this young woman.* With numericals: **Tsyeyàtat tsyakothonwisen**
[tsye-yà:-tat...] *one young woman*; **tekeniyahsen tsyonathonwisen** [te-ke-ni-
yáh-senh tsyo-nat-hon-wí:-senh] *two young women*; **ahsen nikonti
tsyonathonwisen** [áh-sen' ni-kón:-tih tsyo-nat-hon-wí:-senh] *three young women.*

823 **tsyatak** [tsyá:-tak] *seven*
ie. **tsyatak nikon** [...ní:-konh] *(there's) seven of them (onjects)*; **tsyatak nikonti**
[...ni-kón:-tih] *(there's) seven of them (female / animal)*; **tsyatak nihati** [...ni-há:-
tih] *(there's) seven of them (male).* **tsyatak-yawenre** [...-ya-wén:-reh] *seveneen*;
tsyatak-niwahsen [...-ni-wáh-senh] *seventy.* **tsyatak nikatshètake** [...ni-kats-
hè:-ta-keh] *seven bottles*; **tsyatak niwakyen'** [...ni-wák-yen'] *I have seven*;
tsyatak niwaketshètayen' [...ni-wa-kets-hè:-ta-yen'] *I have seven bottles.*

824 **tsyara'se'a** [tsya-ra'-sé:-'ah] *your cousin* (See: onkyara'se'a)

825 **tsyatatenonhkwe** [tsya-tá-te-nonh-kwe'] *your relative*
(See: yakyatatenonhkwe')

826 **tsyatenron** [tsya-tén:-ronh] *your friend* (See: yonkyatenron)

827 **tsyennìto** [tsyen-nì:-toh] *a beaver*

828 **tsyerakewahtha** [tsye-ra-ke-wáh-t-ha'] *an eraser*

829 **tsyeyàtat** [tsye-yà:-tat] *one (female individual)*
ie. **tsyeyàtat yakonkwe** [tsye-yà:-tat ya-kón:-kwe'] *one woman*; **tsyeyàtat
yeksa'a** [tsye-yà:-tat yek-sá:-'ah] *one girl.* **tsyeyàtat ne kononkwe** [tsye-yà:-
tat ko-nón:-kwe'] *one of the women*; **tsyeyàtat ne kontiksa'okonha** [tsye-yà:-
tat ne kon-tik-sa'-o-kón-ha'] *one of the girls.* **Tsyeyàtat wa'ehninònra'.**

[...wa'-eh-ni-nòn:-ra'] *one (of them) went shopping.*

830 **tsyòkawe** [tsyò:-ka-weh] *a crow*

831 **tsyonathonwisen** [tsyo-nat-hon-wí:-senh] *young women; females*
ie. **ne tsyonathonwisen** [ne tsyo-nat-hon-wí:-senh] *the young women;* **thiken'**
tsyonathonwisen [thí:-ken'...] *those young women;* **kiken' tsyonathonwisen**
[kí:-ken'...] *these young women.* (see: tsyakothonwisen)

832 **Tsyothorha** [Tsyo-thór0ha'] *December*

833 **Tsyothorkowa** [Tsyo-thor-kó:-wa'] *January*

834 **tsyowatstakawe** [tsyo-wáts-ta-ka-weh] *a seagull*

835 **tyakenìteron** [tya-ke-nì:-te-ron'] *my spouse, partner*
tesenìteron [te-se-nì:-te-ron'] *your spouse, partner;* **tehnìteron** [teh-nì:-te-ron']
his spouse, partner / her spouse, partner.

836 **tyohton** [tyóh-ton'] *nine*
ie. **tyohton nikon** [...ní:-konh] *(there's) nine of them (onjects);* **tyohton nikonti**
[...ni-kón:-tih] *(there's) nine of them (female / animal);* **tyohton nihati** [...ni-há:-
tih] *(there's) nine of them (male).* **tyohton-yawenre** [...-ya-wén:-reh] *nineteen;*
tyohton-niwahsen [...-ni-wáh-senh] *ninety.* **tyohton nikatshètake** [...ni-kats-
hè:-ta-keh] *nine bottles;* **tyohton niwakyen'** [...ni-wák-yen'] *I have nine;*
tyohton niwaketshètayen' [...ni-wa-kets-hè:-ta-yen'] *I have nine bottles.*

837 **tyohyòtsis** [tyo-hyò:-tsihs] *salt*

838 **tyonnhonhskwaron** [tyonn-hónhs-kwa-ron'] *a cow*
ie. **aketshenen tyonnhonhskwaron** [a-kets-hé:-nenh tyonn-hónhs-kwa-ron']
my cow; **yotinenhrowanen tyonnhonhskwaron** [yo-ti-nen-hro-wá:-nenh...] *a*
herd of cattle; **Tyonnhonhskwaron wakenahskwayen'.** [...wa-ke-náhs-kwa-
yen'] *I have (a) cow(s) / cattle.*

839 **Tyorhenhshàka** [Tyor-henh-shà:-ka'] *the English nation*

840 **tyotahyàkton** [tyo-ha-hyà:k-ton'] *a banana*
ie. **Tyotahyàkton wakekahs.** [...wa-ké:-kahs] *I like bananas.*

841 **tyotkon** [tyót-konh] *always*
ie **Tyotkon ro'nihskwen'onh.** [Tyót-konh ro'-nihs-kwén:-'onh] *He is always*
late.

842 **tyotsha'tayenthon** [tyots-ha'-ta-yént-honh] *it is misty*

843 **tyotskara'kowa** [tyots-ka-ra'-kó:-wah] *pepper*

844 **tyowihsonhtyon** [tyo-wih-sónh-tyonh] *it is hailing*

[842] **tyotsha'tayenthon** [tyots-ha'-ta-yént-honh] *it is misty*

[843] **tyotskara'kowa** [tyots-ka-ra'-kó:-wah] *pepper*

[844] **tyowihsonhtyon** [tyo-wih-sónh-tyonh] *it is hailing*

W

[845] **wahetken** [wa-hét-kenh] *it is ugly*
ie. **wahetken tsi nikaya'tòten'** [...tsi ni-ka-ya'-tò:-ten'] *it is ugly-looking.*

[846] **wahi** [wá-hih] *isn't it; of course*
ie. **Wenhniseriyo, wahi.** [Wenh-ni-se-rí:-yoh, wá-hih] *It's a nice day, isn't it?*
Raonha wahi ne'e ne' nahatyere'. [Rá-on-ha' wá-hih né:-'eh ne' na-há-tye-re'] *He, of course, is the one that did it.*

[847] **wahonnise** [wa-hón:-ni-seh] *a long time (period of time)*
ie. **Wahonnise thikenhne'.** [...t-hi-kénh-ne'] *It's been a long time since I've seen him.*

[848] **wahonnise'kenha** [wa-hon-ni-se'-kén-ha'] *a long time ago*
ie. **Wahonnise'kenha eh nityawen'onh.** [...eh ni-tya-wén:-'onh] *It happened a long time ago.*

[849] **wahsi'kwìserehs** [wah-si'-kwí:-re-rehs] *skidoo*
ie. **Wahsi'kwìserehs rohonwìsere'** [...ro-hon-wì:-se-re'] *He's riding a skidoo.*

[850] **wahskohon** [wah-skó-honh] *a bridge*
ie. **tsi tiwahskohon** [tsi ti-wahs-kó-honh] *at the bridge.* **akta tsi tiwahskohon** [ák-ta' tsi ti-wahs-kó-honh] *near the bridge.* **Akta tsi tiwahskohon thanakere'.** [...t-ha-ná-ke-re'] *He lives / is living near the bridge.* **Ya'tekahskwiya'ks** [ya'-te-kahs-kwí:-ya'ks] *I crossed over the bridge.*

[851] **wahtha** [wáh-tha'] *a sugar maple tree*
ie. **wahtha ohshehs** [...óhs-hehs] *maple syrup.*

[852] **wahyakeri** [wa-hyá-ke-ri'] *fruit juice*

[853] **wahyakhahon** [wa-hyak-há-honh] *tomatoes*

[854] **wakàsen's** [wa-kà:-sen's] *I drop something (accidently)* (A-Stem - Obj.)
onkwàsense' [on-kwà:-sen'-se'] *I dropped...;* **waka'sen'onh** [wa-ka'-sén:-'onh] *I have dropped / did drop.*

855 **wakata'karite** [wa-ka-ta'-ka-rí:-teh] *I am well* (A-Stem - Obj.)
   wakata'karitehkwe' [wa-ka-ta'-ka-rí:-teh-kwe'] *I was well*;
   enwakata'kariteke' [en-wa-ka-ta'-ka-rí:-te-ke'] *I will be-well*;
   aonkwata'kariteke' [a-on-kwa-ta'-ka-rí:-te-ke'] *I would be well / for me to be well.*

856 **wakatera's/wiyo** [wa-ka-te-ra'-swí:-yoh] *I am lucky / fortunate* (A-Stem - Obj.)
   wakatera'swiyohne' [wa-ka-te-ra'-swi-yóh-ne'] *I was lucky*;
   enwakatera'swiyohake' [en-wa-ka-te-ra'-swi-yó-ha-ke'] *I will be lucky*;
   aonkwatera'swiyohake' [a-on-kwa-te-ra'-swi-yó-ha-ke'] *I would be lucky / for me to be lucky.*

857 **wakateryèntare** [wa-ka-ter-yèn:-ta-reh] *I know (about it)* (A-Stem - Obj.)
   wakateryentarehkwe' [wa-ka-ter-yén:-ta-reh-kwe'] *I knew (about it)*;
   enwakateryentarake' [en-wa-ka-ter-yén:-ta-ra-ke'] *I will know (about it)*;
   aonkwateryentarake' [a-on-kwa-ter-yén:-ta-ra-ke'] *I would know / for me to know (about it).*

858 **wakathonte** [wa-ka-thón:-teh] *I hear (a sound / noise)* (A-Stem - Obj.)
   onkwathontene' [on-kwat-hón:-te'-ne'] *I heard...*;   **wakathonte'onh** [wa-ka-thon-té:-'onh] *I have heard / did hear....*

859 **wakatihsayen'** [wa-ka-tih-sá:-yenh] *I am slow to act / do s.t. about* (A-Stem - Obj.) **wakatihsayentahkwe'** [wa-ka-tih-sa-yén:-tah-kwe'] *I was slow to act...*;
   enwakatihsayentakwe' [en-wa-ka-tih-sa-yén:-ta-ke'] *I will be slow to act...*;
   aonkwatihsayentake' [a-on-kwa-tih-sa-yén:-ta-ke'] *I would be / for me to be slow to act....*

860 **wakatihsnore** [wa-ka-tih-snó:-reh] *I am quick to act / do s.t. about* (A-Stem - Obj.) **wakatihsnorehkwe'** [wa-ka-tih-snó:-reh-kwe'] *I was quick to act...*;
   enwakatihsnoreke' [en-wa-ka-tih-snó:-re-ke'] *I will be quick to act...*;
   aonkwatihsnoreke' [a-on-kwa-tih-snó:-re-ke'] *I would be quick / for me to be quick to act....*

861 **wakatkahritsheronni** [wa-kat-ka-hrits-he-rón:-nih] *I am playing* (A-Stem - Obj.) **wakatkahritsheronnihne'** [wa-kat-ka-hrits-he-ron-níh-ne'] *I was playing*;   **enwakatkahritsheronnihake'** [en-wa-kat-ka-hrits-he-ron-ní-ha-ke'] *I will be playing*;   **aonkwatkahritsheronnihake'** [a-on-kwat-ka-hrits-he-ron-ní-ha-ke'] *I would be / for me to be playing*;

862 **wakatshennonni** [wa-kats-hen-nón:-nih] *I am happy* (A-Stem - Obj.)
   wakatshennonnihahkwe' [wa-kats-hen-non-ní-hah-kwe'] *I was happy*;
   enwakatshennonniheke' [en-wa-kats-hen-non-ní-he-ke'] *I will be happy*;
   aonkwatshennonniheke' [a-on-kwats-hen-non-ní-he-ke'] *I would be / for me to be happy.*

863 **wakatyes** [wa-ká-tyes] *I throw (away)* (A-Stem - Obj.)

onkwati' [on-kwá:-ti'] *I threw (away)*; **wakatyonh** [wa-ká-tyonh] *I have thrown / did throw (away)*: **wakathenno'tsheratyes** [wa-kat-hen-no'ts-he-rón-tyes] *I throw a ball*; **wakenhyontyes** *I throw a stick*.

864 **wàke'** [wà:-ke'] *I am going (on my way to some place)* (E-Stem - Obj.)
wakenonh [wa-ké:-nonh] *I have gone / did go*; **wakenònne'** [wa-ke-nòn:-ne'] *I had gone / I was away*; **enwakenonh** [en-wa-ké:-nonh] *I will be gone / will be away*; **aonkwenonh** [a-on-kwé:-nonh] *I would have gone / I would be away / for me to be away*.

865 **wake'nikonhrahseronni** [wa-ke'-ni-kon-hrah-se-rón:-nih] *I am pleased (about it)* (C-Stem - Obj.) **wake'nikonhrahseronnihne'** [wa-ke'-ni-kon-hrah-se-ron-níh-ne'] *I was pleased (about it)*; **enwake'nikonhrahseronnihake'** [wa-ke'-ni-kon-hrah-se-ron-ní-ha-ke'] *I will be pleased (about it)*; **aonke'nikonhrahseronnihake'** [a-on-ke'-ni-kon-hrah-se-ron-ní-ha-ke'] *I would be / for me to be pleased (about it)*;

866 **wake'nikonhraksen** [wa-ke'-ni-kon-hrák-senh] *I am sad* (C-Stem - Obj.)
wake'nikonhraksenhne' [wa-ke'-ni-kon-hrak-sénh-ne'] *I was sad*; **enwake'nikonhraksenhake'** [en-wa-ke'-ni-kon-hrak-sén-ha-ke'] *I will be sad*; **aonke'nikonhraksenhake'** [a-on-ke'-ni-kon-hrak-sén-ha-ke'] *I will be / for me to be sad*;

867 **wake'nikonhrayenta's** [wa-ke'-ni-kon-hra-yén:-ta's] *I understand* (C-Stem - Obj.) **onke'nikonhrayentane'** [on-ke'-ni-kon-hra-yén:-ta'-ne'] *I understood*; **wake'nikonhrayenta'onh** [wa-ke'-ni-kon-hra-yen-tá:-'onh] *I did understand / have understood*.

868 **wakekahs** [wa-ké:-kahs] *I like (the taste of)* (E-Stem - Obj.)
onkekahwe' [on-ké:-kah-we'] *I liked the taste (of it)*; **wakekahonh** [wa-ke-ká-honh] *I did like / have liked the taste (of it)*. ie. **Tekahswàne wakekahs.** [Te-kah-swà:-neh wa-ké:-kahs] *I like (the taste of) pie*.

869 **wakena'khwen'onh** [wa-ke-na'-k-hwén:-'onh] *I am angry* (C-Stem - Obj.)
wakena'khwen'ònne' [wa-ke-na'k-hwen'-òn:-ne'] *I was angry*; **enwakena'khwen'onh** [en-wa-ke-na'k-hwén:-'onh] *I will be angry*; **aonkena'khwen'onh** [a-on-ke-na'k-hwén:-'onh] *I would be / for me to be angry*.

870 **wakenàkhwenhs** [wa-ke-nà:-k-hwenhs] *I get angry (about something)* (C-Stem - Obj.) **onkenàkhwen'** [on-ke-nà:-k-hwen'] *I got angry...*; **wakena'khwen'onh** [wa-ke-na'k-hwén:-'onh] *I did get / have become angry*.

871 **wakenehrakwas** [wa-ke-ne-hrá-kwas] *I am amazed / surprised* (C-Stem - Obj.) **onkenehrako'** [on-ke-neh-hrá:-ko'] *I was amazed*; **wakenehrakwenh** [wa-ke-ne-hrá-kwenh] *I have been amazed*.

872 **wakenonhwaktani** [wa-ke-non-hwák-ta-nih] *I am sick* (C-Stem - Obj.)
wakenonhwaktanihahkwe' [wa-ke-non-hwak-ta-ní-hah-kwe'] *I was sick;*
enwakenonhwaktaniheke' [en-wa-ke-non-hwak-ta-ní-he-ke'] *I will be sick;*
aonkenonhwaktaniheke' [a-on-ke-non-hwak-ta-ní-he-ke'] *I would be / for me to be sick.*

873 **wakenya'tathenhs** [wa-ke-nya'-tát-henhs] *I am thirsty* (C-Stem - Obj.)
onkenya'tathen' [on-ke-nya'-tát-hen'] *I was thirsty;* **wakenya'tathenhonh**
[wa-ke-nya'-tat-hén-honh] *I have been thirsty.*

874 **wàkeren's** [wà:-ke-ren's] *it snows*
ònkerenne' [òn:-ke-ren'-ne'] *It snowed;* **yo'keren'onh** [yo'-ke-rén:-'onh] *It is snowing;* **yo'keren'onhatye'** [yo'-ke-ren'-on-há-tye'] *It is snowing (right along).*

875 **wakitahs** [wa-kí:-tahs] *I am sleeping.* (I-Stem verb: see page)
onkitahwe' [on-kí:-tah-we'] *I was sleeping / slept;* **wakita'onh** [wa-ki-tá:-'onh] *I have slept / have been sleeping.*

876 **wakhteronni** [wak-t-he-rón:-nih] *I am afraid* (C-Stem verb: see page)
wakhteronnihne' [wakh-te-ron-níh-ne'] *I was afraid;* **enwakhteronnihake'**
[en-wakh-te-ron-ní-ha-ke'] *I will be afraid;* **aonkhteronnihake'** [a-onkh-te-ron-ní-ha-ke'] *I would be / for me to be afraid;*

877 **wakyen'** [wák-yen'] *I have* (C-Stem verb: see page)
wakyentahkwe' [wak-yén:-tah-kwe'] *I had;* **enwakyentake'** [en-wak-yén:-ta-ke'] *I will have;* **aonkyentake'** [a-onk-yén:-ta-ke'] *I would have / for me to have.*

878 **wakyenta's** [wak-yén:-ta's] *I acquire / get* (C-Stem verb: see page)
onkyentane' [onk-yén:-ta'-ne'] *I acquired / got;* **wakyenta'onh** [wak-yen-tá:-'onh] *I have acquired / did get.*

879 **wakyo'te** [wak-yó'-teh] *I am working* (C-Stem verb: see page)
wakyo'tehkwe' [wa-kyó'-teh-kwe'] *i was working;* **enwakyo'teke'** [en-wa-kyó'-te-ke'] *I will be working;* **aonkyo'teke'** [a-on-kyó-te-ke'] *I would be / for me to be working.*

880 **wate'nyentenhstahkwa** [wa-te'-nyen-tenhs-táh-kwa'] *a ruler; a measuring stick*

881 **wathyatons** [wat-hyá:-tons] *a pattern*

882 **watya'tarahkwa** [wa-tya'-ta-ráh-kwa'] *an envelope*

883 **wehsènrate** [weh-sèn:-ra-teh] *pink*
ie. **wehsènrate niwahsohkòten'** [...ni-wah-soh-kò:-ten'] *it is pink coloured / dyed pink;* **wehsènrate niyoht** [...ní:-yoht] *it is pinkish / pink-like;* **wehsènrate niwatya'tawi'tsheròten'** [...ni-wa-tya'-ta-wi'ts-he-rò:-ten'] *(it is) a pink coat / dress / shirt.*

884 **wihson kahik** [wíh-sonh ká-hik] *a plum, plums*

885 **wisk** [wíhsk] *five*

ie. **wisk nikon** [...ní:-konh] *(there's) five of them (onjects)*; **wisk nikonti** [...ni-kón:-tih] *(there's) five of them (female / animal)*; **wisk nihati** [...ni-há:-tih] *(there's) five of them (male)*. **wisk-yawenre** [...-ya-wén:-reh] *fifteen*; **wisk-niwahsen** [...-ni-wáh-senh] *fifty*. **wisk nikatshètake** [...ni-kats-hè:-ta-keh] *five bottles*; **wisk niwakyen'** [...ni-wák-yen'] *I have five*; **wisk niwaketshètayen'** [...ni-wa-kets-hè:-ta-yen'] *I have five bottles.*

886 **Wiskhatont** [Wíhsk-ha-tont] *Friday*

ie. **Shiwiskhaton'kenha** [Shi-wihsk-ha-ton'-kén-ha'] *last Friday*; **Wiskhatont nen' ne'e onwa kenh wenhniserate.** [...nen' né:-'eh ón:-wa' kenh wenh-ni-se-rá:-teh] *Today is Friday*; **Wiskhatont nen' ne'e thetenre.** [...nen' né:-'eh t-he-tén:-reh] *Yesterday was Friday*; **Wiskhatont nen' ne'e enyorhenne.** [...nen' né:-'eh en-yór-hen'-ne'] *Tomorrow is Friday.*

Y

887 **yah** [yáh] *no* (Always accompanied by **te-**: see page   )

ie. **Yah tewakyen'.** [Yah te-wák-yen'] *I don't have it.*

a) **yah kaneka** [yah ká-ne-kah] *nowhere; not anywhere*

ie. **Yah kaneka tekayen'.** [Yah ká-ne-kah te-ká:-yen'] *It's not laying about anywhere.*

b) **yah ki' nonwa** [yah ki' nón:-wah] *not right now*

ie. **Yah ki' nonwa teskahtentyonhe'.** [Yah ki' nón:-wah tes-kah-ten-tyón-he'] *I am not going home right now.*

c) **yah nonwa onen** [yah non-wa' ó:-nen] *no longer; not anymore*

ie. **Yah nonwa onen teshènteron'.** [Yah non-wa' ó:-nenh tes-hèn:-te-ron'] *He is no longer living there.*

d) **yah nonwenton** [yah non-wén:-tonh] *never*

ie. **Yah nonwenton tehoyo'tenhs.** [Yah non-wén:-tonh te-ho-yó'-tenhs] *He never works*; **Yah nonwenton tetiwakatkahthonh.** [Yah non-wén:-tonh te-ti-wa-kat-káht-honh] *I have never seen it (before).*

e) **yah onhka** [yah ónh-ka'] *no-one; nobody*

ie. **Yah onhka teyakotkahthonh.** [Yah ónh-ka' te-ya-kot-kát-honh] *No-one saw it.*

f) **yah othenen** [yah ot-hé-nenh] *nothing; not anything*
　　ie. **Yah othenen tetsyotatenron** [Yah ot-hé-nenh te-tsyo-ta-tén:-ron']
　　There is nothing left; **Yah othenen teyonkwawih.** [Yah ot-hé-nenh te-yon-
　　kwá:-wih] *They didn't give me anything.*

g) **yah tekanoron** [yah te-ka-nó:-ronh] *it is inexpensive*
　　ie. **Yah tekanoron kiken' kahyatonhsera ne' wakhninonh.** [Yah te-ka-
　　nó:-ronh kí:-ken' ka-hya-tónh-se-ra' ne' wak-hní:-nonh] *This book I bought is
　　not expensive.*

h) **yah teyohyo'thiye** [yah te-yo-hyo'-t-hí:-yeh] *it is dull; not sharp*
　　ie. **Yah teyohyo'thiye thiken' àshare ne' satstonh.** [Yah te-yo-hyo'-t-
　　hí:-yeh thí:-ken' à:-s-ha-reh ne' sáts-tonh] *That knife you're using is not sharp.*

i) **yah teyokste** [yah te-yóks-teh] *it is light; not heavy*
　　ie. **Yah teyokste thiken' wa'therowanen ne. rokehte'.** [Yah te-yóks-teh
　　thí:-ken' wa'-t-he-ro-wá:-nenh ne' ro-kéh-te'] *That big basket he's carrying is
　　not heavy.*

888 **yahtsi'a** [yah-tsí:-'ah] *your older brother* (See: raktsi'a)

889 **yake'** [yá:-ke'] *I am going there* (E-Stem - Subj.)
　　yewakenonh [ye-wa-ké:-nonh] *I have gone there / did go there*; **yewakenonhne'**
　　[ye-wa-ke-nónh-ne'] *I had gone there / I was there.* ie. **Tsi yonontahere yake'.**
　　[Tsi yo-non-tá-he-reh yá:-ke'] *i am going to the mountain.*

890 **yake'niha** [ya'-ní-ha'] *your father* (See: rake'niha)

891 **yakhi'kenha** [yak-hi'-kén-ha] *our younger sister* (See: khe'kenha)

892 **yakhiyen'a** [yak-hi-yén:-ah] *our daughter* (See: kheyen'a)

893 **yakhsotha** [yah-sót-ha'] *your grandfather* (See: rakhsotha)

894 **yakohonhtariks** [ya-ko-hónh-ta-riks] *a bat*

895 **yakohsatens** [ya-koh-sá:-tens] *a horse*

896 **yakonkwe** [ya-kón:-kwe'] *a female person; a woman*
　　ie. **ne yakonkwe** [ne ya-kón:-kwe'] *the woman*; **thiken' yakonkwe'** [thí:-
　　ken'...] *that woman*; **kiken' yakonkwe** [kí:-ken'...] *this woman*; **kononkwe**
　　[ko-nón:-kwe'] *women.* With numericals: **tsyeyàtat yakonkwe** [tsye-yà:-
　　tat...] *one woman*; **tekeniyahsen tekenonkwe** [te-ke-ni-yáh-senh te-ke-nón:-
　　kwe'] *two women*; **ahsen nikonti kononkwe** [áh-sen' ni-kón:-tih ko-nón:-
　　kwe'] *three women.*

897 **yakyatatenonhkwe** [ya-kya-tá-te-nonh-kwe'] *my relative*
　　tsyatatenonhkwe [tsya-tá-te-nonh-kwe'] *your relative*; **yatatenonhkwe**
　　[ya-tá-te-nonh-kwe'] *his relative (male or female) or her relative (male)*; **kyatatenonhkwe**

[kya-tá-te-nonh-kwe'] *her relative (female)*. ie. **Yah teyakyatatenonhkwe.** [Yah te-ya-kya-tá-te-nonh-kwe'] *We (he & I / her & I) are not related.*

⁸⁹⁸ **yanoha'a** [ya-no-há:-'ah] *your uncle* (See: rakenoha'a)

⁸⁹⁹ **yaokat** [ya-ó:-kat] *it is rough*
ie. **Sotsi yaokat.** [Só-tsih ta-ó:-kat] *it's too rough*; **Akwah tsi yaokat.** [kwah tsi ya-ó:-kat] *it's quite rough*; **Akwah iken' tsi yaokat.** [kwah í:-ken' tsi ya-ó:-kat] *it's very rough*; **Yah e'tho teyaokat** [Yah é'-t-ho te-ya-ó:-kat] *it's not rough enough.*

⁹⁰⁰ **yaote** [ya-ó:-teh] *it is windy*
yaotehkwe' [ya-ó:-teh-kwe'] *it was windy*; **enyaoteke'** [en-ya-ó:-te-ke'] *it will be windy*; **ayaoteke'** [a-ya-ó:-te-ke'] *it would be windy / for it to be windy.*

⁹⁰¹ **yatatenonhkwe** [ya-tá-te-nonh-kwe'] *his (male/female) relative*
(See: yakyatatenonhkwe)

⁹⁰² **yawe'towanen** [ya-we'-to-wá:-nenh] *a lot of (them)*
ie. **yawe'towanen ne kahyatonhsera'okon** [ya-we'-to-wá:-nenh ne ka-hya-tonh-se-ra'-ó:-konh] *a lot of the books*; **yawe'towanen niwakyen'** [...ni-wák-yen'] *I have a lot of (of them).*

⁹⁰³ **yawekon** [ya-wé-konh] *it is good-tasting*
ie. **Yawekon kiken' kana'taronkhonwe.** [Ya-wé-konh kí:-ken' ka-na'-ta-ronk-hón:-weh] *This homemade bread tastes good.*

⁹⁰⁴ **yawenre** [ya-wén:-reh] *...teen*
ie. **ahsen-yawenre** [áh-sen' ya-wén:-reh] *thirteen*; **kayeri-yawenre** [ka-yé:-rih...] *fourteen*; **wisk-yawenre** [wihsk...] *fifteen*; **yayak-yawenre** [yá:-yak...] *sixteen*; **tsyatak-yawenre** [tsyá:-tak...] *seventeen*; **sha'tekon-yawenre** [sha'-té:-kon...] *eighteen*; **tyohton-yawenre** [tyóh-ton...] *nineteen.* Is also used with **enhskat** and **tekeni**: ie. **enhskat-yawenre** [énhs-kat...] *eleven*; **tekeni-yawenre** [té-ke-nih...] *twelve.*

⁹⁰⁵ **Yawentatokenhton** [Ya-wen-ta-to-kénh-tonh] *Sunday*
shiYawentatokenhton [Shi-ya-wen-ta-to-kénh-tonh] *last Sunday*; **Nonwa enyawentatokenhtonke'** [Nón:-wah en-ya-wen-ta-to-kenh-tón:-keh] *next Sunday.*

⁹⁰⁶ **Yawententa'onh** [Ya-wen-ten-tá:-'onh] *Monday*
shiYawententa'onh [Shi-ya-wen-ten-tá:-'onh] *last Monday*; **Nonwa enyawententa'onke** [Nón:-wah en-ya-wen-ten-ta'-ón:-keh] *nest Monday.*

⁹⁰⁷ **yaweronhatye** [ya-we-ron-há-tye'] *no matter*
ie. **Sayo'tenhsek oh yaweronhatye nenyawenne'.** [Sa-yo'-ténh-sek oh ya-we-ron-há-tye' nen-yá:-wen'-ne'] *Keep working no matter what happens.*

⁹⁰⁸ **yayak** [yá:-yak] *six*

ie. **yayak nikon** [...ní:-konh] *(there's) six of them (onjects)*; **yayak nikonti** [...ni-kón:-tih] *(there's) six of them (female / animal)*; **yayak nihati** [...ni-há:-tih] *(there's) six of them (male)*. **yayak-yawenre** [...-ya-wén:-reh] *sixteen*; **yayak-niwahsen** [...-ni-wáh-senh] *sixty*. **yayak nikatshètake** [...ni-kats-hè:-ta-keh] *six bottles*; **yayak niwakyen'** [...ni-wák-yen'] *I have six*; **yayak niwaketshètayen'** [...ni-wa-kets-hè:-ta-yen'] *I have six bottles.*

⁹⁰⁹ **ye'nikhonhkwa** [ye'-nik-hónh-kwa'] *a sewing machine*

⁹¹⁰ **yehnekarahkwa** [yeh-ne-ka-ráh-kwa'] *a water pitcher*

ie. **yehnekarahkwatsherakon** [yeh-ne-ka-rah-kwats-he-rá:-konh] *in the water pitcher.*

⁹¹¹ **yehwihstarahkwa** [ye-hwihs-ta-ráh-kwa'] *a wallet; a bilfold*

ie. **akhwihstarahkwa** [ak-hwihs-ta-ráh-kwa'] *my wallet*; **sahwihstarahkwa** [sa-hwihs-ta-ráh-kwa'] *your wallet*; **akaohwihstarahkwa** [a-ka-o-hwihs-ta-ráh-kwa'] *her wallet*; **raohwihstarahkwa** [ra-o-hwihs-ta-ráh-kwa'] *his wallet.* **raohwihstarahkwatsherakon** [ra-o-hwihs-ta-rah-kwats-he-rá:-konh] *in his wallet*; **Yah tekahwihstare ne raowihstarahkwatsherakon** [Yah te-ka-hwíhs-ta-reh ne...] *There's no money in his wallet.*

⁹¹² **yehyatonhkwa** [ye-hya-tónh-kwa'] *a pen, pencil*
akhyatonhkwa [ak-hya-tónh-kwa'] *my pen...*; **sahyatonhkwa** [sa-hya-tónh-kwa'] *your pen...*; **akaohyatonhkwa** [a-ka-o-hya-tónh-kwa'] *her pen...*; **raohyatonhkwa** [ra-o-hya-tónh-kwa'] *his pen....* **Akwawenk ne akhyatonhkwa.** [A-kwá:-wenk ne ak-hya-tónh-kwa'] *That's my pen*; **Sayen' ken ne yehyatonhkwa.** [Sá:-yen' ken ne ye-hya-tónh-kwa'] *Do you have a pen?*

⁹¹³ **yehyatonhserarahkwa** [ye-hya-tonh-se-ra-ráh-kwa'] *a book case*
ie. **yehyatonhserarahkwatsheràke** [ye-hya-tonh-se-ra-rah-kwats-he-rà:-keh] *on ther bookshelf.*

⁹¹⁴ **yehyatonhstahkwa** [ye-hya-tonhs-táh-kwa'] *a desk; a writing desk*
ie. **yehyatonhstahkwatsheràke** [ye-hya-tonhs-tah-kwats-he-rà:-keh] *on the desk.*

⁹¹⁵ **yekataweyàtha'** [ye-ka-ta-we-yà:-t-ha'] *I go in* (A-Stem - Subj.)
ya'kataweya'te' [ya'-ka-tá:-we-ya'-te'] *I went in*; **yewakataweyàtonh** [ye-wa-ka-ta-we-yà:-tonh] *I have gone in / I did go in / I am inside.*

⁹¹⁶ **yekathsnenhtha'** [ye-kat-hsnenht-ha'] *I descend (from here to there) / go down* (A-Stem - Subj.) **ya'kathsnenhte'** [ya'-kát-hsnenh-te'] *I descended / went down*; **yewakathsnenhtonh** [ye-wa-kat-hsnenh-tonh] *I have descended / gone down / did go down.*

⁹¹⁷ **yekentorahkwa** [ye-ken-to-ráh-kwa'] *a bandage*

918 **yekerathenhs** [ye-ke-rát-henhs] *I climb up (from here to there)* (C-Stem - Subj.) **ya'kerathen'** [ya'-ke-rát-hen'] *I climbed up*; **yewakerathen'onh** [ye-wa-ke-rat-hén:-'onh] *I have climed up / I did climb up.*

919 **yekhonnya'tahkwa** [yek-hon-nya'táh-kwa'] *a cook stove* ie. **yekhonnya'tahkwatsheràke** [yek-hon-nya'-tah-kwats-he-rà:-keh] *on the stove.*

920 **yeksa'a** [yek-sá:-'ah] *a female child; a girl* ie. **ne yeksa'a** [ne yek-sá:-'ah] *the girl*; **thiken' yeksa'a** [thí:-ken'...] *that girl*; **kiken' yeksa'a** [kí:-ken'...] *this girl.* With numericals: **tsyeyàtat yeksa'a** [tsye-yà:-tat...] *one girl*; **tekeniyahsen tekeniksa'a** [te-ke-ni-yáh-senh te-ke-nik-sá:-'ah] *two girls*; **ahsen nikonti kontiksa'okonha** [áh-sen' ni-kón:-tih kon-tik-sa'-o-kón-ha'] *three girls.* With adjectivals: **nihra'a yeksa'a** [ni-hrá:-'ah yek-sá:-'ah] *a small girl*; **yeksa'towanen** [yek-sa'-to-wá:-nenh] *a large girl*; **yeksa'tiyo** [yek-sa'-tí:-yoh] *a good girl*; **yeksa'taksen** [yek-sa'-ták-senh] *a bad girl.* **ratksa'okonha** [ra-tik-sa'-o-kón-ha'] *girls.*

921 **yeksokewàtha** [yek-so-ke-wà:-tha'] *a teatowel*

922 **yekyaken's** [ye-kyá:-ken's] *I go out* **ya'kyakenne'** [ya'-kyá:-ken'-ne'] *I went out*; **yewakyaken'onh** [ye-wa-kya-kén:-'onh] *I have gone out / I did go out / I am outside.*

923 **yena'tsyarahkwa** [ye-na'-tsya-ráh-kwa'] *a frying pan* ie. **yena'tsyarahkwakon** [ye-na'-tsya-ráh-kwa-konh] *in the frying pan.*

924 **yenoharètha** [ye-no-ha-rè:-t-ha'] *soap*

925 **yenon'tarahkwa** [ye-non'-ta-ráh-kwa'] *a milk pitcher* ie. **yenon'tarahkwatsherakon** [ye-non'-ta-rah-kwats-he-rá:-konh] *in the milk pitcher.*

926 **yenon'tararahkwa** [ye-non'-ta-ra-ráh-kwa'] *a soup bowl* ie. **yenon'tararahkwatsherakon** [ye-non'-ta-ra-rah-kwats-he-rá:-konh] *in the soup bowl.*

927 **yesayen'a** [ye-sa-yén:-ah] *your parents* (See: yonkyen'a)

928 **yetsi'tsyarahkwa** [ye-tsi'-tsya-ráh-kwa'] *a flower vase, pot* ie. **yetsitsyarahkwatsherakon** [ye-tsi'-tsya-rah-kwats-he-rá:-konh] *in the flower vase, pot.*

929 **yetsikhe'tarahkwa** [ye-tsi-khe'-ta-ráh-kwa'] *a sugar bowl* ie. **yetsikhe'tarahkwatsherakon** [ye-tsi-khe'-ta-rah-kwats-he-rá:-konh] *in the sugar bowl.*

930 **yo'kènrare** [yo'-kèn:-ra-reh] *it is dusty*

931 **yo'keren'onh** [yo'-ke-rén:-'onh] *it is snowing*
   ie. **yo'keren'onhatye'** [yo'-ke-ren'-on-há-tye'] *it is snowing (right along)*;
   yo'keren'onhne' [yo'-ke-ren'-ónh-ne'] *it was snowing*;   **enyo'keren'onh** [en-
   yo'-ke-rén:-'onh] *it will be snowing / will have snowed*;   **ayo'keren'onh** [a-yo'-ke-
   rén:-'onh] *it would be snowing / would have snowed / for it to be snowing / have snowed.*

932 **yo'nikonhrori** [yo'-ni-kon-hró:-rih] *it is funny, amusing*

933 **yo'shatste** [yo'-sháts-teh] *it is strong, tough*
   ie. **yo'shatstehkwe'** [yo'-s-háts-teh-kwe'] *it was strong, tough*;   **enyo'shatsteke'**
   [en-yo'-s-háts-te-ke'] *it will be strong, tough*;   **ayo'shatsteke'** [a-yo'-s-háts-te-
   ke'] *it would be strong, tough.*

934 **yo'taksen** [yo'-ták-senh] *it is bad; poorly done*
   ie. **yo'taksenhne'** [yo'-tak-sénh-ne'] *it was bad / poorly done*;   **enyo'taksenhake'**
   [en-yo'-tak-sén-ha-ke'] *it will be bad; poorly done*;   **ayo'taksenhake'** [a-yo'-tak-
   sén-ha-ke'] *it would be bad; poorly done / for it to be bad / poorly done.*

935 **yo'tarihen** [yo'-ta-rí-henh] *it is hot, warm*
   yo'tarihenhne' [yo'-ta-ri-hénh-ne'] *it was hot, warm*;   **enyo'tarihenhake'** [en-
   yo'-ta-ri-hén-ha-ke'] *it will be hot, warm*;   **ayo'tarihenhake'** [a-yo'-ta-ri-hén-ha-
   ke'] *it would be hot, warm / for it to be hot, warm.*

936 **yo'tònyote** [yo'-tòn:-yo-teh] *it is piled, heaped up*
   yo'tonhyotehkwe' [yo'-ton-hyó:-teh-kwe'] *it was piled*;   **enyo'tonhyoteke'**
   [en-yo'-ton-hyó:-te-ke'] *it will be piled*;   **ayo'tonhyoteke'** [a-yo'-ton-hyó:-te-
   ke'] *it would be / for it to be piled.*

937 **yohkwennyarahkwa** [yoh-kwen-nya-ráh-kwa'] *a suitcase; closet*
   ie. **yohkwennyarahkwatsherakon** [yoh-kwen-nya-rah0kwats-he-rá:-konh] *in
   the suitcase; in the closet.*

938 **yohnetskha'** [yoh-néts-kha'] *it is soft*

939 **yohniron** [yoh-ní:-ronh] *it is hard, durable*

940 **yohonronte** [yo-hón:-ron-teh] *teakettle*

941 **yohrènton** [yo-hrèn:-tonh] *it is hanging down from, suspended from something*
   ie. **katshe'tènton** [kats-he'-tèn:-tonh] *a hanging light*;   Also: **yohren'tonnyon**
   [yo-hren'-tón-nyon'] *they are hanging down....*

942 **yohskats** [yóhs-kats] *it is beautiful, attractive*

943 **yohsnore** [yoh-snó:-reh] *it is fast; quick*
   ie. **Yohsnore tsi nahatyere'.** [Yoh-snó:-reh tsi na-há-tye-re'] *He did it quick.*

944 **yohstathen** [yoh-stát-henh] *it is dry*
   ie. nominals: **yona'tarathen** [ka-na'-ta-rát-henh] *dried bread*;   **yonenhstathen**

[yo-nenhs-tát-henh] *dried corn*.

945 **yohswen'karohare** [yoh-swen'-ka-ró-ha-reh] *a shelf*
ie. **Tsi yohswen'karohare yaháhsren.** [Tsi yoh-swen'-ka-ró-ha-reh ya-háhs-ren] *Place it up on the shelf.*

946 **yohyo'thiye** [yo-hyo'-thí:-yeh] *it is sharp*
ie. **Sotsi yohyo'thiye** [Só-tsih yo-hyot-hí:-yeh] *it too sharp;* **akwah iken' tsi yohyo'thiye** [kwah í:-ken' tsi...] *it's very sharp.* See: yah teyohyo'thiye)

947 **yokàronte** [yo-kà:-ron-teh] *it has a hole in it*
Also: **yokahronton** [yo-ka-hrón:-tonh] *it has holes in it.*

948 **yokarote** [yo-ká:-ro-teh] *a bill; an account*

949 **yokennoren** [yo-ken-nó:-renh] *it is raining*
yokennoronhatye' [yo-ken-no-ron-há-tye'] *it is raining (right along);*
yokennorahseròron [yo-ken-no-rah-se-rò:-ronh] *it looks like rain.*

950 **yokennores** [yo-kén:-no-rehs] *it rains*
wa'okennore' [wa'-o-kén:-no-re'] *it rained;* **enyokennore'** [en-yo-kén:-no-re'] *it will rain;* **ayokennore'** [a-yo-kén:-no-re'] *it would rain / for it to rain.*

951 **yokerhi'taràse** [yo-ker-hi'-ta-rà:-seh] *a Christmas tree*

952 **yokha's** [yók-ha's] *it leaks*
wa'okhane' [wa'-ók-ha'-ne'] *it leaked;* **yokha'onh** [yok-há:-'onh] *it has leaked / it did leak;* **yokha'onhatye'** [yok-ha'-on-há-tye'] *it is leaking.*

953 **yokste** [yóks-teh] *it is heavy*
yokstehkwe' [yóks-teh-kwe'] *it was heavy;* **enyoksteke'** [en-yóks-te-ke'] *it will be heavy;* **ayoksteke'** [a-yóks-te-ke'] *it would be / for it to be heavy.*

954 **yokwàronte** [yo-kwà:-ron-teh] *it has a bump on it*
Also: **yokwahronton** [yo-kwa-hrón:-tonh] *it has bumps on it.*

955 **yon'wesen** [yon-wé-sen'] *it is pleasant, nice*

956 **yonàkhwat** [yo-nà:-k-hwat] *it is irritating*

957 **yonanawen** [yo-ná:-na-wenh] *it is wet*

958 **yonara'se'a** [yo-na-ra'-sé:-'ah] *her (female) cousin* (See: onkyara'se'a)

959 **yonatenron** [yo-na-tén:-ronh] *her (female) friend* (See: onkyatenron)

960 **yonehrakwat** [yo-ne-hrá-kwat] *it is amazing, surprising*

961 **yonen'tòren** [yo-nen'-tò:-renh] *a white cedar tree*

962 **yonkyara'se'a** [yon-kya-ra'-sé:-'ah] *my cousin*
tsyara'se'a [tsya-ra'-sé:-'ah] *your cousin;* **ronara'se'a** [ro-na-ra'-sé:-'ah] *his*

cousin(s) (male or female) / her cousin(s) (male); **yonara'se'a** [yo-na-ra'-sé:-'ah] *her cousin(s) (female)*

963 **yonkyatenron** [yon-kya-tén:-ronh] *my friend*
tsyatenron [tsya-tén:-ronh] *your friend*; **ronatenron** [ro-na-tén:-ronh] *his friend(s) (male or female) / her friend (male)*; **onatenron** [o-na-tén:-ronh] *her friend (female)*.

964 **yonkyen'a** [yon-kyén-ha'] *my parents*
yesayen'a [ye-sa-yén:-'ah] *your parents*; **ronwayen'a** [ron-wa-yén:-'ah] *his parents*; **yontatyen'a** [yon-ta-tyén:-'ah] *her parents*.

965 **yononhsa'tariha'tahkwa** [yo-nonh-sa'-ta-ri-ha'-táh-kwa'] *a heater, stove*

966 **yonontakàronte** [yo-non-ta-kà:-ron-teh] *a cave; a cavern*
ie. **Tsi yonontakàronte yahayaweya'te'.** [Tsi yo-non-ta-kà:-ron-teh ya-ha-tá:-we-ya'-te'] *He went into the cave.*

967 **yontate'kenha** [yon-ta-te'-kén-ha'] *her younger sister* (See: khe'kenha)

968 **yontatya'tarahkwa** [yon-ta-tya'-ta-ráh-kwa'] *a camera*

969 **yontatyen'a** [yon-ta-tyén:-ah] *her parents / her daughter* (See: yonkyen'a; kheyen'a)

970 **yontorihshentahkwa** [yon-to-rihs-hen-táh-kwa'] *a couch, chesterfield*
ie. **Yontorihshentahkwatsheràke thenskwahere'.** [Yon-to-rihs-hen-tah-kwats-he-rà:-keh t-hents-kwá-he-re'] *He's sitting (up) on the couch.*

971 **yontya'tokewàtha** [yon-tya'-to-ke-wà:-t-ha'] *a bathtowel*

972 **yora'nentaks** [yo-ra'-nén:-taks] *it sticks on, attaches to; it is sticky*
wa'ora'nentake' [wa'-o-ra'-nén:-ta-ke'] *it stuck to it*; **yora'nentakonh** [yo'-ra'-nen-tá:-konh] *it has stuck to it*;

973 **yora'wihstote** [yo-ra'-wíhs-to-teh] *a page (in a book)*

974 **yorahkote** [yo-ráh-ko-teh] *it is sunny*
yorahkotehkwe' [yo-rah-kó:-teh-kwe'] *it was sunny*; **enyorahkoteke'** [en-yo-rah-kó:-te-ke'] *it will be sunny*; **ayorahkoteke'** [a-yo-rah-kó:-te-ke'] *it would be / for it to be sunny.*

975 **yorahkwawerhon** [yo-rah-kwa-wer-honh] *it is shady*

976 **yorakahre** [yo-rá:-ka-hreh] *it is noisy, loud*

977 **yoràse** [yo-rà:-seh] *it is pretty, lovely, nice to look at*

978 **yoresen'** [yó-re-sen'] *it is fat*
Also: **roresen'** [ró-re-sen'] *he is fat*; **yakoresen'** [ya-kó-re-sen'] *she is fat.*

979 **yorharats** [yor-há:-rats] *it is expected; it is promising*

980 **yorihonte** [yo-rí-hon-teh] *it is good for something*

981 **yorihstahniron** [yo-rihs-tah-ní:-ronh] *steel*

982 **yorihwatoken** [yo-ri-hwa-tó:-kenh] *it is dependable*

983 **yoronhyòron** [yo-ron-hyò:-ronh] *it is cloudy*
yoronhyoronhne' [yo-ron-hyo-rónh-ne'] *it was cloudy*; **enyoronhyòronh** [en-yo-ron-hyò:ronh] *it will be cloudy*; **ayoronhyòronh** [a-yo-ron-hyò:-ronh] *it would be / for it to be cloudy.*

984 **yotekha'** [yo-ték-ha'] *it is burning*
wa'oteke' [wa'-ó:-te-ke'] *it burned*; **yotekenh** [yo-té:-kenh] *it has burned / it did burn.*

985 **yoterihonkon** [yo-te-ri-hón:-konh] *it is a nuisance*

986 **yoterihwihson** [yo-te-ri-hwíh-sonh] *it is acceptable, appropriate*

987 **yothore** [yo-thó:-reh] *it is cold*
yothorehkwe' [yot-hó:-reh-kwe'] *it was cold*; **enyothoreke'** [en-yot-hó:-re-ke'] *it will be cold*; **ayothoreke'** [a-yot-hó:-re-ke'] *it would be / for it to be cold.*

988 **yotitsheronnyàtha** [yo-tits-he-ron-nyà:-t-ha'] *a teapot*

989 **yotiwen** [yo-tí:-wenh] *it is thin (skinny)*
ie. **Sotsi yotiwen** [Só-tsih yo-tí:-wenh] *it is too thin (skinny)*; **Akwah iken' tsi yotiwen** [kwah í:-ken' tsi yo-tí:-wenh] *it is really thin (skinny).* **Rotiwen** [Ro-tí;-wenh] *He is thin (skinny)*; **Yakotiwen** [ya-ko-tí:-wenh] *She is thin.* As an adjectival: **Yonahskwatiwen** [yo-nahs-kwa-tí:-wenh] *a thin (skinny) animal.*

990 **yotkate** [yot-ká:-teh] *often*
ie. **Yotkate tsi yokennores tsi niwakennhehs.** [Yot-ká:-teh tsi yo-kén:-no-rehs tsi ni-wa-kénn-hehs] *It often rains during the summer.*

991 **yotkon** [yót-konh] *it is rotten*

992 **yotokenhti** [yo-to-kénh-tih] *it is sacred*

993 **yotsha'ahton** [yots-ha'-áh-tonh] *it is used up*
ie. **Akwekon yeyotsha'ahton** [A-kwé:-kon ye-yots-ha'-áh-tonh] *it's all used up*; **Yah arekho teyotsha'ahston** [Yah á-rek-ho te-yots-ha'-áh-tonh] *It's not used up yet.*

994 **yotsihstohkware** [yo-tsihs-tóh-kwa-reh] *it has spot on it; it's spotted*
ie. **Yotsihstohkware nène akwatyàtawi'.** [Yo-tsihs-tóh-kwa-reh nè:-neh a-kwa-tyà:-ta-wi'] *My coat has a spot on it / there's a spot on my coat.* Also: **yotsihstohkwaronnyon** [yo-tsihs-toh-kwa-rón-nyon'] *there are spots on it / it has*

spots on it.

995 **yotsìtsyonte** [yo-tsì:-tsyon-teh] *it is blossoming, flowering*
Also: **yotsi'tsyonton** [yo-tsi'-tsyón:-tonh] *it has flowers / they are bossoming.*

996 **yotskàra** [yots-kà:-ra'] *it is bitter*

997 **yottakwarihsyon** [yot-ta-kwa-ríh-syonh] *it is straight*

998 **yoweron** [yo-wé:-ronh] *it is thundering*
Also: **yoweronhatye'** [yo-we-ron-há-tye'] *it's thundering (right along)*; **yoweras** [yo-wé:-ras] *it thunders.*

999 **yowihston** [yo-wíhs-tonh] *it is cool*

1000 **yowisarhon** [yo-wi-sár-honh] *it is sleeting*

ENGLISH - MOHAWK

WORD LIST

ENGLISH - MOHAWK

The following pages provide a alphabetical listing of the English interpretations for the Mohawk vocabulary in the first part of this text. Entry numbers accompany each English lsting. Use this number in order to locate the Mohawk entry, which is set up to provide additional usages.

A

aboriginal people **onkwehonwe** *See: 595*

about (to be) **ike's** *See: 132*

accept **kyenahs** *See: 452*

acceptable **yoterihwihson** *See: 986*

account **yokarote** *See: 948*

acid **o'kenhrakeri** *See: 485*

acquire **wakyenta's** *See: 878*

act quickly **wakatihsnore** *See: 860*

act slowly **wakatihsayen** *See: 859*

afraid **waktheronni** *See: 876*

afternoon **entye nikare** *See: 113*

again **are** *See: 51*; **nok are** *See: 481 a)*; **shekon are** *See: 709 a)*

ago **tsi nahe** *See: 810 c)*

airplane **tekatens** *See: 745*

Algonquins **Atirontaks** *See: 79*

all **akwekon** *See: 38*

allow **kerihenhs** *See: 385*

almost **aonsarekon** *See: 50*

already **onen** *See: 569*

also **oni** *See: 590*

always **tyotkon** *See: 841*

amazed **wakenehrakwas** *See: 871*

amazing **yonehrakwat** *See: 960*

amusing **yo'nikonhrori** *See: 932*

and **nok** *See: 481*; **nok are** *See: 481 a)*; **tahnon** *See: 729*

angry **wakena'khwen'onh** *See: 869*

animal (domestic) **katshenen** *See: 318*; **kanahskwa** *See: 213*

ankle(s) **ohsinekòta** *See: 525*

another **oya** *See: 645*

answer **tkherihwa'serakwas** *See: 804*

anything **othenen** *See: 620*

anywhere **kaneka** *See: 222*

apple **sewahyowane** *See: 698*

apply oneslf **katste'nyarons** *See: 322*

appropriate **yoterihwihson** *See: 986*

April **Onerahtokha** *See: 584*

apron **ateniyonta** *See: 64*

arena **tsi teyonto'tsinehtahkwa** *See: 810 w)*

arm(s) **onentsha** *See: 578*

armband **atenentshawi'tanha** *See: 62*

arrange **ikhseronnis** *See: 142*

arrow **kayènkwire** *See: 337*

as **ne'e tsi** *See: 460 b)*

as...as **tsi niyoht ne** *See: 810 m)*; **tsi niyohsnore tsi** *See: 810 l)*; **tsi niyore tsi** *See: 810 o)*; **tsi ok niyore tsi** *See: 810 t)*

ascend **kerathenhs** *See: 381*

ash (black) **ehsa** *See: 100*; (white) **kaneron** *See: 229*

ask (someone) **kheri'wanontonnis** *See: 413*

asleep **wakitahs** *See: 875*

ass **onatsha** *See: 562*

at **tsi** *See: 810*; **nonwe** *See: 484*

attach to something **ikhnerenks** *See: 139*

attaches to **yora'nentaks** *See: 972*

attempt **kate'nyentenhs** *See: 275*

attractive **yohskats** *See: 942*

August **Sehskeha** *See: 697*

aunt **ihsta'a** *See: 130*

away off **a'eren** *See: 3*

axe **atoken** *See: 84*

B

baby animal **owira** *See: 642*; **owira'a** *See: 643*

back **otsi'nohyohsa** *See: 626*; **ohswa** *See: 535*

bad **yo'taksen** *See: 934*

bag **kayare** *See: 334*

ball **athenno'** *See: 75*

banana **tyotahyàkton** *See: 840*

band **kanènra** *See: 227*

bandage **yekentorahkwa** *See: 917*

barn **tsi yetskwa'ehstha** *See: 810 ff)*

barrel **ka'nahkwa** *See: 157*

basket **àthere** *See: 76*

bass **ohskawiyak** *See: 527*

basswood tree **ohohsera** *See: 513*

bat **yakohonhtariks** *See: 894*

bathroom **tsi yotahshetahkwen** *See: 810 kk)*

bathtowel **yontya'tokewàtha** *See: 971*

beans **ohsahèta** *See: 519*; **orhotsheri** *See: 617*

bear **ohkwari'** *See: 503*

beautiful **yohskats** *See: 942*

beaver **tsyennìto** *See: 827*

because **ahse'ken** *See: 9*; **ne'e tsi** *See: 400 b)*

bed **kanakta** *See: 215*

bedroom **tsi yonnonhwetstha** *See: 810 ii)*

beer **katsi'tsyakeras** *See: 319*; **onen'takeri** *See: 571*

believe **tekehtahkwa'** *See: 753*

belt **atya'tanha** *See: 91*

besides **tahnon** *See: 729*

Bible **kahyatonhseratokenhti** *See: 204*

big **kowanen** *See: 443*

bile **otsinekwar** *See: 631*

bill **yokarote** *See: 948*

billfold **yehwihstarahkwa** *See: 911*

bird **tsi'tenha** *See: 811*

bit **ohstonha** *See: 533*

bitter **yotskàra** *See: 996*

black **kahòntsi** *See: 180*

black ash **ehsa** *See: 100*

blanket **ahsire** *See: 16*

blood **onekwenhsa** *See: 566*

blossoming **yotsìtsyonte** *See: 995*

blue **orònya** *See: 619*

board **ohswènkare** *See: 536*

boat **kahonweya** *See: 181*

body **oyàta** *See: 647*; **oyerònta** *See: 654*

bone **ohstyen'** *See: 534*

bonnet **anònwarore** *See: 48*

book case **yehyatonhserarahkwa** *See: 913*

book **kahyatonhsera** *See: 202*

bow **a'enna** *See: 2*

bowl **yenon'tarahkwa** *See: 925*; **yetsikhe'tarahkwa** *See: 929*

box **karontotshera** *See: 265*

boy **raksa'a** *See: 658*; **ratiksa'okonha**

See: 62

bracelet **atenentshaanha** *See: 61*

brain **onònwara** *See: 607*

branch **o'nhahte** *See: 487*

bread **kanàtaronk** *See: 218*

break something **tekhrihtha'** *See: 763*

brick **o'tara** *See: 492*

bridge **wahskohon** *See: 850*

bright **teyohswathe'** *See: 786*

brother (older) **raktsi'a** *See: 659*

brother (younger) **ri'kenha** *See: 669*

brown **athehsa** *See: 74*

bucket **kanàtsyonk** *See: 221*

bug **otsi'nowa** *See: 627*

building **kanonhsa** *See: 238*

bump **yokwaronte** *See: 954*

bundle **atakwari** *See: 55*

bundle something up **katakwariks**
  See: 270

burden **kahryèna** *See: 184*

burning **yotekha'** *See: 984*

bush(es) **okwire** *See: 558*

but **nok** *See: 481*; **ne ok tsi** *See: 458 b)*;
  nok are *See: 481 a)*

butter **owihstohsera** *See: 641*

butterfly **tsiktsinonnawen** *See: 819*

buttermilk **kanon'tihsa** *See: 237*

buttock(s) **ohohkwa** *See: 512*; **onatsha**
  See: 562

button **otsihkwa** *See: 628*

buy **khninons** *See: 421*

by what **tsi nahòten** *See: 810 d)*

C

calculate **kahseta's** *See: 187*

camera **yontatya'tarahkwa** *See: 968*

cane **atennits** *See: 67*

canoe **onake** *See: 561*

car **kàsere'** *See: 268*

carcass **oyerònta** *See: 654*

carpet **kentskare** *See: 372*

carrots **otsinekwar ohtera** *See: 632*

carry on oneself **ikhawe'** *See: 128*

carry (with oneself) **khawis** *See: 398*

cat **takohs** *See: 731*

catch **kyenahs** *See: 452*

catepillar **kanontatsti** *See: 243*

cave **yonontakàronte** *See: 966*

cavern **yonontakàronte** *See: 966*

Cayuga nation **Kayonkwe'hàka** *See: 341*

cedar **yonen'tòren** *See: 961*

cedar (red) **onen'takwenhton** *See: 572*

chair **ennitskwàra** *See: 111*

change **tektenyes** *See: 767*

chant **karenna** *See: 248*

cheap **yah tekanoron** *See: 887 g)*

cheek(s) **ohohkwa** *See: 512*

cherry **eri** *See: 117*

chesterfield **yontorihshentahkwa**
  See: 970

child **eksa'a** *See: 101*

children **eksa'okonha** *See: 102*;
  ratiksa'okonha *See: 662*

chin **ohyotsha** *See: 546*

chipmunk **orhyoken** *See: 618*

choose **kerakwas** *See: 380*

Christianity **Karihstyahne** *See: 255*

Christmas tree **yokerhi'taràse** *See: 951*

church **Ononhsatokenhti** *See: 601*

circle **okahkwènta** *See: 548*

city **kanatowanen** *See: 220*

clan **o'tara** *See: 492*

clay **o'tara** *See: 492*

clean off **kerakewas** *See: 380*

climb up **kerathenhs** *See: 381*;
  tkerathenhs *See: 803*; **yekerathenhs**
  See: 918

close the door **kenhotons** *See: 358*

closet **yohkwennyarahkwa** *See: 937*

clothes **ahkwennya'** *See: 7*

clothing **ahkwennya'** *See: 7*;
  athseronnya' *See: 7*

cloudy **yoronhyòron** *See: 983*

clown **attsihstohkwa** *See: 90*

club **otsihkwa** *See: 628*

coat **atyàtawi'** *See: 92*

coffee **teyohsahe'tahnekonnyàtha**
  See: 784; **kahwe** *See: 784*

coffee pot **kahwetsheronnyàtha** *See: 198*

cold **yothore** *See: 987*

collection **otyohkwa** *See: 638*

colouring **ahsohkwa** *See: 17*

comb **atkerothiya** *See: 81*

come **take'** *See: 730*

come down **tkathsnenhtha'** *See: 799*

come in **tkataweyàtha'** *See: 798*

come out **yekataweyàtha'** *See: 915*

Confederacy (Iroquois) **Rotinonhsyonni**
  See: 690

consent **kathontats** *See: 293*

consequently **kati** *See: 298*

conserve **kateweyèntons** *See: 292*

contains **ikare** *See: 127*

control **tkennonhtons** *See: 802*

cook **kehrihtha'** *See: 344*; **kekhonnis**
  See: 346

cook stove **yekhonnya'tahkwa** *See: 919*

cool **yowihston** *See: 999*

copy **tekhna'neta's** *See: 762*

corn **onenhste** *See: 575*

corn seed **onenha** *See: 573*

corn soup **onenhsto** *See: 576*

corn soup (lyed) **kanenhstohare**
  See: 226

corner **tsi teyothyohsate** *See: 810 z)*

costume **kanena** *See: 225*

cottontail **kwa'yenha** *See: 446*

couch **yontorihshentahkwa** *See: 970*

cough **kahshakha'** *See: 188*

councillor **ratsyenhayens** *See: 667*;
  ratitsyenhayens *See: 665*

cousin **yonkyara'se'a** *See: 962*

count **kahseta's** *See: 187*

cover (for a pail, basket, etc...)
  atenon'teksta *See: 68*

cover something **kerhòroks** *See: 384*

cow **tyonnhonhskwaron** *See: 838*

Creator **Shonkwaya'tihson** *See: 716*

Cree **Ratirhakonha** *See: 664*

creek **nikahyonha'a** *See: 467*

cricket **taraktarak** *See: 733*

crooked **teyotshàkton** *See: 790*

crow **tsyòkawe** *See: 830*

crying **tekahshenthos** *See: 739*

cucumber(s) **kanon'onhserakeras**
  See: 236

cupboard **tsi yeksayentahkwa**
  See: 810 dd)

curved **teyotshàkton** *See: 790*

cushion **atkònsera** *See: 82*

customarily **ens** *See: 112*

cut in half **tekya'ks** *See: 768*

cut off (of) **ikya'ks** *See: 151*

cut (open) **khrenahs** *See: 425*

D

dance **kanonnya** *See: 241*;
tekenonnyahkwa' *See: 761*; tsi
tetkanonnyahkwa *See: 810 v)*

dangerous **teyoteryen'thara** *See: 788*

damage something **katyesàtha'** *See: 326*

dark-coloured **kahòntsi** *See: 180*

daughter **kheyen'a** *my daughter See: 417*

day **tsi niwenhniserehs** *See: 810 i)*

dear **kanoron** *See: 244*

December **Tsyothorha** *See: 832*

deer **ohskennonton** *See: 528*

definitely **se'** *See: 695*

depart **kahtentyes** *See: 193*

dependable **yorihwatoken** *See: 982*

descend **kathsnenhtha'** *See: 295*;
yekathsnenhtha' *See: 916*

desk **yehyatonhstahkwa** *See: 914*

detest **ikhswenhs** *See: 144*

devote oneslf to **katste'nyarons** *See: 322*

dining room **tsi teyontskàhons**
See: 810 y)

direction **kenh nonkati** *See: 352 b)*;
eh nonkati *See: 99 e)*

dirt **o'kènra** *See: 486*

dish **kaksa** *See: 210*

dislike **ikhswenhs** *See: 144*

distant **inon niyore** *See: 153 a)*

do something **nikyerha'** *See: 475*;
nikatyerha' *See: 470*

doesn't matter **Thiyaweronhatye'**
See: 794

dog **erhar** *See: 115*

doll **kaya'tonni** *See: 332*

dollar **skahwihstat** *See: 720*

door **kanhoha** *See: 231*

doorway **tsi kanhokàronte** *See: 810*

dough **ohsherha** *See: 522*

doughnuts **kahsherhonni** *See: 189*

downtown **kanathen** *See: 219*

drag **katèseres** *See: 290*

draw **kerahstha'** *See: 378*

drawing **karahsto** *See: 247*

dress **o'whahsa** *See: 497*; **atyàtawi'**
See: 92

dress up **ikhseronnis** *See: 142*;
kathseronnis *See: 294*

drink (soft) **kahnekakon** *See: 166*

drink **khnekirha'** *See: 420*

drinking water **ohnekanos** *See: 508*

drive **katoris** *See: 315*

drop (by accident) **wakàsen's** *See: 854*

drop down **ka'senhtha'** *See: 157*

dry **yohstathen** *See: 944*

duck **sorak** *See: 728*

dull **yah teyohyo'thiye** *See: 887 h)*

duplicate **tekhna'neta's** *See: 762*

durable **yohniron** *See: 939*

during **tsi nikarìwehs** *See: 810 f)*; tsi
niwenhnìtehs *during the month See: 810
j)*; **tsi niwenhniserehs** *during the day
See: 810 i)*; **tsi niwahsontehs** *during the
night See: 810 h)*; **tsi niyohserehs**
during the year See: 810 k)

dust **o'kènra** *See: 486*

dusty **yo'kènrare** *See: 930*

dye **ahsohkwa** *See: 17*

E

eagle **akweks** *See: 39*

ear **ohonhsa** *See: 514*; **ohonhta** *See:
515*

early **orhen'kehtsi** *See: 615*

earring **ate'wahsare** *See: 58*

eat a meal **tekatskàhonhs** *See: 749*

eat **ikeks** *See: 134*

eat soup **kathsoris** *See: 297*

eat **katekhonnis** *See: 278*

effort **kahkwihsrons** *See: 164*

egg **o'nhonhsa** *See: 488*

eight **sha'tekon** *See: 700*

elastic **ohnatirontha** *See: 504*

elbow **ohyohsa** *See: 545*

elm **akaratsi** *See: 26*

employment **kayo'tenhsera** *See: 340*

encourage **khehretsyarons** *See: 400*

English nation **Tyorhenhshàka** *See: 839*

ensemble **atahkwennya'** *See: 54*

enter **kataweyàtha'** *See: 274*

envelope **watya'tarahkwa** *See: 882*

erase **khyatonhkwas** *See: 426*

eraser **tsyerakewahtha** *See: 828*

evergreen(s) **onènta** *See: 577*

everything **akwekon** *See: 38*; **akwah tsi ok nahòten** *See: 37 j)*

everywhere **akwah tsi ok nonwe** *See: 37 k)*

examine **katkènse's** *See: 305*

examine **ikka'ènyons** *See: 145*

exit **kyaken's** *See: 499*

expect **katerharats** *See: 286*

expected **yorharats** *See: 979*

expensive **kanoron** *See: 244*

extinguish (a fire / light) **kahswàtha'** *See: 192*

eye(s) **okàra** *See: 551*

eyelash(es) **okahrehta** *See: 549*

F

face **kakonhsa** *See: 209*

face **okònwara** *See: 555*

fall (a season) **kannenna'kène** *See: 234*

fall **kyaten's** *See: 451*

fall from **kya'tyènen's** *See: 448*

family **kahwatsire** *See: 195*

far **inon** *See: 153*; **eh niyore tsi** *See: 99 c)*; **to niyore** *See: 806 e)*; **tsi niyore tsi** *See: 810 o)*; **tsi ok niyore tsi** *See: 810 t)*

far away **a'eren** *See: 3*; **inon niyore** *See: 153 a)*

fast **oksa** *See: 556*; **yohsnore** *See: 943*; **akwah ken' niyohsnore tsi** *See: 37 f)*; **eh niyohsnore tsi** *See: 99 d)*; **tsi niyohsnore tsi** *See: 810 l)*

fast runner **tewakeka** *See: 773*

fat **yoresen'** *See: 978*

father **rake'niha** *my father See: 655*

February **Ennihska** *See: 107*

feed (someone) **khenontens** *See: 407*

feet **ohsìta** *See: 526*

femur **ohahsa** *See: 500*

fence **aten'ènra** *See: 60*

few **tho ok nikon** *See: 795*

field **kahehta** *See: 160*

fight **kateriyos** *See: 288*

find **ketshenryes** *See: 390*

finger nail(s) **otsi'era** *See: 625*

finger(s) **ohsnonhsa** *See: 529*

firewood **oyente** *See: 652*

fish **kentsyonk** *See: 376*

fist **otsihkwa** *See: 628*

five **wisk** *See: 885*

fix **ikkwatakwas** *See: 147*

fix up **ikhseronnis** *See: 142*

fixed up **katkwatakwas** *See: 307*

floor **ohson'karàke** *See: 532*

floor matt **kentskare** *See: 372*

flour **athèsera** *See: 621*

flower vase **yetsi'tsyarahkwa** *See: 928*

flower pot **yetsi'tsyarahkwa** *See: 928*

flower bed **katsi'tsyayenthon** *See: 320*

flowering **yotsìtsyonte** *See: 995*

fly **tsiks** *See: 818*

fly about **kitye's** *See: 432*

follow **ikhseres** *See: 140*

follow someone **khehseres** *See: 402*

food **kakhwa** *See: 207*

foot **ohsìta** *See: 526*

footware **ahta'** *See: 26*

for **iken'** *See: 135*

forehead **okonkwara** *See: 553*

forehead **okontstara** *See: 554*

fork **ahsikwe** *See: 14*

fortunate **wakatera'swiyo** *See: 856*

four **kayeri** *See: 338*

fox **tsitsho** *See: 821*

freeze something
   kenennyo'kwanenhstha' *See: 351*

fresh meat **o'wahràse** *See: 495*

Friday **Wiskhatont** *See: 886*

fried fish **kentsyakehrìta** *See: 376*

fried meat **ka'wahrakehrìta** *See: 159*

fried potatoes **kahnenna'takehrìta**
   See: 167

friend **yonkyatenron** *my friend See: 963*

frog **tsikeren'tanhnyaks** *See: 815*

fruit **kahik** *See: 163*

fruit tree **kerhite** *See: 383*

fruit (to pick) **kahyakwas** *See: 200*

fruit juice **wahyakeri** *See: 852*

fry **ktakerìta's** *See: 444*

frying pan **yena'tsyarahkwa** *See: 923*

full **kanànon** *See: 216*

funny **yo'nikonhrori** *See: 932*

G

gamble **tekyens** *See: 769*

game **okahrìtshera** *See: 550*

gas station **tsi kenhyenahninons**
   See: 810 B)

gather up **keròroks** *See: 387*

get **wakyenta's** *See: 878*

get into **katita's** *See: 299*

get out of **katitahkwas** *See: 300*

get up **katketskwas** *See: 306*

get used to **kerennha's** *See: 382*

gift **atatawi** *See: 56*

girl **yeksa'a** *See: 920*

girl friend **akya'tasetshera** *See: 40*

girls **kontiksa'okonha** *See: 440*

give (someone) **kheyawis** *See: 416*

glass **owise** *See: 644*

glasses **atkahranha** *See: 80*

gloves **a'nyanawen'** *See: 5*

glue **teyekhahstha** *See: 781*

go in **tkyaken's** *See: 805*

go out **yekyaken's** *See: 922*

goat **kaya'takeras** *See: 330*

God **Rawenniyo** *See: 668*

going **ike'** *See: 131;* **wàke'** *See: 864;*
   yake' *See: 889*

gold **ohwihstanoron** *See: 541*

good **awiyo** *See: 95*

good at **keweyenhon** *See: 392*

good for something **yorihonte** *See: 980*

good (smelling) **kahserakon** *See: 186*

good-tasting **yawekon** *See: 903*

goose **onahsakenra** *See: 560*

grain **enhnekeri** *See: 104*

grandfather **rakhsotha** *See: 657*

grandmother **akhsotha** *See: 31*

grape(s) **onenharatase** *See: 574*

grass **ohonte** *See: 517*

grasshopper **tsihstarare** *See: 813*

green **ohonte** *See: 517*

groceries **atennàtshera** *See: 65*

grocery store **tsi yekhwahninons** *See: 810 cc)*

group (organized) **kanènra** *See: 227*

group **otyohkwa** *See: 638*

guard **ikenonhne'** *See: 136*

gum **ohnehta** *See: 505*

gun **kahonre** *See: 169*

H

hailing **tyowihsonhtyon** *See: 844*

hair **ononhkwise** *See: 600*

hand(s) **ohsnonhsa** *See: 529*

handbag **kenhnàta** *See: 355*

handful **othsyana** *See: 622*

Handsome Lake religion **Karihwiyo** *See: 258*

hang up **kharha'** *See: 397*

hanging down **yohrènton** *See: 941*

happens **niyawen's** *See: 478*

happy **wakatshennonni** *See: 862*

hard to come by **kanoron** *See: 244*

hard **yohniron** *See: 939*

harvest **kyenthokwas** *See: 454*

hat **anònwarore** *See: 48*

hatchet **atoken** *See: 84*

hate **ikhswenhs** *See: 144*

have **wakyen'** *See: 877*

have a knack for **keweyenhon** *See: 392*

have on oneself **ikhawe** *See: 128*

have to **tkakonte** *See: 797*

hawk **karhakonha** *See: 250*

hay **enhnekeri** *See: 104*

he **raonha** *See: 661*

head **onontsi** *See: 606*

headband **atenonhwaranha** *See: 69*

headdress **kahstowa** *See: 191*

heaped up **yo'tònyote** *See: 936*

hear **kahronkas** *See: 182*; **wakathonte** *See: 858*

hearing **ohonhsa** *See: 514*

heart **aweryahsa** *See: 94*

heat **o'tarihenhsera** *See: 493*

heat up **ka'tarihàtha'** *See: 158*

heater **yononhsa'tariha'tahkwa** *See: 965*

heavy **yokste** *See: 953*

help (someone) **kheyenawa's** *See: 418*

hemlock **onen'ta'onwe** *See: 570*

her **akaonha** *See: 25*

here **kenh nonwe** *See: 352 c)*

here **kèntho** *See: 371*

here **kenh ki' nonwe** *See: 352 a)*

hereabouts **kenh nonwe tsi niwat** *See: 352 d)*

heron **kentsyokwas** *See: 375*

hide (something) **kahsehtha'** *See: 185*

hide **katahsehtha'** *See: 269*

hill **ononta** *See: 603*

him **raonha** *See: 661*

hockey rink **tsi teyonto'tsinehtahkwa** *See: 810 w)*

hoe **atshòkten** *See: 88*

hole **yokàronte** *See: 947*

hole **ohshonwa** *See: 523*

honey **ohshehs** *See: 521*

hope for **katerharats** *See: 286*

horse **yakohsatens** *See: 895*

hospital **tsi yakoheyon'tayentahkwa**
  See: 810 aa)

hot **yo'tarihen** *See: 935*

house **kanonhsa** *See: 238*

household **kanahkwa** *See: 212*

how **to** *See: 806*

  how far **to niyore** *See: 806 e)*

  how is it **to niyoht** *See: 806 d)*

  how long **to niyenhs** *See: 806 c)*

  how long **to nikarìwehs** *See: 806 a)*

  how many **to nikon** *See: 806 b)*

huckleberry **àyok** *See: 96*

hundred **tewen'nyawer** *See: 779*

hungry **katonhkarya'ks** *See: 312*

hunt **katorats** *See: 313*

hunter **ratorats** *See: 666*

hurry **tewakhsterihenh** *See: 775*

hurt someone **khekahrewahtha'** *See: 403*

husband **rone** *See: 680*

I

I **i'i** *See: 126*

ice **owise** *See: 644*

if **tokat** *See: 808*

ill-tempered **ikhserohen** *See: 141*

indeed **se'** *See: 695*

Indian tobacco **oyen'kwahonwe** *See: 648*

inexpensive **yah tekanoron** *See: 887 g)*

insect **otsi'nowa** *See: 627*

instead **nène yawet** *See: 463 a)*; **khere
  ken'en** *See: 410*; **kheken** *See: 404*

Iroquois Confederacy **Rotinonhsyonni**
  See: 690

irritating **yonàkhwat** *See: 956*

isn't it **wahi** *See: 846*

it **aonha** *See: 49*

it is **iken'** *See: 135*

it is that... **ne'e** *See: 460*

J

jack rabbit **taonhtaneken** *See: 732*

January **Tsyothorkowa** *See: 833*

job **kayo'tenhsera** *See: 340*

juice **wahyakeri** *See: 852*

July **Ohyarihkowa** *See: 544*

jump **tekenni'tsyonhkwahkwa'** *See: 760*

June **Ohyariha** *See: 543*

K

keep **katerakwas** *See: 284*

kill **keryos** *See: 386*

kitchen **tsi yekhonnyàtha** *See: 810 bb)*

knee **okwitsha** *See: 559*

knife **àshare** *See: 53*

know **wakateryèntare** *See: 857*

know how to **keweyente** *See: 393*

know (someone) **kheyenteri** *See: 419*

L

lacrosse (game) **attsihkwa'e** *See: 89*

ladder **kanekòta** *See: 223*

lake **kanyatare** *See: 245*

lamp **ohahsera** *See: 501*

land **onhwentsya** *See: 589*

last night **shiyòkarahs** *See: 711*

later **onwahtsi ok** *See: 610*

laying down **katya'tyonni'** *See: 324*

laying on **kayen'** *See: 336*

laying down (on) **kaya'tyonni** *See: 333*

leaf **onerahte** *See: 583*

leaks **yokha's** *See: 952*

learn **keweyentehta's** *See: 394*

leave **kahtentyes** *See: 193*

leaves **onerahte** *See: 583*

leg(s) **ohsina** *See: 524*

let go **katkawas** *See: 303*

let it be **kenhak** *See: 353*

lettuce **onerahtakate** *See: 582*

lid (for a pail, basket, etc...)
  atenon'teksta *See: 68*

lie **onowen'** *See: 608*

life **atonnhets** *See: 86*

light **yah teyokste** *See: 887 i)*

light **ohahsera** *See: 501*

light-coloured **kenraken** *See: 368*

lightning **tewennine'karahwanyon's**
  See: 780

like **kenònwe's** *See: 367*

like the taste **wakekahs** *See: 868*

like (someone) **khenònwe's** *See: 408*

lips **ohsa** *See: 518*

liquid **ohneka** *See: 507*

liquor **kahneka'shatste** *See: 165*

little **ohstonha** *See: 533*

little bit **nikonha** *See: 473*

live in a place **kenakeres** *See: 349*

living room **tsi kanonhsiyo** *See: 810 a)*

load **kahryèna** *See: 184*

lock something **keniyontarhos** *See: 359*

log **karonta** *See: 263*

long **iyenhs** *See: 155*; **to nikarìwehs**
  See: 806 a); **to niyenhs** *See: 806 c)*

long for **kenònwaks** *See: 366*

long time **akwah ken' nikarìwehs**
  See: 37 c)

long time ago **wahonnise** *See: 847*

longhouse **kanonhsehs** *See: 239*

Longhouse religion **Kanonhsehsneha**
  See: 240

look **katkahthos** *See: 301*

look after **kateweyèntons** *See: 292*

look at **katkènse's** *See: 305*

look at **tekkanere'** *See: 765*

look for **kesaks** I look for / looking for
  See: 388

lot **eso** *See: 118*

lot of **yawe'towanen** *See: 902*

loud **yorakahre** *See: 976*

love (someone) **khenoronhkwa'** *See: 409*

lovely **yoràse** *See: 977*

lower something down **ka'senhtha'**
  See: 157

lunch **atennàtshera** *See: 65*

lucky **wakatera'swiyo** *See: 856*

lump **yokwaronte** *See: 954*

lye **o'kenhrakeri** *See: 485*

M

make **konnis** *See: 436*

make from **konnyàtha'** *See: 437*

make use of **katstha'** *See: 321*

male **rohskenhrakehte** *See: 674*

males **rotihskenhrakehte** *See: 688*

man **ronkwe** *See: 681*

many **eso** *See: 118*; **to nikon**
  See: 806 b)
maple **wahtha** *hard maple See: 851*;
  kahtha'kenra *soft maple See: 194*
March **Ennihskowa** *See: 108*
marriage **kanahkwa** *See: 212*
mask **kakonhsa** *See: 209*
matt **kentskare** *See: 372*
May **Onerahtokkowa** *See: 585*
maybe **tokat nonwa** *See: 808 a)*
me **i'i** *See: 126*
meadow **kahènta** *See: 161*
measure **kate'nyentenhstha'** *See: 276*
measuring stick **wate'nyentenhstahkwa**
  See: 880
meat **o'wàronk** *See: 496*;
  ka'wahrakehrìta *fried meat See: 159*;
  o'wahràse *fresh meat See: 495*
medicine **ononhkwa'** *See: 599*
men **rononkwe** *See: 84*
mend **ke'nikhons** *See: 342*
metal **karihstatsi** *See: 253*
mid-town **kanathen** *See: 219*
Mid-winter **Anonhwarori** *See: 45*
midnight **ahsonthen** *See: 19*
milk **onònta** *See: 604*
milk pitcher **yenon'tarahkwa** *See: 925*
minnow **kaniyonta** *See: 233*
mirror **atatken** *See: 57*
mistake **tekenera'ks** *See: 754*
misty **tyotsha'tayenthon** *See: 842*
mittens **a'nyanawen'** *See: 5*
mitts **a'nyanawen'** *See: 5*
moccasin(s) **ahtahkwa'onwe** *See: 23*
Mohawk nation **Kahnyen'kehàka**
  See: 168
Monday **Yawententa'onh** *See: 906*

money **ohwihsta** *See: 539*
month **tsi niwenhnìtehs** *See: 810 j)*
moose **ska'nyonhsa** *See: 719*
morning **orhen'kène** *See: 616*
moss **awerahsa** *See: 93*
mother **ake'nihstenha** *my mother See: 27*
mouse **tsinowen** *See: 820*
mouth **ohsakàra** *See: 520*
move over **katkwìtha'** *See: 309*
mud **onawatsta** *See: 563*
muskrat **anókyen** *See: 44*

N

nail **karonware** *See: 266*
native **onkwehonwe** *See: 595*
native way of doing **onkwehonwehneha**
  See: 596
nearly **thoha** *See: 796*
necessary **teyotonhwentsyohon** *See: 789*
neck **onyàra** *See: 611*
necklace **ennihtyakstha** *See: 110*
necktie **teyontenyàteren'** *See: 787*
need **tewakatonhwentsyoni** *See: 772*
need (be in need of) **tekatkaryas**
  See: 747
needle **karonware** *See: 266*
net **a'are** *See: 1*
never **yah nonwenton** *See: 887 d)*
nice **yon'wesen** *See: 955*
nice **yoràse** *See: 977*
night **shiyòkarahs** *See: 711*;
  tsi niwahsontehs *See: 810 h)*;
  ahsonthènne' *See: 20*
night time **ahsonthènne'** *See: 20*
nine **tyohton** *See: 836*

no yah / yahten *See: 887*

no longer **yah nonwa onen** *See: 887 c)*

no matter **yaweronhatye** *See: 907*

no one **yah onhka** *See: 887 e)*

nobody **yah onhka** *See: 887 e)*

noisy **yorakahre** *See: 976*

nose **o'nyonhsa** *See: 489*

not right now **yah ki' nonwa** *See: 887 b)*

not yet **arekho** *See: 52*

nothing **yah othenen** *See: 887 f)*

nourishment **kakhwa** *See: 207*

November **Kenkenhkowa** *See: 370*

now **onen** *See: 569;* **nonwa** *See: 483*

nowhere **yah kaneka** *See: 887 a)*

nuisance **yoterihonkon** *See: 985*

number of **nikon** *See: 472;* **nihati** *See: 465;* **nikahwihstake** *See: 466;* **nikonti** *See: 474*

nut(s) **ohsòkwa** *See: 531*

O

oak (red) **karihton** *See: 256*

oak (white) **otokenha** *See: 624*

obstinate **katerahya'tahkwa'** *See: 283*

October **Kentenha** *See: 369*

of course **wahi** *See: 846*

often **yotkate** *See: 990*

oil **kènye'** *See: 377*

old man **rokstenha** *See: 677*

old men **rotiksten'okonha** *See: 689*

old people **rotiksten'okonha** *See: 689*

old woman **akokstenha** *See: 35*

old women **kontiksten'okonha** *See: 441*

older sister **aktsi'a** *See: 36*

one **enhskat** *See: 105*

one animal **skayàtat** *See: 724*

one female **tsyeyàtat** *See: 829*

one male **shayàtat** *See: 707*

one who **tsi nikayen'** *See: 810 g)*

Oneida nation **Onenyotehàka** *See: 581*

onions (cooking) **anonk** onions (cooking onions) *See: 46*

onions (green) **anonkshera** *See: 47*

only **ok** *See: 547;* **ne ok ne'e** *See: 458 a);* **akwah ne ok ne'e** *See: 37 g)*

Onondaga nation **Ononta'kehàka** *See: 605*

open the door **kenhotonkwas** *See: 357*

or **netens** *See: 464;* **katon** *See: 311*

or else **netens** *See: 464*

orange **otyarènta** *See: 637*

other side **ihsi nonkati** *See: 129 b);* **ihsi nonwe** *See: 129 a)*

other(s) **otya'ke** *See: 636*

otter **tawine** *See: 734*

outfit **atahkwennya'** *See: 54*

over there **ken' nonwe t-** *See: 348 a)*

owl **tsihstekeri** *See: 814*

P

pack **kahryèna** *See: 184*

package **atakwari** *See: 55*

package something **katakwariks** *See: 270*

page **yora'wihstote** *See: 973*

pail **kanàtsyonk** *See: 221*

pair **oyana** *See: 646*

pants **athahsteren'** *See: 73*

paper **kahyatonhsera** *See: 202*

parents **yonkyen'a** *my parents See: 964*

parrot **tekahstya'ks** *See: 740*

partidge **ahkwesen** *See: 8*

partner **tyakenìteron** *See: 835*

pasture **kahènta** *See: 161*

pathway **ohaha** *See: 499*

pattern **wathyatons** *See: 881*

peace **skennen** *See: 725*

peacefully **skennenha** *See: 726*;
  skennenhahson'a *See: 727*

pear **katshe' kahik** *See: 317*

peas **onekwa** *See: 565*

pen **yehyatonhkwa** *See: 912*

pencil **yehyatonhkwa** *See: 912*

pepper **tyotskara'kowa** *See: 843*

perch **oyenhèta** *See: 649*

perhaps **tokat** *See: 808*; **onhte** *See: 588*

person **oyàta** *See: 647*; **onkwe** *See: 594*

persons **ononkwe** *See: 602*

pet **katshenen** *See: 318*

pick fruit **kahyakwas** *See: 200*

pick something up **tekehkwa'** *See: 752*

pickerel **skakahraksen** *See: 721*

picture **kayàtare** *See: 335*

pig **kweskwes** *See: 447*

pike **tsikonhses** *See: 817*

pile **o'tonwa** *See: 494*

piled up **yo'tònyote** *See: 936*

pillow **atkònsera** *See: 82*

pine tree **ohnehta'kowa** *See: 506*

pink **wehsènrate** *See: 883*

pipe **ohonrota** *See: 516*

pitch **ohnehta** *See: 505*

pitcher **yehnekarahkwa** *See: 910*;
  yenon'tarahkwa *See: 925*

place **eh nonwe** *See: 99 f)*; **kanakta**
  See: 215

plank **ohswènkare** *See: 536*

plant **kyenthos** *See: 455*

plantain **atenneha** *See: 66*

plate **akèra** *See: 30*

play cards **tekyens** *See: 769*

playing **wakatkahritsheronni** *See: 861*

pleasant **yon'wesen** *See: 955*

pleased **wake'nikonhrahseronni**
  See: 865

plentiful **kennakere** *See: 361*

plum(s) **wihson kahik** *See: 884*

pole **kanakare** *See: 214*

poorly done **yo'taksen** *See: 934*

pop (soda) **kahnekakon** *See: 166*

porcupine **anèntaks** *See: 41*

pot **yetsi'tsyarahkwa** *See: 928*

potatoes **ohnennàta** *See: 510*

potatoes (fried) **kahnenna'takehrìta**
  See: 167

pour **kawerons** *See: 329*

practice **kateweyenhstha'** *See: 291*

prayer **aterennayent** *See: 72*

present **atatawi** *See: 56*

presently **nonwa** *See: 483*

pretty **yoràse** *See: 977*

profit from **tekatèntsha's** *See: 746*

promising **yorharats** *See: 979*

proper **tkayeri** *See: 801*

provisions **atennàtshera** *See: 65*

pull **tkatirontha'** *See: 800*

puppy **eris** *See: 116*

purple **oharennahta** *See: 502*

purse **kenhnàta** *See: 355*

pursue **ikhseres** *See: 140*

put around the neck **kennihtya'ks**
  See: 363

put away **kateweyèntons** *See: 292*

put effort into **kahkwihsrons** *See: 164*

put inside **keta's** *See: 389*

put out (a fire / light) **kahswàtha'**
See: 192

Q

quick **oksa** *See: 556*; **akwah oksa ok**
See: 37 h); **yohsnore** *See: 943*

quick to act **wakatihsnore** *See: 860*

quickly **oksa ok** *See: 556 a)*

quietly **skennenhahson'a** *See: 727*;
skennenha *See: 726*

quit **katkawas** *See: 303*

quite **akwah tsi** *See: 37 i)*; **akwah**
See: 37

quiver **ahtatshera** *See: 24*

R

rabbit **kwa'yenha** *See: 446*;
taonhtaneken *See: 732*

raccoon **atiron** *See: 78*

radio **kawennokwas** *See: 327*

raining **yokennoren** *See: 949*

rains **yokennores** *See: 950*

raspberries **skanekwenhtarati** *See: 722*

rattle **ahstawen** *See: 21*

read aloud **kewennahnotha'** *See: 391*

read to oneself **kataterihonnyennis**
See: 271

reason **karihonni** *See: 251*

reasonable **kattokha'** *See: 323*

receive **kyenahs** *See: 452*

red **onekwenhtara** *See: 567*

red cedar **onen'takwenhton** *See: 572*

red oak **karihton** *See: 256*

refrigerator **kakhwawihstonhtha**
See: 208

relative **yakyatatenonhkwe** *See: 897*

remember **kehyàra's** *See: 345*; **keyahre'**
See: 395

remove from **ktahkwas** *See: 445*

reserve **onkwehonwène'** *See: 597*

rest **katorihshenhs** *See: 314*

restaurant **tsi teyontska'honhkwa**
See: 810 x)

ribbon **kanheks** *See: 230*

rifle **kahonre** *See: 169*

right **tkayeri** *See: 801*

ring **ennihsnonhsawi'** *See: 42, 109*

river **kahyonhowanen** *See: 205*

road **ohaha** *See: 499*

roast something **ke'skontha'** *See: 343*

robin **tsihskoko** *See: 812*

rock **otstènra** *See: 635*

roof **ahskwa** *See: 16*

root(s) **ohtera** *See: 538*

rope **ahseriye'** *See: 12*

rotten **yotkon** *See: 991*

rough **yaokat** *See: 899*

rubber **ohnatirontha** *See: 504*

ruler **wate'nyentenhstahkwa** *See: 880*

run **iktakhe's** *See: 150*; **tewakeka**
See: 773

run away **katekwas** *See: 279*

run out of **tekatkaryas** *See: 747*

run short of **katòktha'** *See: 310*

S

sacred **yotokenhti** *See: 992*

sad **wake'nikonhraksen** *See: 866*

salt **tyohyòtsis** *See: 837*

salty **teyohiyòtsihs** *See: 783*

Saturday **Tsi Yenaktohares** *See: 810 ee)*

say **katon'** *See: 311*

scarf **teyontenyàteren'** *See: 787*

score a goal **tekatèntsha's** *See: 746*

seagull **tsyowatstakawe** *See: 834*

see **katkahthos** *See: 301*; **ikkens**
  See: 146; **khekens** *See: 405*

seed(s) **kanen** *See: 224*

self **oyàta** *See: 647*

sell **katenhninons** *See: 280*

Seneca nation **Shotinontowane'hàka**
  See: 717

September **Sehske'kowa** *See: 696*

set down **ikyens** *See: 152*

set up on **kherha'** *See: 411*

set upright **khnyotha'** *See: 423*

seven **tsyatak** *See: 823*

several **tohka** *See: 807*

sew **ke'nikhons** *See: 342*

sewing machine **ye'nikhonhkwa**
  See: 909

shady **yorahkwawerhon** *See: 975*

sharp **yohyo'thiye** *See: 946*

she **akaonha** *See: 25*

sheep **siksik** *See: 718*

shelf **yohswen'karohare** *See: 945*

shiney **teyohstarathe'** *See: 785*

shirt **atyàtawi'** *See: 92*

shoe(s) **ahta'** *See: 22*

shoot **karontats** *See: 264*

shoot with a bow **kiyaks** *See: 434*

short **niyenhsha'** *See: 479*

short time **nikarihwehsha'** *See: 468*;
  ken' ok nikarihwehsha' *See: 348 b)*

short ways off **ken' niyore'a** *See: 348 c)*

short while **nikarihwehsha'** *See: 468*

shoulder(s) **ohnenhsa** *See: 509*

shovel **karihstohare** *See: 254*

show someone **khena'tonnis** *See: 406*

sick **wakenonhwaktani** *See: 872*

side (toward this) **karo nonkati** *See: 262
  b)*; (this side) **karo nonwe** *See: 262 a)*;
  (other side) **ihsi nonwe** *See: 129 a)*;
  (other side) **ihsi nonkati** *See: 129 b)*

silk **kanheks** *See: 230*

silver **ohwihstakenra** *See: 540*

since **tsi nahe** *See: 810 c)*; **tsi nen nahe**
  See: 810 e)

sing **katerennotha'** *See: 285*

sister (older) **aktsi'a** *See: 36*

sister (younger) **khe'kenha** *See: 399*

sit down **katyens** *See: 325*

sitting **kìteron'** *See: 429*

sitting down on **kitskote'** *See: 430*

sitting up on **kitskwahere'** *See: 431*;
  kentskwahere' *See: 374*; **kahere**
  See: 162

sitting upright **kentskote** *See: 373*

six **yayak** *See: 908*

skate **tekato'tsinehtha'** *See: 748*

skate(s) **ato'tsinehta** *See: 83*

skidoo **wahsi'kwìseres** *See: 849*

skinny **yotiwen** *See: 989*

skirt **kakhare** *See: 206*; **o'whahsa**
  See: 497

skunk **anìtas** *See: 43*

sky **karònya** *See: 267*

slacks **athahsteren'** *See: 73*

sleeping **wakitahs** *See: 875*

sleet **yowisarhon** *See: 1000*

slice **kakwe'taratshera** *See: 211*;
  ikkwètarons *See: 148*

slow to act **wakatihsayen** *See: 859*

small **niwa'a** *See: 476*

smell good **kahserakon** *See: 186*

smell (sniff at) **katehswàtha'** *See: 277*

smoke **kathsokwas** *See: 296*

smoke (from a fire) **oyènkwara** *See: 651*

snake **onyare** *See: 612*

sneeze **tewaki'tsyonkha'** *See: 777*

snowing **yo'keren'onh** *See: 931*

snows **wàkeren's** *See: 874*

snowshoe(s) **kahwènkare** *See: 197*

snowsnake **aterahwènta** *See: 71*

snowstorm **tekanyen'kwatase** *See: 742*

so **e'tho** *See: 97*; **eh niyore n(i)-** *See: 99 b)*

so far **akwah ken' niyore** *See: 37 d)*; **akwah ken' niyore'a** *See: 37 e)*; **ken' niyore'a** *See: 348 c)*

so then **kati** *See: 298*; **se ok** *See: 695 a)*

soap **yenoharètha** *See: 924*

sock(s) **karis** *See: 260*

soda pop **kahnekakon** *See: 166*

sofa **yontorihshentahkwa** *See: 970*

soft drink **kahnekakon** *See: 166*

soft **yohnetskha'** *See: 938*

softly **skennenha** *See: 726*; **skennenhahson'a** *See: 727*

soil **onhwentsya** *See: 589*

somemore **shekon** *See: 709*

someplace **tsi ok nonwe** *See: 810 u)*

something **nahòten ok** *See: 457 a)*; **tsi ok nahòten** *See: 810 r)*; **ok nahòten** *See: 547 a)*

sometime **katke ok** *See: 304 a)*; **sewatyeren** *See: 699*

somewhere **ka' ok nonwe** *See: 156 d)*; **tsi ok nonwe** *See: 810 u)*

son **riyen'a** *See: 670*

song **karenna** *See: 248*

soon **akwah ken' nahe'a** *See: 37 b)*; **onen thoha** *See: 569 a)*

soot **o'kènra** *See: 486*

soul **atonnhets** *See: 86*

soup **kanòntara** *See: 242*

soup bowl **yenon'tarahkwa** *See: 926*

speak **katatis** *See: 272*

spear **ahsìkwara** *See: 13*

spill **kawerons** *See: 329*

spoon **atokwa** *See: 85*

spot **yotsihstohkware** *See: 994*

spotted **yotsihstohkware** *See: 994*

spouse **rone** *See: 680*; **tyakenìteron** *See: 835*

spout **ohsa** *See: 518*

Spring **kenhkwitène** *See: 354*

spring **tsi yohnawate** *See: 810 gg)*

spring water **ohnekanos** *See: 508*

spruce **o'sora** *See: 491*

squash **onon'onhsera** *See: 598*

squash blossoms **otyarènta** *See: 637*

stand up **tekta's** *See: 766*

standing **ikete'** *See: 137*

standing upright **kànyote** *See: 246*

steal **kenenhskwas** *See: 350*

steel **yorihstahniron** *See: 981*

stick **kanhya** *See: 232*

sticks on **yora'nentaks** *See: 972*

sticky **yora'nentaks** *See: 972*

still **shekon** *See: 709*

still again **shekon are** *See: 709 a)*

stir something **tekawenryehs** *See: 750*

stomach **ohsyehònta** *See: 537*; **onekwènta** *See: 568*

stone **onenya** *See: 580*

stop **tekta's** *See: 766*

store **tsi yekhwahninons** *See: 810 cc)*;
tsi yontenhninontha *See: 810 jj)*

stove **yekhonnya'tahkwa** *See: 919*;
yononhsa'tariha'tahkwa *See: 965*

straight **yottakwarihsyon** *See: 997*

strawberries **niyohontehsha** *See: 480*

stream **kahyonha** *See: 204*;
nikahyonha'a *See: 467*

string **ahseriye'** *See: 12*

string beans **orhotsheri** *See: 617*

strong **yo'shatste** *See: 933*

strong wind **kawera'shatste** *See: 328*

study **katerihwayenhstha'** *See: 287*

succeed **katkwenyes** *See: 308*

sugar **otsikhèta** *See: 630*

sugar bowl **yetsikhe'tarahkwa** *See: 929*

sugar maple **wahtha** *See: 851*

suit **atahkwennya'** *See: 54*

suit of clothes **athseronnya'** *See: 77*

suitcase **yohkwennyarahkwa** *See: 937*

Summer **akennha'kène** *See: 29*

Sunday **Yawentatokenhton** *See: 905*

sunny **yorahkote** *See: 974*

surprising **yonehrakwat** *See: 960*

surprized **wakenehrakwas** *See: 871*

suspended from **yohrènton** *See: 941*

sweet **teyottsikhètare** *See: 791*

swim **katawenhs** *See: 273*

syrup **ohshehs** *See: 521*

T

table **atekhwàra** *See: 59*

take care of **kateweyèntons** *See: 292*

take care of someone **kheyateweyèntons**

See: 415

take out **iktahkwas** *See: 149*

take down **khnyotakwas** *See: 422*

take down from **khrakwas** *See: 424*;
khahrakwas *See: 396*

take one's time **katennihskwahtha'**
See: 282

take out of **ktahkwas** *See: 445*

talk **katatis** *See: 272*

taste **katkènse's** *See: 305*

tea **oti** *See: 623*

tea (loose-leaf) **kanerahta'kerha**
See: 228

teach (someone) **kherihonnyennis**
See: 413

teakettle **yohonronte** *See: 940*

teapot **yotitsheronnyàtha** *See: 988*

teatowel **yeksokewàtha** *See: 921*

-teen **yawenre** *See: 904*

teeth **onawira** *See: 564*

television **kaya'tarha** *See: 331*

tell **khehroris** *See: 401*

ten **oyeri** *See: 653*

tent **atosera** *See: 87*

than **tsi niyoht tsi** *See: 810 n)*

that **thiken'** *See: 793*; **tsi** *See: 810*;
nène *See: 463*

the **ne** *See: 458*

them **rononha** *See: 683*; **kononha**
See: 438

then **e'thòne** *See: 98*; **se ok** *See: 695 a)*;
nen *See: 461*

there **e'tho** *See: 97*; **eh nonwe** *See: 99 f)*;
eh ki' nonwe *See: 99 a)*; **ken' nonwe t-**
See: 348 a)

thereabouts **eh nonwe tsi niwat** *See: 99 g)*

they **rononha** *See: 683*; **kononha**

See: 438

thick **katenhs** *See: 281*

tie to something **ikhnerenks** *See: 139*

thin **nikatenhsha'** *See: 469*; **yotiwen**
  See: 989

things **naho'tenhson** *See: 456*

think about **kennonhtonnyons** *See: 364*

this **kiken'** *See: 428*

this direction **kenh nonkati** *See: 352 b)*

this place **kèntho** *See: 371*

this spot **kèntho** *See: 371*

this way **kenh nonkati** *See: 352 b)*

thousand **tewen'nyawe'ehseron** *See: 778*

thread **ahseriye'** *See: 12*

three **ahsen** *See: 10*

thristy **wakenya'tathenhs** *See: 873*

throat **ohnyàtha** *See: 613*; **ohnyàsa**
  See: 511

throw away **wakatyes** *See: 863*

thumb **oweyonhkara** *See: 640*

thundering **yoweron** *See: 998*

Thursday **Kayerihatont** *See: 339*

tibia **orenhsa** *See: 614*

time **e'thòne** *at that time See: 98*;
  karìwehs *a long time See: 261*; **ken' ok**
  nikarihwehsha' *just a short time See:*
  348 b); **nikarihwehsha'** *a short time*
  See: 468; **wahonnise** *a long time*
  See: 847

tin **karihstakenra** *See: 252*

tire **okahkwènta** *See: 548*

tired **tewakhwihshenheyon** *See: 776*

to **tsi** *See: 810*

to the place of **nonwe** *See: 484*

toad **tsikhnennàtaks** *See: 816*

tobacco **oyènkwa** *See: 650*

today **kenh wenhniserate** *See: 352 e)*;

onwa kenh wente *See: 609 a)*

toe(s) **ohyakwira** *See: 542*

tomato(es) **wahyakhahon** *See: 853*

tomorrow **enyorhenne'** *See: 114*

too **oni** *See: 590*

tooth **onawira** *See: 564*

tornado **tekaweratase** *See: 751*

tough **yo'shatste** *See: 933*

tounge **en'nahsa** *See: 103*

toward **nonkati** *See: 482*

town **kanata** *See: 217*

toy **okahrìtshera** *See: 550*

train **teyo'seretsheràka** *See: 782*

tranquility **skennen** *See: 725*

travel **tekatawenryehs** *See: 744*

tree **kerhite** *See: 383*

troupe **kanènra** *See: 227*

truck (tree) **karonta** *See: 263*

truly **tokenhske'** *See: 809*

try **kate'nyentenhs** *See: 275*

try harder **kahkwihsrons** *See: 164*

Tuesday **Tekenihatont** *See: 756*

turkey **skawerowane** *See: 723*

turn around **katkarhatenyes** *See: 302*

turnips **otsihkwa ohtera** *See: 629*

turtle **a'nowara** *See: 4*

twenty **tewahsen** *See: 771*

two **tekeni** *See: 755*

two children **tehniksa'a** *See: 735*

two dollar bill **tekahwihstake** *See: 741*

two girls **tekeniksa'a** *See: 757*

two old men **tehnikstenha** *See: 736*

two old women **tekenikstenha** *See: 758*

two people **tehniyahsen** *two males See:*
  738; **tekeniyahsen** *two females See: 759*

-ty **niwahsen** *See: 477*

typewriter **tekarihstoraraks** *See: 743*

U

ugly **ikhserohen** *See: 141*; **wahetken**
  See: 845

uncle **rakenoha'a** *See: 656*

understand **wake'nikonhrayenta's**
  See: 867

understand (a language) **kahronkha'**
  See: 183

uniform **kanena** *See: 225*

unlock something **keniyontahrakwas**
  See: 360

until **tsi niyore** *See: 810 p)*;
  tsi ok niyore *See: 810 s)*

upper part of leg **ohahsa** *See: 500*

upright **kànyote** *See: 246*

us **i'i** *See: 126*

use **katstha'** *See: 321*

used up **yotsha'ahton** *See: 993*

useful **kahstha'** *See: 190*

usually **ens** *See: 112*

V

vase **yetsi'tsyarahkwa** *See: 928*

vegetables **a'sehson'a** *See: 6*

vehicle **kàsere'** *See: 268*

very **akwah iken' tsi** *See: 37 a)*

village **kanata** *See: 217*

voice **owenna** *See: 639*

W

wagon **kàsere'** *See: 268*

walking **ike'** *See: 131*

walking stick **atennits** *See: 67*

wall **ahsonhta** *See: 18*

wallet **yehwihstarahkwa** *See: 911*

want **tewakatonhwentsyoni** *See: 772*

want to **ikehre'** *See: 133*

warm **yo'tarihen** *See: 935*

warmth **o'tarihenhsera** *See: 493*

warrior **rohskenhrakehte** *See: 674*

warriors **rotihskenhrakehte** *See: 688*

was **kènne'** *See: 362*

wash **kenohares** *See: 365*

washing machine **kanohares** *See: 235*

watch **kateròroks** *See: 289*

watch over **ikenonhne'** *See: 136*

watch (someone) **kheyateròroks**
  See: 414

water **ohneka** *See: 507*; **ohnekanos**
  See: 508

water pitcher **yehnekarahkwa** *See: 910*

way (this) **kenh nonkati** *See: 482 b)*;
  (that way) **eh nonkati** *See: 482 a)*; (over
  this way) **karo nonkati** *See: 262 b)*

we **i'i** *See: 126*

wears out **karihwènta's** *See: 257*

Wednesday **Ahsenhatont** *See: 11*

weed **kahontaksen** *See: 170*

weigh **kate'nyentenhstha'** *See: 276*

well **tsi yohnawate** *See: 810 gg)*

well **wakata'karite** *See: 855*

wet **yonanawen** *See: 957*

what **oh nahòten** *See: 498 b)*; **tsi
  nahòten** *See: 810 d)*; **nahòten** *See: 457*

wheel **okahkwènta** *See: 548*

when **katke** *See: 304*; **onen** *See: 569*;
  ne onen *See: 458 c)*; **tsi** *See: 810*;
  ne nen *See: 458 e)*

whenever **katke** *See: 304*

where **ka' nonwe** *See: 156 a)*; **tsi**
See: 810; **tsi nonwe** *See: 810 q)*

whereabouts **ka' nonwe tsi niwat**
See: 156 c)

which **ne nahòten** *See: 458 d)*

which one **ka' nikayen'** *See: 156 b)*

while **nikarihwehsha'** *See: 468*

whiskey **kahneka'shatste** *See: 165*

white **kenraken** *See: 368*

white ash **kaneron** *See: 229*

white cedar **yonen'tòren** *See: 961*

white oak **otokenha** *See: 624*

White people **O'seronni** *See: 490*

who **tsi nikayen'** *See: 810 g)*

who **nène** *See: 463*

who all **onhkare'okon** *See: 587*

whoever **onhka ki' ok** *See: 586 b)*

whole thing **akwekon** *See: 38*

why **oh niyotyeren** *See: 498 e)*

wife **rone** *See: 680*

will be **enkenhake** *See: 106*

win **katkwenyes** *See: 308*

wind (strong) **kawera'shatste** *See: 328*

window pane **otsisera** *See: 633*

window **tsi yohsonhtakàronte**
See: 810 hh)

windy **yaote** *See: 900*

winter **kohsera'kène** *See: 435*

wipe **kerakewas** *See: 380*

wire **karonware** *See: 266*

wise **kattokha'** *See: 323*

with what **tsi nahòten** *See: 810 d)*

with something **tsi ok nahòten** *See: 810 r)*

wolf **okwaho** *See: 557*

woman **yakonkwe** *See: 896*

women **kononkwe** *See: 439*

wood **oyente** *See: 652*

woods **karhakon** *See: 249*

word **owenna** *See: 639*

work **kayo'tenhsera** *See: 340*

working **wakyo'te** *See: 879*

would be **akenhake'** *See: 28*

wrap up **katakwariks** *See: 270*

wrap-around skirt **o'whahsa** *See: 497*

wrist **onentshawìtha** *See: 579*

wristband **atenentshawìtha** *See: 63*

write **khyatons** *See: 427*

writing desk **yehyatonhstahkwa** *See: 914*

written **kahyaton** *See: 201*

Y

yard **atenoseràke** *See: 70*

year **tsi niyohserehs** *See: 810 k)*

yellow **otsinekwar** *See: 631*

yes **hen'en** *See: 123*

yesterday **thetenre** *See: 792*

yet again **shekon are** *See: 709 a)*

you **ise** *See: 154*

young man **ranekenhteron** *See: 660*

young men **ratinekenhteron** *See: 663*

young woman **tsyakothonwisen** *See: 822*

young women **tsyonathonwisen** *See: 831*